INTELLECTUAL
WARFARE

INTELLECTUAL WARFARE

Jacob H. Carruthers

THIRD WORLD PRESS   CHICAGO

Printed in the United States of America

06 05 04 03 02 01 00 99   5 4 3 2 1

Cover design by Angelo Williams

Library of Congress Cataloging-in-Publication Data

Carruthers, Jacob H.
            Intellectual Warfare/Jacob H. Carruthers.
                    p. cm.
        Includes bibligraphical references and index.
        ISBN 0-88378-160-3 (cloth: alk. paper).
        ISBN 0-88378-180-8 (pbk.: alk. paper).
            1. Africa—Civilization. 2. Afro-Americans. 3. Afrocentrism. 4.
Eurocentrism. 5. Civilization, Western—Philosophy. 6. Civilization,
Western—African influences. 7. Multicultural education—United
States. I. Title.
DT14.C38   1999
960—dc21   97-29817
                                                            CIP

                        Third World Press
                        7822 S. Dobson
                        Chicago, IL 60619

To John Henrik Clarke

C O N T E N T S

Preface

These essays reflect the thought of the "Chicago group" and the "African Community of Chicago." I was simply a vehicle through whom ideas flowed. Even the mistakes are our mistakes rather than mine alone. The conceptualization of our work as *Intellectual Warfare* emerged out of the actual battles in which we were engaged.

Some of us have been based at the Center for Inner City Studies (CICS) of Northeastern Illinois University. In our effort to keep the Center open and to develop a community oriented curriculum, we have been involved in continuous warfare. The battle to hold and expand our intellectual turf has been unremitting.

The success of our efforts is reflected, to some extent, in the organizations which we have launched and those which have nurtured us at CICS. These include the Communiversity, the Association of African Historians (AAH), the National Black United Front (NBUF), the Kemetic Institute (KI), the Temple of the African Community of Chicago (TACC), and the Association for the Study of Classical African Civilizations (ASCAC). Our publications have included several books, a journal, several newsletters, and the current *Kemetic Voice*, a bi-monthly bulletin.

The organizational bases have enabled us to provide some direction and structure for the development of a battle plan to continue the project that we inherited from our elders and ancestors. These projects would not have come into being without the instruction and guidance of our elders Chancellor Williams, John Henrik Clarke and Yosef ben-Jochannan. Nor would we have gone very far had we not consulted the works of our intellectual ancestors such as David Walker, Martin Delany, Henry Highland Garnet, Edward Wilmot Blyden, and Henry McNeal Turner. We were also inspired by the ideas of Carter G. Woodson, Marcus Garvey, Leo Hansberry, Drusilla Dunjee Houston, George G. M. James, and, of course, Malcolm X.

Vital components in the production of these ideas are the

students at CICS and members of the KI, TACC, NBUF, and ASCAC. Significant revisions were made in response to questions and concerns raised by members of this extended family.

This work is tendered as a tribute to our ancestors, a testimony of our office, and a gift of life to the coming generations.

Acknowledgments

In addition to the acknowledgments implicit in the Preface and Introduction, special recognitions are in order for a few individuals:

John Henrik Clarke, who not only is my elder and role model but who has always encouraged me to produce and offered specific advice for this project;

Anderson Thompson, who not only converted me to Nationalism but also raised questions and provided insights that provoked much of what is written here;

Conrad Worrill, who has perused and promoted these essays;

Haki R. Madhubuti, who has always encouraged and provided opportunities for publishing thoughts like these;

Bobbie Womack and Carol Moses, who deciphered my chicken scratch and typed the manuscripts pro bono;

Leon Harris, the Kemetic Institute editor who made many suggestions which made the text more intelligible;

Gwendolyn Mitchell and Melissa Moore, Third World Press editors who greatly brought this project to fruition;

Donn Bailey, the director of the Center for Inner City Studies, whose support has been so vital for the success of our projects; and

Ife and Tawa, my wife and my daughter, who not only graciously shared my time with the project but who also served as backup typists, editors, and advisors.

Credits

I would like to thank the following publishers for kind permission to use articles published by them:

Black Books Bulletin
Institute of Positive Education—Chicago

Critical Commentaries
The Association for the Study of Classical African Civilizations—Los Angeles

African or American: A Question of Intellectual Allegiance
The Kemetic Institute—Chicago

Introduction

The seventeen pieces in this collection are written versions of speeches uttered over a fifteen year period. Some of them have been presented several times. Most of them were spoken from outlines on first delivery and were subsequently written down as they appear here. Slightly different versions of some of them have been published elsewhere or widely circulated within the Association for the Study of Classical African Civilizations (ASCAC) community. However, the revisions and variations have not resulted in any substantial change of the ideas which I attempted to convey.

Intellectual Warfare, which is the focus of these efforts, is discussed in historical context in the title essay. The speech was an address at the Eighth Annual National ASCAC Conference in 1991. The argument was intended as a challenge to African thinkers to decisively continue our project to dismantle the European intellectual campaign to commit historicide against African peoples. The European atrocity which has been continuous for two and one half centuries must be unconditionally halted.

The second essay, "Reflections on the History of the Afrocentric Worldview," is the oldest of the speeches. It was first spoken and written in 1979 and published in Vol. 7, No. 1 of *Black Books Bulletin*. Here the nature of intellectual rebirth is explored. The next three essays, written between 1981 and 1986, explore various dimensions of the alien terrain. These probes into the European worldview are designed to help us define the nature of the war. Unfortunately, many brave African thinkers and warriors have fought the wrong battles simply because the nature of the enemy has been disguised.

The focus of Part II is more specific. Here attention is drawn to some of the contemporary strategies, including attempts to de-Africanize significant moments of African civilization used by the European defenders of the European way to explain aspects of African history and culture. These critiques were developed during the early 1990s as a response to the escalation of the war by European intellectuals who had begun to feel the bite of the African-centered education movement. "A Critique of Eurocentric Comparisons of the Cultures of Tricontinental Antiquity" and "Reflections on the Question of the Race of the Ancient Egyptians," essays in the second section, were presented to participants in "Extending the Great Conversation," an event that was funded by the National Endowment for Humanities, but conceived by the Kemetic Institute. The project was based upon an exploration of the literature of Tricontinental Antiquity and also included several European-American professors as presenters. The deconstruction of modern European intellectual "generals" is a necessary phase of our battle plan. We have divided these intellectuals into two camps: the hard-liners and the soft-liners. Some intellectuals from the latter group appear to be siding with us, but let us beware.

Part III focuses on the internal warfare among African thinkers and speakers. While some significant differences are to be expected in any project of considerable scope, we are confronted by a group of African thinkers who have pledged allegiance to European intellectuals and are, in effect, black defenders of white supremacy. The submission to Western civilization and its most outstanding offspring, American civilization, is, in reality, surrender to white supremacy. Such acceptance is one way to "solve" the so-called race problem and is certainly acceptable to the white supremacists. The focus on two "African-American" thinkers in this category should not obscure the intergenerational context of this internal intellectual struggle. We are, after all, battling for the African mind, which, as Anderson Thompson notes, is the struggle of the twenty-first century. All three essays were written in 1994, the first two were published by the Kemetic Institute under the title "African or American: A Question of Intellectual Allegiance."

Part IV is devoted to the challenge given by "The Master," Cheikh Anta Diop, who, having dedicated the last forty years of his life to our project, is truly the champion of African-centered thought. His ideas gave us the ammunition to wage this most difficult phase in the long and brutal war. It was Diop who invited all African scholars, especially those of us in the diaspora, to enroll in this mighty army. Dr. Diop was the youngest of our mentors, but held his own in the company of Chancellor Williams, John Jackson, John Henrik Clarke, and Yosef ben-Jochannan.

The speeches in the final section put forth proposals for the victory campaign. Indeed we must take over the education of African people and develop an African-centered curriculum. We also must build the foundation of our renewed educational establishment on the African worldview. We must draw our ideas from the deep well of our heritage. We must build institutions to foster our careers. To this foundation we may add whatever stands the test of truth and propriety. In other words, we must recreate a universe of African establishments to encompass every phase of life.

Restoration of African civilization is not possible without a return to African spirituality. Therefore we must revisit African theology. Cultivation of the relationships among divinity, cosmos, nature, society, and humanity is the office of all conscious Africans. Indeed, Kemetic theology is synonymous with the concept of human speech. The words *Medew Netcher* mean Divine Speech. *Medew Netcher* thus is a metaphor for our spiritual project. In other words, the road to African liberation begins at the door of that "Good Old African Spirit."

—Jacob H. Carruthers

PART I

THE NATURE OF THE WAR

1

Intellectual Warfare

The Battle for Kemet

Throw away the image of the god of the whites who has so
often brought down our tears and listen to liberty which
speaks in all our hearts.

—Bookman Dutty

In 1791, Bookman Dutty articulated the African declaration
of spiritual, intellectual, and cultural freedom, and on August
14 of that same year, he launched the war against the most
brutal project in the history of humanity. This prayer, which evoked
the Haitian Revolution, should always guide us as we wage war against
our oppression. It should be a constant reminder that the military
victory against biological genocide must be consummated by a final
triumph over the cultural tyranny that has been imposed on the life
and history of African peoples.

The intellectual aspect of the struggle became accentuated as soon
as the military campaign ended. Two interrelated reactions to the
victory of the Haitian people over the Spanish, and British, as well as
the French army of Napoleon revealed the protracted nature of the final
phase of the intellectual war. One reaction was the European
intellectual denial that Africans of Haiti had done what they did.
Africans had conceptualized and successfully executed the most
significant event in recent history. Thus, they began to fabricate
explanations that accorded with the New Orthodoxy (which I will
explain below). One fabrication was that misguided and disaffected
Europeans had stirred up the slaves; another was that the Africans
"copied" the French Revolution; another was that the unanticipated

advent of a yellow fever plague so vitiated the French forces that victory literally fell into the hands of the Africans. Since these theories could not stand in the light of sharp scrutiny, the European intellectuals buried the event in the corners of history and covered it with a heroic picture of Toussaint L' Ouverture which had been abstracted from reality. In other words, the European deep thinkers tried to do intellectually what Napoleon had failed to do militarily—destroy the Haitian campaign to dismantle slavery and reenslave the Africans.

The other reaction posed an even greater challenge to African independence. This reaction came from Haitians who, even though they sooner or later joined in the military campaign for biological freedom, never were persuaded to give up the image of the white man's god. These Haitians wanted and fought only to be treated as equals in a modified European world order. Needless to say, these assimilationists formed an alliance with the upholders of the European worldview with its twin pillars—Western civilization and white supremacy. Of course, most African devotees to Western civilization would deny that they favor white supremacy. Yet, how is it possible to separate the two. Not only are they joined at the body, but they share the same vital organs, including the heart and mind.

Thus, those who have been waging the long war to liberate African history and culture have been fighting the following two battles: (1) an international war against the European intellectuals and (2) a civil war against the colonized African spokespersons who are trained by Europeans to undermine African independence. The war is truly, as Anderson Thompson says, a battle for the African mind, or as Asa Hilliard and the First World Alliance put it, a battle to free the African mind.

Winning the civil war is the essential condition for victory. When African peoples reunite with African history and culture, solutions to the other problems will be possible. The point to emphasize here is that the victory will occur when and only when African teachers (the Mwalimu), who have drunk deeply from the deep well of the African heritage, take over the preservation, cultivation, reconstruction, and dissemination of African history and culture as the vital core of African education. This is the project that was pioneered by Bookman, Jean Jacques Dessalines, Prince Hall, P. V. Vastey, Prince

Sanders, David Walker, Hosea Easton, Henry Highland Garnet, and Martin Delany. This is the project that launched the Association for the Study of Classical African Civilizations (ASCAC). Since the founding of ASCAC, and perhaps because of our work, the war has significantly escalated. Today we are facing the top guns of the European intellectuals with their state-of-the-art weapons, that is, their retooled disciplines of archaeology, Egyptology, linguistics, history, and anthropology. Their main forces, the uncompromising defenders of Western civilization, are buffered by the practitioners of what Anderson Thompson calls "sambo historiography," for example, the Africans trained to fight against African freedom fighters, and the even more troublesome liberal and radical European intellectuals who assert they are on our side and only want to help us refine our strategy and tactics, but who in fact have drunk a swig or two from our deep well to better defend Western civilization.

From this perspective, I would like to first briefly explain the New Orthodoxy which invented the doctrine of white supremacy and its corollary, Negro inferiority. (In this Eurocentric context, Negro is synonymous with Black and African.) Second, I would like to outline the African response to this campaign of cultural genocide. Third, I would like to make some observations about the opposition. Fourth, I would like to highlight some of the features of our position in the current phase of the war. By "our" I mean the Kemetic Institute and at least some other members of ASCAC and some individuals outside of ASCAC.

The New Orthodoxy

As an introduction to the explanation of the New Orthodoxy, let me comment on the origin and nature of the intellectual tyranny. First, the predisposition to battle is deeply embedded in the clashing world views as explained in Cheikh Anta Diop's Two Cradle Theory. Leonard Jeffries describes it as the difference between the people of the sun and the people of the ice. The incipient stages of the conflict emerged in ancient history. The occasional negative statements by the classical and Hellenistic Greeks, the Jews, and the Romans who often sought ancient African ideas reveal a potential for the modern

European project. Perhaps the most direct antecedent of the New Orthodoxy was the Talmudic tradition which fabricated a connection between the biblical curse of Ham and the cultural inferiority of African people. Shakespeare's Moors and Bacon's "foul little Ethiop" are extensions of this tradition.

The doctrine of white supremacy which I call the New Orthodoxy, however, begins with the explicit declaration of biological inferiority of Negroes in relationship to whites. As I read history, this occurs in the middle of the eighteenth century and can best be seen in the thoughts of David Hume and Charles Montesquieu. Hume (1987) on his part drew the conclusion that Negroes were: "Naturally inferior to the whites" (p. 214). He charged any evidence of accomplishments by Negroes as exaggerations of feats that were comparable to talking parrots. He also asserted: "You may obtain anything of the Negroes by offering them strong drink; and may easily prevail with them to sell, not only their children, but their wives and mistresses, for a cask of brandy" (p. 214). Hume seemed also to anticipate the apparent contradiction between his assertions about Negroes and the tradition concerning Kemetic civilization. He therefore asserted:

> All the arts and the sciences arose among free nations...*Egyptians*, notwithstanding their ease, opulence, and luxury, made but faint efforts towards a relish in those finer pleasures, which were carried to such perfection by the *Greeks*. (p. 89)

Hume's solution to the Nile Valley contradiction was simply to knock Kemet down a few pegs!

Montesquieu, for his part, offered a more apparent reason for his argument about Negro inferiority. After offering several reasons related to the physical repulsiveness of Negroes, Montesquieu (1949) asserted "it is natural to look upon color as the criterion of human nature." He concluded: "It is impossible for us to suppose these creatures to be men, because, allowing them to be men, a suspicion would follow that we ourselves are not Christians" (pp. 238–239).

Montesquieu, who was a pioneer in the establishment of the typology for the Eurocentric notion of social evolution, separated mankind into three stages of social development: savage, barbarian, and

6

civilized (pp. 276, 332). His classification of Africans is provided here:

> The greatest part of the people on the coast of Africa (the only ones with whom most Europeans were acquainted in the mid-eighteenth century) are *savages* and *barbarians*...They are without industry or arts...They have gold in abundance which they receive immediately from nature. Every *civilized* state is *therefore* in a condition to traffic with them to advantage, by raising their esteem for things of no value, and receiving a very high price in return.
>
> (p. 332)

Thus, Montesquieu justified the rape of the African continent and its peoples.

Montesquieu did not share Hume's concern with the tradition concerning Kemet because he stated in the section on "Slavery of the Negroes" that "Egyptians [were] the best philosophers in the world." He did, however, accuse them of color prejudice against presumably "fair skinned" red-haired men (p. 239).

The problem of the reputation and fame of Kemet as one of the cradles of civilization, if not *the cradle* of human wisdom, posed a great embarrassment to these advocates of Negro inferiority. The ancient Greeks, on whom the eighteenth-century intellectuals were founding their myth of white supremacy, had expressed great respect and admiration for Africans. As indicated above, Hume was unlimited in praise of the perfection of the arts and sciences among the Greeks. Montesquieu, a bit more subtly (or more objective *s'il vous plaît*), used the Greek institutions and social thinkers profusely to clarify his theories. Therefore, this troublesome problem had to be explained away if the doctrine was to stick.

Napoleon's 1798 invasion of Kemet paved the way for the solution. When Napoleon entered Kemet he took an intellectual army along with his soldiers. These intellectuals, charged with the responsibility of investigating and reporting on the remains of the amazing ancient Nile Valley civilization, placed the surviving works of the African ancestors into captivity, carting much off to Europe and holding the remainder in bondage in the land of its origin. Thus emerged the modern Pan European discipline of Egyptology which has monopolized access to the greatest body of evidence on African civilization presently known.

From this vantage point the intellectuals of Europe became the directors of Egyptian antiquities and the experts on the nature, meaning, and identity of the Kemetic nation and its people. But it was a nineteenth-century German philosopher who best articulated the complete New Orthodoxy and thus offered the solution to the problem. Georg Wilhelm Friedrich Hegel in his *Philosophy of History* (1956) asserted that the Negro in Africa:

> Exhibits the natural man in his completely wild and untamed state...there is nothing harmonious...with humanity to be found in this type of character. (p. 93)

He further concluded that the condition of Africans "is capable of no development or culture" and that enslavement to more advanced Europeans is necessary to the "increase of human feeling among the Negroes" and is an advance towards becoming participants in a higher morality...a phase of education" (p. 98).

> At this point we leave Africa not to mention it again. *[*He does, however, manage to mention it again.]* For it is not a historical part of the world; it has no movements or development to exhibit. Historical movements in it—that is in its northern part—belong to the Asiatic or European world. Carthage displayed there an important transitionary phase of civilization; but, as a Phoenician colony, it belongs to Asia. Egypt will be considered in reference to its Western phase, but it does not belong to the African Spirit. What we properly understand by Africa is the unhistorical, undeveloped spirit, still involved in the conditions of mere nature, and which had to be presented here only as on the threshold of the world's history. (Hegel, p. 99) [*Author's insertion]

He also noted that Egypt, which was somewhat impressive, was flawed because it was in the vicinity of "African stupidity." Hegel proclaimed the alienation of Egypt from Africa and Africans from Egypt. This feat ultimately required the manufacture of two Africas—

Black Africa and non-Black Africa. A more recent innovation has been the creation of the notion that Egypt was a part of a nonexistent continent called the Middle East. The upshot was that Kemet could not be connected with African culture, or rather nonculture, because Africans were not capable of producing civilization. Since Africans had not evolved from the lowest stage of humanity (i.e., Montesquieu's savages), Africans had to be removed from history. In other words, from the standpoint of historiography, Africans were depicted as mere animals who since the beginning had perennially done the same inane things.

This magical solution was echoed by the Egyptologists who had the task of making facts conform to theory. One bothersome fact was the tendency of Kemetic artists to paint pictures of themselves with black and brown skin and some other people with pink, pale, and swarthy skin. According to Diop, the brother of the European scholar who is credited with deciphering the Kemetic written language finally attempted to silence some Europeans who chose to follow the evidence of their senses rather than the incredible New Orthodoxy. Champoleon Figeac asserted in 1837:

> The two physical traits of black skin and kinky hair are not enough to stamp a race as Negro and Volney's conclusion as to the Negro origin of the ancient population of Egypt is glaringly false and inadmissible. (Diop, *General History*, p. 40)

Seventy-two years later, James Breasted, the American Egyptologist who founded the Oriental Institute at the University of Chicago, found it necessary to reassert the unbelievable. He proclaimed that "the conclusion maintained by some historians that the Egyptian was of African Negro origin is now refuted" (Breasted, 1937, p. 26). This (of course) had to be the case since Breasted insisted that *all* civilizations were founded by the great "White race" (p. 43).

All of these ideas were put forth as sound philosophic and scientific truth. Therefore all European disciplines dealing with humanity including anatomy, physiology, medicine, physical anthropology, and physical education incorporated the myth into their analytical frameworks. Certainly this inclusion can clearly be seen in

Freudian psychology, Durkheimian sociology, the political science of John Burgess, and the political economy of Karl Marx. In other words, the theory is deeply and inextricably intertwined with the principles that govern the social universe under the dominion of the Europeans.

Today, we are arrayed in a great war to determine whether the doctrine and practice of white supremacy shall be overthrown. Recently, the war, which is as old as the European intellectual riot (i.e., 250 years old), has escalated. Our ancestors in the eighteenth, nineteenth, and early twentieth centuries defended us amazingly well considering the imbalance in weapons. Those guerrillas, or "old scrappers" as Anderson Thompson used to call them, developed a mighty strategy which we must consult as we begin the final battle. We are ready because they prepared the way.

The Repetition of the Birth

It is interesting to note that both of Napoleon's precursory moves, prior to initiating his objective of dominating world history, were directed against Africans. The invasion of Egypt in 1798 was designed to rob Africans of the *idea* of civilization to complement what Chancellor Williams called *The Destruction of Black Civilization*. The previously mentioned invasion of Haiti was designed to reenslave the Africans so that the notion that Africans were capable of self-emancipation could be effaced from the memory of humankind. It also is interesting to note that both projects ultimately failed! The schemes failed because African thinkers found a formula by which to protect the African mind against the mania spread by the New Orthodoxy. The formula anchored the African Freedom Movement on the twin pillars of Kemet and the Haitian Revolution. Martin Delany articulated the connection in 1854 when he proclaimed:

> The Island of Haiti [is] peopled by as brave and noble descendants of Africa as they who laid the foundation of Thebes, or constructed the everlasting pyramid...of Egypt. A people who have freed themselves by the might of their own will, the force of their own power, the unfailing

strength of their own right arms, and their unflinching
determination to be free. (Delany, p. 337)

What Delany implied was a repetition of the spirit of Kemet in
the Haitian victory. This echoed the Horus name taken by the
Pharaoh Amen-M-Hat in 1990 B.C. when he established the glorious
Twelfth Kingdom. The name was "Weheme Mesu," which means
either "Repetition of the Birth," "Rebirth,"or "Renaissance"—perhaps
the true origin of the idea.

In fact, the connection between ancient African civilization and
the freedom struggle was articulated during the Haitian Revolution by
Prince Hall who, in addressing the African Masons whom he
organized, lectured them that their major duty was to work for the
liberation of African people from slavery. In framing his mandate he
said:

> My brethren, let us not be cast down under these and many
> other abuses we at present labour under; for the darkest is
> before the break of day: My brethren, let us remember
> what a dark day it was with our African brethren six years
> ago, in the French West-Indies. Nothing but the snap of
> the whip was heard from morning to evening; hanging,
> broken on the wheel, burning, and all manner of tortures
> inflicted on those unhappy people, for nothing else but to
> gratify their masters pride, wantonness and cruelty; but
> blessed be God, the scene is changed; they now confess that
> God hath no respect of persons, and therefore receive them
> as their friends, and treat them as brothers. Thus doth
> Ethiopia begin to stretch forth her hand, from a sink of
> slavery to freedom and equality. (Hall, 1970, p. 49)

Hall placed the liberation struggle, in general, and the Haitian
war, in particular, within the context of the ancient Africans as reported
in the Bible.

Such a construction was followed by the leading contemporary
Haitian historian of the Revolution, P. V. Vastey, who had the task of
defending the image of the Haitian Revolution from the detractors
mentioned above. He reminded the "traducers" that not only were the
Egyptians the teachers of the Greeks, but that the Taharka of the Bible
was an Ethiopian pharaoh of Kemet. In the same context, Prince

11

Sanders, who emigrated to Haiti, asserted that "the Egyptians and Ethiopians [were] our ancestors" (Sanders 1816, p. 219).

David Walker was perhaps the first to articulate the philosophy of history implicit in the diasporic African response to the New Orthodoxy. Concerning the revolution he proclaimed:

> Haiti [is] the glory of the Blacks and terror of tyrants...one thing which gives me joy is that they are men who would be cut off to a man before they would yield to the combined forces of the whole world—in fact, if the whole world was combined against them it could not do anything with them. (Walker, 1965, p. 21)

In turning to Kemet, Walker outlined the argument followed by our thinkers from Prince Hall to Diop, to my mentor John Henrik Clarke. Concerning the identity of the Kemites he said:

> The Egyptians were Africans...such as we are...some of them yellow and others dark...a mixture of Ethiopians and the natives of Egypt...about the same as you see the coloured people of the United States at the present day. (Walker, 1965, p. 47)

Therefore, people of African descent as they struggle for freedom should:

> Take a retrospective view of the arts and sciences—the wise legislators—the Pyramids and other magnificent buildings—the turning of the channel of the river Nile, by the sons of Africa or Ham among whom learning originated and was carried thence into Greece. (p. 48)

Based upon such a study, a philosophy of history emerges. Walker summarized it thusly:

> The whites have always been an unjust, jealous, unmerciful, avaricious and blood-thirsty set of beings, always seeking after power and authority. We view them all over the confederacy of Greece where they were first known to be

12

anything (in consequence of education), we see them there, cutting each other's throats—trying to subject each other to wretchedness and misery—to effect which, they used all kinds of deceitful, unfair, and unmerciful means....In fine, we view them all over Europe, together with what were scattered about in Asia and African, as heathens, and we see them acting more like devils than accountable men. (p. 56)

Walker then addressed the ethos of Africans and Asians:

Some may ask, did not the Blacks of Africa, and the mulattoes of Asia; go on in the same way....I answer no— they were not half so avaricious, deceitful and unmerciful as the whites. (p. 56)

Walker's summary contains all the essential moments of our view of history—the priority of Kemetic civilization and the diametric opposition between Kemetic culture and European culture or what we call Diop's Two Cradle Theory. Walker also anticipated Diop's concept of the zone of confluence to designate the cultural and biological mixture of Indo-European and African peoples in Western Asia. This theory has directed our educational strategy for two hundred years. It has been the weapon by which we have defended the African mind from the massive assault of white supremacy and genocide.

The method by which we wage this war as outlined by David Walker is simple to state but difficult to do. The method of liberation is to free the African mind through research, creative production, spiritual development, and education—the Association for the Study of Classical African Civilizations agenda.

The Four Commissions

Isn't it embarrassing when we witness non-Africans taking the lead in researching our heritage? Isn't it embarrassing to have to consult the Cambridge series on history? As a critical response to these questions the ASCAC agenda is divided into four commissions. The Research Commission's task is to take over the production of knowledge not only about us but about the world—at least that which is disseminated to African peoples. Not only do we need to correct the misinterpretations of our oppressors but we also need to restore the messages of our ancestors so that we can have access to the deep well of African wisdom and guidance as we continue our upward march. The winning of the research battle is thus a vital phase of the war.

The second commission is Creative Production. We need a substantial number of creative intellectuals to tap into the artistic culture of African antiquity and reproduce the values for the aesthetic development of our peoples. Painting, sculptures, drama, songs, and dances can incorporate those ancient themes in ways which will enrich, enlighten, and inspire the African imagination. Brother Ausbra Ford's recent works are outstanding examples of the possibilities in this regard.

The reevaluation of spirituality is the task of the third commission, Spirituality. Certainly we need to heed Bookman's plea to "throw away the image of the white man's god," and begin to celebrate with our God who has given us life, power, and health and commanded us to do likewise. We need to seek the divine speech through good speech which is so divine that we can achieve our human purpose. This is the arena of deep thought where we must begin to reconstruct our way of thinking about the way things are and the way they should be. Divine speech is our answer to the destructive import of European philosophy and science.

It is through the Education Commission that we must take command of education. Our people are subjected to an educational process and content that, either by design or as an unavoidable by-product, deforms most African minds. This is so whether the individual student fails or succeeds vis-`a-vis the standard imposed by the system. That is, the 'A' student is as much if not more damaged than the 'F' student. In fact the miseducated are probably more disadvantaged than the diseducated. Therefore the battle to reestablish African education under the conceptualization and direction of African teachers is the sine qua non.

ASCAC, with its four commissions, has merely refined our battle plan. If we develop it we will win—the alternative is unthinkable.

B e w a r e   t h e   G r e e k   G i f t

Historically, our intellectual leaders have been so preoccupied with the campaigns against the hard-line white supremists who make no compromise in their flaunting of Western civilization that we have sometimes overlooked the more subtle attack from the mild mannered and friendly acting liberal intellectuals. We have become quite skilled at exposing and disposing of the arguments of the Humes, Montesquieus, Hegels, Mortimer Adlers, and Alan Blooms. We even recognize the false facade of the Diane Ravitchs and Frank Yurcos. Diane Ravitch, who professes to be a multiculturalist of the pluralistic variety, offered us the movie *Glory* as an outstanding example of the best in multicultural education. She never thought that many of us put *Glory* in the same category as *Gone With the Wind*, the latter the southern white man's version, and the former the northern white man's version of the Civil War. In both cases, Africans were subjected to the command of white supremacists.

For his part, Yurco offered us a few black Egyptians but lectured us about the evils of attaching racial labels to the Kemites. I respond by saying that we didn't start the race war but we will decide when it has ended and upon what terms. In other words, we want complete victory and unconditional surrender. No negotiations, no compromise.

While many Kemetic scholars are well aware of the soft-line approach of giving us a few tokens, such as a white-approved black hero or two and even a trio of Pharaohs, some of us are not aware of the even more awesome threat posed by Martin Bernal—a European who runs into our camp with a white flag and shouts that he would rather fight on our side. As proof of his fidelity to our cause he offers us a gift entitled *Black Athena* (read: Black Greeks) and praises our visionary George G. M. James for converting him to the path of truth. As a point of reference, I recall that at the first and founding ASCAC conference we laughed off the podium a brother who was reading a paper entitled "Black Zeus." Let us also understand that notwithstanding Bernal's evocation of our trailblazer, George G. M. James never wrote a letter of recommendation for Dr. Bernal, who is the grandson of Alan Gardiner.

Reread Bernal's book and you will discover that while he praises

Brother James, he damns most of the rest of us including Yosef ben-Jochannan, Cheikh Anta Diop, and myself. He implies that we are anti-Semitic scholars obsessed with proving the blackness of the Kemites and who are ignorant of the protocols of scholarly research. Furthermore he declares his allegiance to the African intellectuals who are most willing to compromise the issue.

Maulana Karenga correctly pointed out that Bernal's focus on Greece still obstructs the real question, which is the African identity of Kemet. Indeed, Bernal's not-so-obvious interest in rehabilitating the Jewish influence on Western civilization is probably paramount. Thus, Martin Bernal turns out to be perhaps the softest of the soft-liners. He nonetheless must be treated as a defender of Western civilization and white supremacy (although he is a less arrogant defender).

Whatever the case, we must not allow these neoabolitionists to take over or intrude into our research and educational projects. Their Greek gifts of a few heroes and a one-sided alliance are merely tokens which they are willing to give up in order to make a super-profit through our surrender.

The Current State of the War

Since the takeover of the education of Africans is a necessary condition for our liberation from intellectual and cultural tyranny and genocide, we are advocating an African-centered curriculum. Such a curriculum must be fueled by research centers which have as a prime objective the production of an African history of the world. The African-centered curriculum must be undergirded by classical African academies as alternative and supplemental models and headed by an African university to, among other things, establish criteria and standards for the curriculum. African parents, teachers, and administrators must use their power to establish an African curriculum in all schools attended by African children. We must take over and direct the multicultural education movement or dismantle it because as it is presently structured, it is designed to destroy us. Finally, we must continue and expand the study group movement among all segments of the African population of the world. These tasks are primary responsibilities of ASCAC's Research and Education Commissions.

In the domain of culture, our artists must paint, sculpt, write, sing, and dance the themes of Africa with a greater emphasis on antiquity. Just as Shakespeare drew from the Greek playwrights so must our artists dramatize our classical moments. We must fill our theaters, music, exhibition halls, bookshelves, and television and movie screens with images of African glory. We must adorn our bodies with African clothes; our necks, fingers, and arms with African jewelry. We must nourish our stomachs with African food. "Made in Africa" must be as common and profitable among us as "Made in America" and "Made in Japan" are to Eurasians. These are responsibilities assigned to ASCAC's Commission on Creative Production.

Not only must we build African temples and celebrate African liturgies and rituals, we must begin the reconstruction of our deep thought to reproduce the African vision of the cosmos. African explanations of the meaning of life and of correct social relations and governance must inform the way we approach the understanding and utilization of the natural world, including our bodies. Such studies will provide the foundation for the revitalization of African medicine, African engineering and architecture, and African mathematics. This is the responsibility of ASCAC's Commission on Spiritual Development.

We have a great deal of work to do, but we have come a long way. The reason the opposition is so fierce today is because suddenly it became aware of the impact of what we have been doing for the last half-century. Starting after World War II, the advance guard consisting of visionaries such as George G. M. James, Cheikh Anta Diop, John Henrik Clarke, John G. Jackson, and Yosef ben-Jochannan began their teachings. The response was at first barely detectable amidst the din of the decolonization of Africa and the civil rights and Black Power revolts. But the movement to free the African mind and liberate African history and studies emerged in places like Chicago's Communiversity and the First World Alliance of New York. The study tours to Africa led by the Center for Inner City Studies, Yosef ben-Jochannan, Asa Hilliard, Leonard Jeffries, and others were part of a great mobilization drive. We have recruited not only college teachers and artists, we also have enlisted physicians, lawyers, judges, engineers, mothers, and plumbers.

Our army is deep. The enemy sharpshooters cannot stop us by focusing on a lone leader. When they attack John Clarke, an army pounces on them with deadly weapons. We are ready, but we must continue to build our army and retool our weapons.

When Pharaoh Piankhy liberated Memphis, he included in his army engineers and artists, as well as archers. We must do likewise as we retake Kemet, the gateway to African liberation. Let us again celebrate the bicentennial of the Haitian Revolution, that is the repetition of the birth. Let us again evoke the prayer of Bookman:

> Throw away the image of the god of the whites who has so often brought down our tears and listen to liberty which speaks in all our hearts.

R E F E R E N C E S

Bernal, Martin. 1986. *Black Athena: The Afroasiatic Roots of Classical Civilization.* Vol. I. The Fabrication of Ancient Greece 1785–1985. New Brunswick: Rutgers University Press.

Breasted, James Henry. 1937. *A History of Egypt: From the Earliest Times to the Persian Conquest.* New York: Charles Scribner and Sons.

Carruthers, Jacob H. 1985. *Irritated Genie: An Essay on the Haitian Revolution.* Chicago: Kemetic Institute.

Clarke, John Henrik. 1991. *Africans at the Crossroads: Notes for an African World Revolution.* Trenton, N.J.: Africa World Press.

Diop, Cheikh Anta. 1974. *The African Origin of Civilization: Myth or Reality.* Westport: Lawrence Hill.

—. 1981. "The Origin of the Ancient Egyptians," *General History of Africa*, Vol. II. G. Mokhtar, ed. London: Heinemann.

Drake, St. Clair. 1990. *Black Folk Here and There.* Los Angeles:Center for Afro-American Studies, University of California, Los Angeles. Vol. 2.

Hall, Prince. 1970. "A Charge." *Afro-American History: Primary Sources*, ed. Thomas R. Frazier. New York: Harcourt Brace and World, Inc.

Hegel, Georg Wilhelm Friedrich. 1956. *The Philosophy of History.* New York: Dover.

Hume, David. 1987. *Essays: Moral, Political, and Literary.* Indianapolis: Liberty Classics.

James, George G. M. 1976. *Stolen Legacy.* San Francisco: Julian Richardson Associates.

Montesquieu, Charles. 1949. *The Spirit of the Laws.* New York: Hafner.

Rollin, Frank A. 1969. *Life and Public Services of Martin R. Delany.* New York: Kraus Reprint Co.

Sanders, Prince, ed. 1816. *The Haytian Papers.* London.

Thompson, Anderson. 1975. "Developing an Afrikan Historiography." *Black Books Bulletin*, vol. 3, (Spring).

Walker, David. 1965. *David Walker's Appeal.* New York: Hill and Wang.

Williams, Chancellor. 1976. *The Destruction of Black Civilization.* Chicago: Third World Press.

2

Reflections on the History of
the Afrocentric Worldview

I would first of all like to disentangle the concept of an Afrocentric worldview from any connotation of ideology. Since ideology is largely associated with the rationalization of class interests, it does not encompass the idea of a worldview which includes the way a people conceive the fundamental questions of existence and organization of the universe. While those who merely parrot European theorists may not be able to see nor appreciate the difference, they will, if and when they stop regurgitating and start studying and thinking. The upshot is that Afrocentrism is a misnomer. All of the current "isms" and ideologies accept the Western worldview—they share the same cultural orientation, the same view of history, the same view of science, and so on.

The Afrocentric worldview is based upon two basic truths which have been transmitted by our ancestors:

1. There is a distinct and universal African worldview. This concept is best illustrated by the idea presented in Cheikh Anta Diop's book, *The Cultural Unity of Black Africa*, which I would modify to include the idea of the Cultural Unity of Black African people throughout the world.

2. The African worldview, modified to account for modern conditions, is the only viable foundation for African liberation. Wherever records still exist the wisdom of the African people proclaims the necessity of the restoration of the African worldview as the

necessary condition for liberation. An assessment of history demonstrates that when the principle has been followed, liberation struggles have gone forward. In contrast retrogression has taken place when the principle has been abandoned.

First, I will place each of these assumptions in historical perspective. Fortunately, we have the works of our great mentors Cheikh Anta Diop, Yosef ben-Jochannan, John G. Jackson, John Henrik Clarke, and a host of our ancestors including Martin Delany, Chancellor Williams, Edward Blyden, Henry McNeal Turner, and Marcus Garvey to guide us in this task.

The Universal African Worldview

The African worldview is distinct and universal among African people who have been uncorrupted by foreign influence. This fact was emphasized by Delany and Blyden who did field studies in Africa before the partition of 1884-85. This universality applies to time as well as space. The comparison between ancient Ethiopian-Egyptian civilization and contemporary Africa has been a part of the tradition of modern Afrocentric scholarship since the early nineteenth century (Easton, 1969).

From a sociological viewpoint, the distinction is made in terms of the contrast of the nature of cultural orientation between African societies and Eurasian societies. Through time and space African people are found to have created peaceful, cooperative societies, stressing the moral obligations among fellow men; Eurasian societies are depicted as being nomadic, violent, aggressive, and egocentric. This truth is repeated again and again in the documents and studies of African intellectuals. For example, in the Ninth Dynasty of ancient Egypt during the twenty-first century B.C., the pharaoh Merikare passed on the following wisdom to his heir:

Be skillful in speech that you may be strong.
Words are more powerful than fighting ...
Comfort the weeper
do not oppress the widow
do not take a man's inheritance away
do not degrade your subordinates
do not punish wrongfully
do not kill

Lo the miserable Asiatic
He is wretched because of the place he's in
Short of water, bare of wood,
It's paths are many and painful because of
mountains.
He does not dwell in one place,
Food propels his ego,
He fights since the time of Horus.

(Lichtheim, 1975, p. 104)

This ancient text touches all aspects of the Afrocentric world:

1. Right compels the individual (other texts require the same conduct of all citizens) to assume as a primary responsibility for the welfare of all other citizens, especially those who are in distress.

2. Peace is the basis of social order.

3. Justice must be based upon the supremacy of law. (Obviously the "European and Arabian philosophers" stole these ideas from the Egyptians, as George G. M. James asserted in *Stolen Legacy*. The difference is that the Egyptians actually lived according to these ideas while the Eurasians only professed them, as Khaldun and Machiavelli pointed out.)

4. The Asiatics (Europeans as a distinct group had not yet arrived in the Egyptian world) were nomadic, violent, and basically savage. What is also apparent is

the fact that the worldview of the ancient Black
Egyptians contained the formulation of what emerges
in Cheikh Anta Diop as the Two Cradle Theory.
Diop's idea has been summarized as: "Existence was
so easy in the valley of the Nile...that the Egyptians
tended to believe that Nature's benefits poured down
from the sky...(Diop, 1974, p. 230) [and thus the]
Ethiopians and the Egyptians created and raised to an
extraordinary stage of development all the elements of
civilization" (Diop, 1974). In contrast, the "Eurasians
were still steeped in barbarism" (p. 230). Their spirit
was basically one of "rapine and conquest" because
they lived in a country "Unfavored by Nature" (p.
230). Thus, we find a continuity of this view from
the twentieth century B.C. throughout the twentieth
century A.D.

The African Worldview

The second assumption that the African worldview is the only
viable base for African liberation is equally supported by ancient and
continuous tradition. Conversely, when the leadership abandons these
principles the results have been disastrous. The truly great pharaohs of
ancient Egypt are all associated with the restoration of the ancient
world orientation. The last of these truly great restorers was perhaps
Shabaka of the so-called Twenty-fifth Dynasty, about 750 b.c.
Shabaka, one of the so-called Ethiopian pharaohs who established a
new capitol farther south than previous lineages, in ordering the
restoration of an ancient text (which the Egyptologists identify as the
Memphile theology) asserted:

> This writing was copied out anew by his majesty in the
> house of his father...for his majesty found it to be a work of
> the ancestors which was worm-eaten. (Lichtheim, 1975, p.
> 52)

Throughout the history of ancient Egypt the literature identified the period of disorder (yisfit) as the abandonment of the right way or *Maat*. The "prophets" always prophesied a restorer who would reestablish Maat—the ancient African world order.

While there is a great amount of controversy over the cause of the fall of Egypt, there are two factors that are undeniable: the infiltration of Eurasians and Eurasian cultural traits into the core of Egyptians in the Eighteenth Dynasty and the final overthrow of civilian priestly power by the military elite at the end of the Eighteenth Dynasty with the assassination of Tut Ankh Amun. The ancient wisdom, which always dictated the explusion of Asiatics and the triumph of *Horus* over *Seth* as the governing principle, was thus abandoned. This latter principle was a part of *Maat*. That is that rulership combined both right and *might*, but that *right* must always triumph over *might*. This principle was dramatized by the two crowns of upper and lower Egypt. The white crown of upper Egypt was the embodiment of *right* and was always worn by Osiris. The red crown of lower Egypt was symbolic of *might* and was worn along with the white crown by the living embodiment of power, the pharaoh. This principle was achieved through actual governance by a civilian prime minister symbolized by Jehewty, the divine manifestation of articulate speech (which, as previously stated, was mightier than fighting).

Although the lineage which included Shabaka was the last major defense of Egypt before the Eurasian onslaught, the restoration of the African world order continued through the successive rise of Meroe, Axum, Ghana, and the other African empires of more recent times in West, Central, Southern, and Eastern Africa. The documentary evidence is sparse and generally of a non-primary nature, but implicit in what is known of these great centers of civilization is the fact that they were built on the foundation of what the ancient Egyptians called *Maat*. Chancellor Williams' great work *The Destruction of Black Civilization* (1987) traces this historical phenomenon [see also John G. Jackson, *Introduction to African Civilizations* (1974)].

While it is conventionally popular to stress the superiority of European military technology, mainly fire power (e.g., the gun) as the major determining factor, historical accuracy impels us to take a closer examination. The gun does not account for the conquest of Egypt by

Assyria or of Sudan by the Arabs. It appears that in each successive ✱ instance of substantial African defeat, the abandonment of the principles of African social order made the societies vulnerable to foreign conquest. That theme has been very brilliantly dramatized by Ayi Kwei Armah's *Two Thousand Seasons* (1973), in which the abandonment of reciprocity and the toleration of crippled leaders are depicted as the conditions that caused the shame of Africa. The lust for power of these leaders at the expense of the African social order was the port of entry for Arab and European alike. The toleration and indulgence of these leaders must also include the masses of African people within these societies. Thus, while the corruption of the leaders was the major factor, the sympathy of the people was at least on the order of contributory negligence.

The one flaw in the ancient worldview which may have persisted seems to be the inability of African wisdom to account for the nature of the Eurasian. To return to Merikare, is it the "place he is in" which is "short of water (and) bare of wood" that makes him nomadic and makes him aggressive? The same question may be put to Diop. Does not history deny the possibility of really civilizing and humanizing those who by nature are barbarian?

✚ ✱ When the foundation for the modern African liberation movement was being prepared at the beginning of the triumph of Haiti over France, Britain, and Spain in August of 1791, Bookman, the architect of Haitian independence, taught:

> The god of the white man inspires him to crime. But our God orders us to do good work. Our God who is good to us orders us to revenge our wrongs. He will direct our arms and aid us. Throw away the image of the white man's god...and listen to Liberty which speaks in all our hearts.

Bookman's revolutionary principles were thus dedicated not only to military victory, but also to cultural restoration. ✱✚

Unfortunately, Toussaint abandoned the Bookman principle. Though he brought about a brilliant military victory over the three most powerful European superpowers of the day, his attempt to convert Saint Dominique into the first neocolonial subordinate of the New France proved to the masses of blacks, who had won their freedom

26

from slavery in a sea of blood, that Toussaint, at heart, was a Francophile and not a champion of the African world order. When Toussaint's naive love of French prestige led to his destruction, Dessalines arose from the shadows of semiobscurity and brought to fruition the revolutionary principles of Bookman. "Independence or Death" was his battle cry, and thus he rallied the African people to the triumph that destroyed the flower of Napoleon's great army. After the military victory, Dessalines asserted that never again would a European enter Haiti as a proprietor or colonist. He also raised the question: "What have we in common with that bloody-minded people?" He continued by asserting: "Their cruelties compared with our moderation...plainly tell us they are not our brethren; that they will never become such" (Stewart 1914, p. 239). This statement is the key to a modern African worldview. That is why Africa must be independent. Brotherhood or equality cannot exist between the Eurasian mentality and the African, therefore Africa cannot be dependent on European or Asian powers. We may play them against each other as Toussaint and Dessalines did, but history gives us no reason to believe that we can sit down as equals and negotiate a world order that will result in true African liberation.

Conclusion

I would like to conclude this historical sketch by briefly tracing out the nineteenth and twentieth century continuity of the African worldview. The major concepts of the African worldview can be seen in the thought of Hosea Easton who in 1837 traced out the history of the world as basically a clash between the bellicose Europeans and Asians on the one side and the peaceful African people on the other. Ironically Easton's own thought exhibited the problem of modern black thought because while he articulated the historical problem he also believed that the black man of the diaspora had been totally severed from the African cultural heritage. This tradition was also articulated by Henry Highland Garnet who said in 1848:

Numerous...instances...indicate the ancient fame of our ancestors. A fame which arose from every virtue, and talent that render mortals pre-eminently great. From the conquests of love and beauty, from the praisers of their arms, and their architecture, poetry, mathematics, generosity, and piety. (Bracey 1970, p. 120)

It was Garnet who five years earlier had issued the call for a slave rebellion, echoing the "Appeal" of David Walker in 1828.

Martin Delany was perhaps the most consistent advocate of this position from the early 1850s through the Civil War. Not only did he write consistently on the African world struggle, he was also prominent among the leaders of unilateral African struggle against slavery and European imperialism. This position was carried into Africa itself by Edward Wilmot Blyden, who was born in the West Indies and traveled to the United States before repatriating to West Africa. Blyden was perhaps the most active force for nationalism and Pan Africanism in West Africa before the rise of the more formal Pan African movement at the turn of the century.

The AME Bishop Henry McNeal Turner took up the mantle of Delany in the United States. Not only did he advocate the African worldview, but he was instrumental in forming institutional ties between Africans on the continent and North America. He was also an organizer and advocate of the Back to Africa Movement that was later revitalized by Marcus Garvey. During this period the African connection was so compelling that many of the assimilationists rallied to the formal Pan African organizations. Authentic African restoration had to be waged largely outside the inner circle of Negro celebrities who had not just abandoned the African principle, but were largely ignorant of its existence.

Neocolonialism besieged Africa at the very moment of political "independence" precisely because the African leaders had been nurtured on foreign ideologies and alien principles. Africa has thus become the battlefield for the world supremacy of Eurasian powers and the true interests of African people are all but ignored. It is this last fact that has been the major focus of those of us in the Association of African Historians (AAH) for the last several years. What we are simply saying is that the only appropriate social theory for African

28

people is one that is based solely on our interests which are summarized as the African worldview outlined in this essay.

R E F E R E N C E S

Armah, Ayi Kwei. 1973. *Two Thousand Seasons.* Nairobi: East African Publishing House.

ben-Jochannan, Yosef. 1972. *Black Man of the Nile.* New York: Alkebu-land Books.

Blyden, Edward W. 1967. "African Life and Customs" and "A Liberal Education for Africans," in *Christianity, Islam and the Negro Race.* Edinburgh: University of Edinburgh Press.

Bracey, John Jr., et al., eds. 1970. *Black Nationalism in America.* New York: Bobbs-Merrill.

Clarke, John Henrik. 1974. "Cheikh Anta Diop." *Freedom Ways,* fourth quarter.

Delany, Martin R. 1991. "International Policy of the World Toward Africa," in Frank Rollin, *The Life and Public Services of Martin R. Delany.* Lotham: University Press of Anenew.

—. 1991. *The Origin of Races and Color.* Baltimore: Black Classic Press.

Diop, Cheikh Anta. 1974. *The African Origin of Civilization: Myth or Reality.* Westport: Lawrence Hill.

Easton, Hosea. 1969. "A Treatise on the Intellectual Character and Civil and Political Condition of the Colored People of the United States." *Negro Protest Pamphlet,* ed. Dorothy Porter. New York: Ayer.

Jackson, John G. 1974. *Introduction to African Civilizations.* Secaucus, N. J.: The Citadel Press.

James, George G. M. 1954. *Stolen Legacy.* New York: Philosophical Library.

Khaldun, Ibin. 1967. *The Muqaddimah: An Introduction to History.* Translated by Franz Rosenthal, and edited by N.J. Dawood Princeton Bollingen Series.

Lichtheim, Miriam. 1975, 1976, 1980. *Ancient Egyptian Literature.* Berkeley: University of California, Berkeley Press.

Machiavelli, Niccolo. 1950. *The Prince and other Discourses.* New York: McGraw.

Stewart, T.G. 1914. *History of the Haitian Revolution, 1791–1804.* New York: Thomas-Newell.

Williams, Chancellor. 1976. *The Destruction of Black Civilization.* Chicago: Third World Press.

3
Thinking About European Thought

African intellectuals have never been amazed at the apparent contradictions in European or Western words and deeds. The Athenian love for democracy and slavery seem contradictory, as does the contemporary Western advocacy of democracy, equality, and freedom on the one hand and their maintenance of slavery, colonialism, and white supremacy on the other. These contradictions within the traditional Western camp have also been noticed among the Eastern radical opponents of the Occidental Tradition. Thus, Marx and Engels have been accused of racism (Carlos Moore 1973); and the communist movement as a whole has been criticized for its practice of white supremacy (Harold Cruse 1967).

A closer examination reveals that the contradictions and inconsistencies are more apparent than real, and that the traditional black perspective is somewhat simplistic. The European quest for omnipotence and omniscience seems to be at odds with freedom, the work ethic, and the scientific method; but they are quite unified at a deeper level. Those themes have also been consistent with significant aspects of European thought in antiquity. Obviously, insight into the historical and philosophical relationships among these aspects of European thought will be of significant interest to African people as we attempt to liberate ourselves from enslavement to Europeans. The actual liberation must be preceded by the liberation of our minds from intellectual tyranny. When we understand the mind of the oppressors then we can develop a successful plan.

A few preliminary remarks are appropriate before undertaking this examination of the European mind. We will abandon the misleading and inaccurate division between Europe and Asia, West and East, Occidental and Oriental. Linguistic, cultural, and biological data suggest that the Northwestern Europeans who have dominated the world for the last five hundred years are of the same stock as the Irano-Indians and Greeks of antiquity. In antiquity, these people identified themselves as Aryans, which means the Lords or Master people. Since that cultural motif has survived from prehistoric to contemporary times, it is quite appropriate that we recognize the Aryan people and culture as properly including the people who inhabit the Eurasian continent. This is especially significant since Europe is not a continent but an extension of the huge Northern continent. The differences between the Western and Eastern Aryans have been the constant theme of modern dialogue; the unity has often been ignored.

We will also abandon the traditional Western emphasis on the difference between the thoughts of Europeans of antiquity and those of modern Occidental man. For us the similarities between Plato and Marx, Aristotle and Adam Smith are much more important than their differences. Indeed, the similarities between the mythology and lore of Hesiod and the scientific philosophy of Francis Bacon are startling to those who have been anesthetized by European intellectual intrigues.

For the last two hundred years, black thinkers have examined Aryan thought as it relates to racism and the racial behavior of our oppressors. Such analysis has been invaluable, but repetitive. It is time now to recede from the periphery of race relations and prejudice and focus on the core of Aryan thought, that is, the Aryan worldview. Such a focus takes us away from the question, why do white folks treat us the way they do? Instead, we address the question, why do Aryans think and act as they do? This formulation in the long run is a more useful one because it will take us away from a debate which has consumed so much of our time. We have argued enough about which group of whites are more or less prejudiced, more or less brutal, more or less tolerant. Let us rather begin to analyze the Aryan, period. By so doing we will end another white monopoly, that is, the sacred field of critical European thought. No one is alarmed when white scholars become experts on black thought because whites are generally considered qualified to study blacks. But when a black scholar becomes an expert on white thought, a truly unique phenomenon will have arrived.

Work   and   the

European   Worldview

The value of work or labor has received universal acceptance among modern European thinkers. According to both capitalists and communists, work is the source of economic value and moral virtue. Indeed, Max Weber saw the work ethic and the spirit of capitalism as synonymous terms. Marx made no secret of the fact that the workers are the only revolutionary class within modern industrial society, and the *Communist Manifesto* issues the call to revolution in the name of "Workingmen" (no male chauvinism intended by either Marx or me).

Ironically, the capitalists, who proclaim the virtue of work the loudest, do not work, yet they receive all the value. Furthermore, under the capitalist regime, the workers receive no value as the *Manifesto* points out (Marx 1959, pp. 335–388). We must also remark, in passing, that the leaders and spokesmen for communism, like the capitalists, do not work. It seems that work, though highly valued, is reserved for the masses while the elites concentrate on ruling. But let us not too hastily confirm the contradiction. Perhaps there is a closer relationship between work and dominion than the satisfaction of the appetites of the ruling classes.

The contradiction, however, does appear awesome. The work ethic is said to have reached its peak in modern times among a people who in antiquity were famous for "loving indolence" (Tacitus 1970, p. 114). Tacitus asserts that concerning the German, "He thinks it tame and spiritless to accumulate slowly by the sweat of his brow (work) what can be got quickly by the loss of little blood" (p. 114). In fact, Tacitus attributes this in part to the following inherent characteristic: "They are less able to endure toil or fatiguing tasks" (p. 104). "When not engaged in warfare they spend a certain amount of time in hunting but much more in idleness" (p. 114). The Germans "have no taste for peace" (p. 113) and their major source of wealth was plunder. Yet in spite of the natural disinclination of the German people to toil, and even though the elites avoid labor, work is enthroned. The love of conquest and dominion, which seem to be the ethos of the Northwestern Europeans, would naturally lead to the opposite result, a praise of indolence, for example. One notices the same nature

35

characterized in the folk literature of other Aryan people such as the ancient Iranians and the classical Greeks (Avestas 1977, Theogony 1973). From whence then cometh the work ethic?

The answer to this question can be found in the early myth and lore of the Aryan people themselves. Everywhere among them we find that their leaders and prophets, who are worshiped as conquerors, are the patrons of industry and hard work (Hesiod 1973).

Before proceeding with the review of Aryan antiquity with respect to the work ethic, let us focus on the differences between the Aryan worldview and the African worldview. Diop has summarized the contrast thusly:

> The Meridional (African) Cradle...is characterized by the matriarchal family, the creation of the territorial state...the emancipation of woman in domestic life, xenophilia, cosmopolitanism,...collectivism,...a material solidarity of right for each individual.... In the moral domain, it shows an ideal of peace, of justice, of goodness and an optimism which eliminates all notion of guilt or original sin. (Diop, p. 195)

In contrast:

> The Northern Cradle...is characterized by the patriarchal family, by the city-state...xenophobia, individualism, moral and material solitude, a disgust for existence...an ideal of war, violence, crime and conquests (and) a feeling of guilt and of original sin, which causes pessimistic religious or metaphysical systems to be built. (Diop, p. 195)

Diop's conclusions about the character of the Aryan cultural orientation is compatible with Father Mongameli Mabona who asserted that Aryan philosophy was based on: a quest for illumination, polytheism, and a belief in divine origin of their race.

Work and Domination in
Aryan Antiquity

In Aryan life, the curious relationship between work with its aura of peace and dominion with its aura of violence is probably a function of the transition from nomadic to sedentary culture. This transition was recognized by the writers of classical Greek antiquity (Thucydides 1943, pp. 350–351). The Zarathustrian Revolution in Iranian history seems also to be a movement against the traditional nomadic culture in favor of establishing a sedentary agricultural society (Avestas, vol. 3; Yasna, p. xxix). The same may be said of changes in the Hindu culture. The cause of the transformation may well have been the impact of African civilization on the Aryan culture of antiquity as George G. M. James and Cheikh Anta Diop have stated. Certainly the emergence of Greek philosophy was largely a reaction of certain Hellenic sages to their Egyptian education (James 1954). Diop said: "It is impossible to stress all that the...Hellenistic world...owed to the Egyptians. The Greeks merely continued and developed, sometimes partially, what the Egyptians had invented" (p. 230). Thus, it may have been that sedentary values like work were engrafted onto the cultural ethos of the Aryans after they made contact with the high civilizations of the Indian Peninsula, Mesopotamia, and the Nile Valley.

Whatever the source, we find the work ethic in the earliest recorded thoughts side by side with the mosaic of fundamental Aryan orientations. A review of these themes will clarify the matrix from which the work ethic emerges.

Cosmic disorder is the pervading theme of Aryan myth and the emergence of the goddess Gaea (Earth) preceded by Chaos in Greek mythology is the epitome of the phenomenon (Hesiod, p. 27). Gaea spawned order (i.e., the sky, mountains, ocean, and ultimately humanity) while Chaos gave birth to black night and Erebos (underworld, darkness and ultimately blame, distress, Nemesis, deceit, old age, strife, and wretched work) (pp. 27–30). Thus, in Hellenic myth, one encounters duality as in Iranian and Germanic myths. Conflict between two diametrically opposed forces is the basis of Aryan polytheism. Order is opposed by an irreconcilable antiorder. The idea of constant wars between these principles leading to an inevitable

37

Armageddon is ensconced in the ethos of Aryan culture. Conflict emerges as the basic orientation to relationship.

This cosmic conflict is reflected in the relationship between the gods and goddesses. The strife between Gaea (mother Earth) and Ouranus (father Sky) led to the downfall of Ouranus; the conflict between their son and daughter, Kronos and Rhea, who became mates, led to the downfall of Kronos. In turn, Zeus and Hera, the children of Kronos and Rhea, were constantly at odds. The theme of male-female conflict is undoubtedly related to the lowly status of women in Aryan cultures which Diop analyzes in *The Cultural Unity of Black Africa*.

This deadly conflict between motherhood and fatherhood leads directly to conflict between father and son. Thus, Kronos becomes his father's enemy and literally emasculates him at the bidding of his mother. Likewise, Zeus becomes the chief of the gods by violently dethroning his father Kronos. These acts of would-be patricide were preceded by acts of would-be infanticide on the part of the fathers.

Even in the realm of order, deceit, disloyalty, and brutality constantly plague the celestial realm of the gods. Warfare is a way of life and the military victor is praised for his success, regardless of his means. The brutal war between the gods and Titans is a war between brothers. The same is true of the daily battles in Asgard from Nordic myth and of the Bhagavad-Gita from Hindu lore.

In the midst of divine discord, Zeus, who "had become king in heaven" (Hesiod 1973, p. 25) stands above the rest. The most important thing about Zeus is his freedom. As Aeschylus put it in *Prometheus Bound,* "all things are a burden save to rule over the gods, for none is free but Zeus" (Aeschylus, p. 40). Zeus is viewed as having arbitrary power over men and the other gods. Although he cannot kill his fellow gods who, like him, are immortal, "through his great will...each is famous or unknown" (Hesiod 1973, p. 59). Zeus, with his enormous will and power over men and gods, is the model for all European concepts of freedom. Freedom, in its broadest operational sense, is the power to do what one wants. This includes using other beings for one's selfish whims.

The human condition is founded upon divine disharmony and caprice of the most powerful divinity. As the king of gods, Zeus had the power to distribute the good things according to his will. As

Aeschylus put it:

> To diverse gods, diverse goods he gave...but of miserable
> men, recked not at all, rather it was his wish to wipe out
> man. (Aeschylus, p. 42)

Hesiod reiterates that "Zeus will destroy this race of men." The human condition willed by Zeus is miserable. "Fathers...have no common bond with son, neighbor with neighbor...guest with host, nor friend with friend brother-love (is) gone. Men dishonor...parents who grow old too quickly...men...destroy the towns of other men, the just...(are) dispersed but men will praise the bad...might (is) right" (Hesiod, p. 64) Originally, mankind, though given hardly anything with which to survive, was at least "apart from sorrow and from painful work, free from disease" (p. 61). All of this changed when the god Prometheus, against the will of Zeus, used trickery in an attempt to improve man's lot. Prometheus asserted:

> I took from man expectancy of death...(and) conferred the
> gift of fire (so that man could) master many arts thereby.
> (Aeschylus, p. 42)

As punishment, Zeus created woman, Pandora, who was given:

> A face like an immortal goddess...
> the lovely figure of a virgin girl,
> sly manners and the morals of a bitch... (Hesiod, p. 61).

Lies were "put in her breast" and she was given "persuasive words and cunning ways." So equipped, she became the "ruin of mankind" (p. 61). She opened up the box "and scattered pains and evils among men" (p. 62).

Mankind is thus doomed to misery because they "love this ruin in their hearts" (p. 61). Women, who are indispensable to man's enjoyment, can never be trusted. Hesiod warns, "Don't let a woman, wiggling her behind and flattering and coaxing take you in...woman is just a cheat" (p. 70). The theme of divine discord, which emphasizes the conflict between the male and female divinities, is inherent in human life.

It is from this mythological conception of the miserable human condition that the work ethic arises in Greek antiquity. Ironically, the work ethic emerges out of a general depreciation of work. Work is "painful" (Hesiod p. 61). "By day men work and grieve unceasingly" (p. 64). The golden race which was the first and most noble race fashioned by the gods was "untouched by work or sorrow" (p. 62).

But as degraded as work is, it offers the only salvation to the present race of mankind. Thus, there is a work imperative inherent in the human condition. Furthermore, the spirit of strife is a part of human nature. "Strife was set by Zeus...in the roots of earth [and is] an aid to men [because] she urges even lazy men to work." As a result of this tendency, competition is the basis of human interaction. As Hesiod put it:

> A man grows eager, seeing another rich from ploughing, planting, and ordering his house. So neighbor vies with neighbor in the rush for wealth; this strife is good for mortal men. Potter hates potter, carpenters compete, and beggar strives with beggar, bard with bard. (p. 59)

Miserable work is thus ironically the key to success and the good life because "Badness can be caught in great abundance easily...But good is harder, for the gods have placed in front of her much sweat...and thus from working men grow rich...and dearer to the deathless gods" (pp. 67–68). Therefore there is no shame in work, rather shame lies in idleness (p. 68). Work is indeed better because "the gods have given work to men" (p. 71). As a consequence, a man should always stay busy and resist the opportunity to "put work off for another day" (p. 72) and "wile away time by gossip" (pp. 74–75). Clearly then, in European antiquity, the work ethic emerges as the foundation of progress and the good life. The competitiveness and individualism found so valuable in modern European life are rooted in the values of the Hellenes who are credited with the birth of Western civilization.

Let us hasten to point out that the good man is saved from ceaseless toil because he is advised to first get an unmarried female slave to help in the fields (p. 71) and is instructed on the proper use of his slaves for maximum productivity. In fact, the good man seems to be involved not so much in menial work himself but with the organization of work for his slaves (p. 68). Thus, though mankind is doomed to work, some men are masters who supervise menials who in turn do the actual work. Thus, the men who are "dearer to the gods" (Hesiod, p. 68) appear to be god-like in that they, like the gods, arrange tasks or ordeals for other men.

One of the clearest renditions of the total and endemic cosmic conflict which characterizes early Aryan thought can be found in the *Avestas* of Iran. Between the two conflicting forces in this high stakes battle, men must choose the right side, the side that will win.

> the primeval spirits who as a pair...
> have been formed (as) a better thing...
> and a worse, as to thought, as to work and
> as to deed...between these two let the wisely
> acting choose aright (because) the two spirits
> come together at the first to make life and
> shall at the last be...for the wicked the worst
> life, for the holy the best mental state.
>
> [*Zend Avestas* Part III, pp. 29–30]

Another verse tells us that those who:

> cleave unto the Victorious Saoshyant (the Savior) and his
> helpers when he shall restore the world...will (thenceforth)
> never grow old and never die...the dead will rise, when life
> and immortality will come (but) the Drug (evil) shall
> perish, though she may rush on every side to kill the holy
> beings; she and her hundredfold brood shall perish, as it is
> the will of the Lord.
>
> [*Zend Avestas* Part II, pp. 306–7]

Thus, in the end, Armageddon will engulf the entire creation including the cosmos and man, and the good and bad will be locked in a war to the finish. This is the thrust of all Aryan mythology and this is especially so with European mythology. Examples of these myths are the *Eddas*, Greek and Roman mythology, the *Avestas* of Iran and the *Vedas* of India. The outcome of this final confrontation is predicted as good in some accounts (the *Avestas*) and bad in others (the *Eddas*).

In sum, the Aryan worldview of antiquity, which includes the classical Greeks, is based upon a fundamental assumption of cosmic conflict, hostility between male and female principles, patricide, infanticide, alienation between god and man, warfare between man and nature, competition and strife among men, and slavery as a natural human institution. This Eurasian orientation, that is deeply embedded in the Aryan worldview, can be called fundamental alienation. This is the context of the work ethic that requires work for the achievement of success, progress, and the Good Life but which permits some men to live the Good Life by dominating others who do the hard work but do not themselves achieve the Good Life. Such is the legacy of ancient Western culture. Man must rework or dominate nature in order to survive and prosper. Thus, work is "bossing" others who do the really necessary work.

Dominion and Work in the Modern Western Philosophy of Science

The reduction of work to tertiary status by Plato and Aristotle echoed the general Aryan practical solution to the disdain for work and the recognition that work was a necessary activity for somebody else to do. The Aryan Indians also relegated the working citizens to the third caste behind the priests and administrator warriors; the more menial work was reserved for the outcasts. The work ethic, which was obscured by the protocols of the Greco-Roman and feudal orders, emerged to new heights among the northwestern Europeans as they began their rise to world dominion (see Max Weber, *The Protestant Ethic and the Spirit of Capitalism*).

The work ethic is not only the "spirit of capitalism" and communism, as I have already indicated, but it is also the essential spirit of modern Western science. Francis Bacon was one of the earliest articulators of the reformation of European thought which emerged from the Renaissance and the Protestant Reformation. He taught that the Good Life could be achieved only by a conscientious, thorough, and continuous working over of nature, similar to the way in which a master craftsman works over his raw materials to make a precision product. For Bacon, the wedding of knowledge and work is based upon the biblical wisdom of Solomon. Bacon wrote that "the Glory of God is to conceal a thing; the glory of (man is) to search it out" (Bacon, p. 538). Thus, the most noble ambition for Bacon was "to establish and extend the power and dominion of the human race...over the universe" (p. 539). In other words, man must work to achieve an "empire of man over things" because the ultimate object is to "command nature" (p. 539). Hesiod's assertion that "the gods hid the stuff of life from men" is thus restated as a cornerstone of the new science. Bacon's assertion that "knowledge and power are synonymous" (p. 46) is the essence of modern science. The careful working over of nature is thus equated with exercising power, or dominion, over things. The scientist must be a master craftsman creating a precise model of nature to obey the will of man. Bacon thought Europeans who had developed this workmanship like orientation were gods in comparison to the peoples of cultures who had not developed the work ethic (p. 538).

Bacon's scientific thought was based upon a number of assumptions. The first was that nature was basically devious or subtle. He felt that undisciplined intelligence was no match for nature. Therefore, the seeker of the secrets of nature had to submit to a rigorous and arduous regime, first surrendering to nature and later seducing from nature her secrets. Bacon consciously drew an analogy between nature and woman (pp. 459, 522, 531). Men who wanted to penetrate her secrets had to do more than speculate, argue, and orate; they had to actually outwit her through rigid discipline and hard work. In this endeavor man could take nothing for granted. He must work every step of the way.

Thus, for Bacon, science was not so much a body of knowledge to be uncovered by human insight but rather a process of knowing. Bacon assumed that man could know nothing unless that knowledge proceeded out of the experiential world. The major problem of human thought was thus an epistemological problem. What can be known and how can it be known? This casual science is easily reduced to the following formula: I know it because I can control it; I can control it, therefore I know it.

Bacon emphasized the inductive method of knowing and

established the rationale for the modern concept of the experimental method which is the epitome of modern science. This method is, as Bacon pointed out, easy to state but hard to practice. What it requires is that the scientist first of all surrender to nature by the endless observation of minutia. Finally, after such discipline, he/she must take the thing from nature and put it in a laboratory where it can be subjected to the will of the scientist who can then torture from it its secrets. The changing of nature's nature is the ultimate object of science. As long as nature goes her own way, according to Bacon, man will benefit scarcely.

While engaged in this very important work, scientists must free themselves from the pressures to produce useful results, although the ultimate and final justification for the pursuit of knowledge must be "none other than...that human life be endowed with new discoveries and power" (Bacon, p. 499). The work of the scientist is to search for the truth of causation. He or she must therefore pursue experiments of light rather than those of fruit (pp. 516–517, 530–531). In other words, the scientist must stick to his business and leave political, social, and economic affairs alone.

All of this is necessary so that nature, or things, can be "duly investigated...verified...counted, weighed and measured." This is because for Bacon "the secrets of nature reveal themselves more readily under the vexations of art than when they go their own way" (p. 516). Humans are in a deadly contest against nature for survival and prosperity, like the capitalistic entrepreneur and therefore must take a risk and "stake all on the victory of art over nature in the race" (p. 528).

Here we can see clearly that the principle of balance with which the African worldview approaches nature is abandoned. Any negotiation with nature in the European mind is merely a strategy, a subterfuge to gain an advantage toward nature's unconditional surrender. Africans treat nature as an equal. Europeans treat nature as a defiant slave to be broken. Again, the real good life for the European is to be the "boss."

Bacon advised that he was "building in the human understanding a true model of the world" which requires "a very diligent dissection and anatomy of the world" because "whatever deserves to exist deserves also to be known, for knowledge is the image of existence" (pp. 430,

534). Such work will lead to "new creations and imitations of God's works" (p. 538). The scientific man and those who share his culture will become men who are "God to man...in regard of aid and benefit [and] by a comparison of condition" (p. 538). So European man becomes the master of men from the "barbarous districts" of the world.

This view of science reached its peak three hundred years later during the early twentieth century in the thought of Sigmund Freud, the father of the modern Western science of psychology. Freud proclaimed: "Our best hope for the future is that intellect, the scientific spirit, reason—may in process of time establish a dictatorship of the mental life of man" (Freud, p. 171). He further asserted: "Truth cannot be tolerant...it admits of no compromises or limitations, (scientific) research regards every sphere of human activity as belonging to it and...it must be relentlessly critical of any of it" (p. 160).

Freud's view of modern science is the logical extension of Bacon's more modestly put formulation. He pointed out that modern science:

> asserts that there are no sources of knowledge of the universe other than the intellectual working over of carefully scrutinized observations—in other words, what we call research—and alongside of it no knowledge derived from revelation, intuition or divination. (p. 159)

Thus, science is the master discipline and modern science is, as stated elsewhere, the "Science of Oppression" (Carruthers, p. 18). This "matter-of-fact" knowledge is compatible with the character of modern Europeans who "are to a peculiar degree capable of an impersonal dispassionate insight into the material facts with which mankind has to deal" (Veblen, p. 1). One of the obvious bases for the wedding of the scientific viewpoint with the work ethic is the new organization of work in the modern era. The machine-like organization of labor is the model par excellence for modern science. While science did little to improve industry until quite recent times, it nonetheless developed along the same path. Modern science thus:

> Is the Master's science, not only in the sense that he uses it to control his subjects, but also in the sense that it was

established through and for oppression. That is, the original assumptions *are* oppression, suppression and repression. Thus, the science or methodology is not neutral or objective; it is the science of control through intervention and/or the unnatural alteration (if possible) of all objects. When intervention and modification are successful, then the hypothesis is proved; if not, then impurification in the application of the methodology is alleged (either because of limited primary knowledge or bias). Thus, the conquest of Africa is not basically different from the conquest of uranium. Both started with a theory about harnessing certain forces and subduing certain oppositions to the desired change. Both required laboratory experiments (cyclothrons for uranium and the West Indies slave system for Africans). Both resulted in the unnatural re-ordering of the behavior of the objects. Less the analogy be depreciated, we must realize that social science or philosophy occupies almost the same position *vis-`a-vis* governance or social policy as does pure science *vis-`a-vis* applied science or technology. (Carruthers, p. 3)

Work and the War Against Nature

Although Marxists are the modern champions of the workers, insisting on the dignity of labor and asserting that the workers will inherit the earth, it is to the pioneers of modern capitalism that credit should go for elevating the work ethic to the heights of philosophic insight. One of the most articulate holders of the position was John Locke who viewed men as the "workmanship of one omnipotent and infinitely wise maker...sent into the world by his order, and about his business—they are his property whose workmanship they are" (Locke 1952, pp. 5–6). Locke's reasoning was based on the premises that originally the earth and its fruits were "given to mankind in common," (p. 16) but, because the fruits belong to all men in common, men would starve to death, so "there must...be a means to appropriate" the fruits. The right to appropriate for private consumption for Locke is based upon the fact that individuals must labor or work to take the fruit from nature for their nourishment. About the individual who exerts himself, Locke points out:

> The labor of his body and the work of his hands...are properly his. Whatsoever...he removes out of...nature...is his own...it is his property. (p. 17)

Work is thus the basis of property, and property is the *sine qua non*, the alpha and omega of the good life. The promotion of work was the underlying motive that bid some men to "enclose" or fence off some land for their private use. According to Locke, the enclosure of land "improved" the conditions of man because "of the products of the earth useful to the life of man, nine tenths are the effects of labor" (p. 25). According to this view "labor makes the far greatest part of the value of things we enjoy in this world."

> Land that is left wholly to nature...is called...wasted; and...the benefit of it amount(s) to little more than nothing. (p. 25)

Locke's position, therefore, was that "God commanded man...to labor [and] to subdue the earth, (i.e., improve it)" (p. 20). He also pointed out that subduing or cultivating the earth, (i.e., working it over) and having dominion are synonymous (p. 21). The natural condition of man, which required that man work or exercise dominion over the earth, would result in very little work because "God has given us all things richly." Thus most of the potentially valuable things would not be produced because, as Hesiod had put it twenty-three hundred years earlier, a man could "work for a day and earn a year's supplies," or, as Locke himself put it, man would have no "reason...to enlarge his possessions beyond the use of his family" (p. 29). Therefore, the conditions among men would be substantially equal, but somewhat bland if not meager. So the goodies had to be better hidden from men in order to make them work more, so that Bacon's dream of human dominion over nature could be realized. In other words, man had to declare war against nature.

The invention which permitted this beneficent act to occur was,

47

for Locke, money, which "gave [men] the opportunity to continue and enlarge" their possessions (p. 28). Because most men irrationally placed a value on "gold and silver," which were useless to fill man's natural needs, "it is plain...that men have agreed to a disproportionate and unequal possession of the earth" (p. 29). Thus, some men took these worthless shiny objects in exchange for food and land, and implicitly not only lost the land but lost the money as well. A few men wound up with most of the land, and money thus brought about a condition of inequality.

Implicitly, according to Locke, it was men who made the "stuff of life" scarce. This resulted in artificial scarcity and alternation of nature. Men who by nature would have worked very little now have to work a very great deal more in order to "earn a year's supplies." In fact most men are forced to toil ceaselessly for the same sustenance which they enjoyed before nature was tampered with.

Thus, Locke not only "found a way how a man may *fairly* possess more than he himself could use," he also found a way that the most successful men of all can own everything without working. Such a fraud-like operation is explained in part by the fact that "different degrees of industry are apt to give men possessions in different proportions" (p. 28). In Locke's view, when the money game is invented the "industrious and rational" (p. 20) evidently get the upper hand and wind up with the goodies and the money. These nonworking, godlike owners provide the opportunity for the rest of mankind to fulfill God's command by working to improve the products of the earth.

The work ethic, which has been extolled since the time of Homer, was finally put into perspective by the modern European thinkers who interwove the work ethic with an aspiration to dominate all others and all things. Work was necessary in order to subdue the earth. The godlike men who direct this activity do not themselves have to work. This explains how work is viewed as miserable and noble at the same time. This modern European ethos was summed up by Henri de Saint-Simon who proclaimed that this new spirit is "called upon to link together the scientists, artists, and industrialists, and to make them the managing directors of the human race" (Saint-Simon, p. 105).

Since Europeans are the only portion of mankind that have

achieved this level of industry, they are godlike when compared to others. Even the lowest ranks of Europeans are masters *vis-`a-vis* other people because, as Locke put it, "a king of a large and fruitful (non-European) territory…feeds, lodges, and is clad worse than a day-laborer in England" (Locke, p. 25). Thus, the elite among Europeans dominate other Europeans who all together dominate all other portions of mankind who in turn, with their masters directing them, will exercise dominion over nature. So it goes, God (Zeus) is free in relation to all others; godlike men are free in relationship to all other Europeans; Europeans are free in relationship to all other men; and mankind is free in comparison to nature, which, like the cheese in the children's game "The Farmer in the Dell," stands alone. The children's rhyme dramatizes how the farmer in the dell takes a wife, the wife takes a child, the child takes a cat, the cat takes a rat, the rat takes some cheese, and the cheese stands alone. Notice the hierarchy of dominance in this nursery rhyme, which was also a game that was part of the rearing culture of European children for generations.

Implicit in Thomas Hobbes' political thought is the necessity for man to wage war against nature because, according to the Eurocentric prospective, man in the state of nature lives a violent and short life which would ultimately destroy the species. Work is one level of conquest designed to solve the problem, while "bossing" is how some men escape the misery of work.

The Borrowed Legacy

The irony of European thought is that so much of it was borrowed from ancient African people. James' analysis shows clearly that what was called philosophy by the ancient Greeks began as an attempt to incorporate the mystery system of the Egyptians into Hellenic culture (James 1954). European thinkers succeeded in grafting African ideas on a diametrically opposed worldview. Diop explains this seldom mentioned African connection:

> It is impossible to stress all that…the Hellenistic world owed the Egyptians. The Greeks merely continued and developed, sometimes partially, what the Egyptians had

invented. By virtue of their materialistic tendencies, the
Greeks stripped those inventions of the religious, idealistic
shell in which the Egyptians had enveloped them...the
worldly genius of the Greeks, emanating basically...from
their religious indifferences, favored the existence of a
secular, worldly science. (pp. 230–31)

Added to the irony of borrowing from the diametrically opposed
African way, the European thinker, while generally suppressing insight
concerning the African connection and debasing black culture, exuded
a veiled admiration for ancient African civilization.

Bacon's conclusions are instructive. Although he asserted that
"the sciences which we possess come...from the Greeks," he agreed
with the "judgement...concerning the Greeks by the Egyptian
priest—they were always boys, without antiquity of knowledge or
knowledge of antiquity" (Bacon p. 491). Bacon was quoting from
Plato (*Timaeus*), who two thousand years earlier had also given the
Egyptians subdued praise. Bacon also cryptically applauded the
"Egyptians who rewarded inventors with divine honors and sacred
rites" (p. 492). For Bacon, the Egyptians exemplified the correct
judgement of antiquity and demonstrated that "the introduction of
famous discoveries...had by far the first place among human actions
(which) was the judgement of the former ages" (p. 537). Bacon did
not deal with the context of such Egyptian cultural practices, but, as
expected, he interpreted them from the Eurocentric perspective. The
African orientation to invention was one of cooperation and
negotiation with nature rather than conquest and dominion over
nature.

Added to this double irony of European cultural plunder and
concealed admiration is the fact that many modern black thinkers have
borrowed the European perspective for their own intellectual guidance.
Most of these conforming black intellectuals have taken issue with
some aspects of the European position, yet their objection to European
thought, for the most part, has been concerned with what I consider
the periphery of the European worldview. They have concentrated on
racism, this is, for example, why do European scholars hold such
demeaning views and hostile opinions towards black people? The last
chapter of W.E.B. Du Bois' *Black Reconstruction* is a good example of

this trend. In his examination of what he calls the "Propaganda of History," Du Bois accuses the American historians of abandoning scientific methods in their dealing with blacks and substituting their racist biases, which have had a detrimental effect on race relations (Du Bois pp. 711–728). It is interesting to note what Du Bois said of one of the most prominent white scholars who was guilty of this practice: "Subtract from Burgess his belief that only white people can rule, and he is in essential agreement with me" (p. 726). A similar sentiment has guided most black intellectual concern with white thought. The position of black sociologist, Robert Staples, who distinguishes between white sociology and general sociology, follows this Du Boisian pattern.

Those who have taken a different path *vis-`a-vis* European thought have usually joined forces with European radical critics of the European tradition such as Marx. Gerald McWorther, in "The Ideology of Black Social Science" (1973), revises the Marxist theory in analyzing the problem of racist thought in the social sciences (pp. 173–189). However, in a more balanced assessment, Dennis Forsythe points out that radical Marxist, as well as traditional European theories are implicitly, if not explicitly racist, and must be approached with caution (Forsythe 1973, pp. 213–233).

The ultimate purpose of such critiques of white intelligentsia is to assess the impact of racist ideas on social reality. The methodological issue involved in such critiques is the extent to which the European intellectual framework can be used to overcome the oppression caused by those same ideas. Most black intellectuals have tended to hold the opinion that European research methods can be used fruitfully by black intellectuals, provided they are suitably modified to eliminate racism. Needless to say these studies have not dealt directly with the study of European thought at its core.

These black thinkers have been aptly described by E. Franklin Frazier who, for the most part, worked well within the tradition which he criticized. In 1973 Frazier said:

> The American Negro intellectual goes his merry way discussing such matters as the superficial aspects of material standard of living among Negroes and the extent to which they enjoy civil rights...Negro intellectuals have failed to achieve any intellectual freedom. (pp. 270–271)

51

According to Frazier, this absence of intellectual freedom among black thinkers has resulted in Blacks having "no philosophers or thinkers who command the respect of the intellectual community at large" (p. 273). Frazier's own enslavement to white judgement thus blinded him to the fact that we do have "men who have reflected upon the fundamental problems which have always concerned philosophers such as the nature of human knowledge and the meaning or lack of meaning of human existence" (p. 273) and equally important matters.

Intellectual Freedom

Most black scholars who are enslaved by European intellectuals have been shunted to the periphery of the European worldview and participate in what Anderson Thompson calls "sambo historiography" (Thompson 1975, p. 7). This occupation has led to a considerable body of literature in which the black scholars take issue with the findings of white research into slave rebellions. This is the crux of Du Bois' work on reconstruction and John Hope Franklin's work on "Negro" history.

The rejection of this tradition is long and honorable. The Black thinkers who have analyzed the core of the European worldview have, as it were, become intellectual maroons. Like the maroons who declared their freedom in fact through their actions, the intellectual maroons have declared their freedom through their publicly stated thoughts.

This historical, independent concern, with the thought and behavior of the Eurasians emerged centuries later in the Haitian Revolution, which was perhaps the most brutal war in modern history, but one that Blacks won decisively. Dessalines, the liberator of the Haitian people, queried concerning the French: "What have we in common with that bloody-minded people?" (Rainsford 1805, p. 483). Indeed, the deeds of the French in that encounter were so devoid of human decency that many European commentators made negative evaluations.

In the United States this tradition of black analysis continued throughout the nineteenth century. Hosea Easton wrote a brief historical sketch of the history of African-European relations in which he said, the Europeans:

> Were in the deepest state of heathenish barbarity. A
> continual scene of bloodshed and robbery was attendant on
> the increase of their numbers. Their spread over different
> countries covered almost an entire extinction of all civil and
> religious governments, and of the liberal arts and sciences.
> And even since that period, all Europe and America have
> been little else than one great universal battle field. (p. 18)

Edward Wilmot Blyden described the phenomenon as "the harsh
and stern fiber of the Caucasian races" (Blyden 1971, p. 278). More
recently Mongameli Mabona, analyzing the basic patterns of European
thought stated thusly:

> Three fundamental characteristics of the European emerge:
> (a) [the] search for illumination; (b) belief in the
> multiplicity of gods; (c) belief in the divine origin of his
> race…this basic orientation is towards clearness of logic and
> truth. (p. 63)

These insights, coupled with the analysis by Diop, give us a basic
Afrocentric grasp of the real European mind. From this perspective we
can stop taking issue with the European intellectuals, the biases, blatant
effronteries, and inaccuracies of slave rebellion research. We can ignore
slave rebellion research and turn to the more relevant task of
researching the oppressor. In recent years, a handful of black
psychologists have joined that tradition of intellectual freedom by
studying the European. A very stimulating essay in this regard was
entitled "Voodoo or I.Q." and written by Clark, McGee, Nobles, and,
Weems (*Journal of Black Psychology*, 1975). The works of Bobby
Wright are also brilliant insights into the collective psyche of the
Europeans (see *The Psychopathic Racial Personality*, 1984). Joseph
Baldwin has also contributed to this great effort (see "Education and
Oppression in the American Context," *Journal of Inner City Studies*,
1979).

Conclusion

This essay has explored the core of the European worldview. While there are significant differences among Europeans which were not emphasized in this study, we may still safely conclude that whatever their place in time or position on the ideological spectrum, all recognized European thinkers:

> See mastery of nature including human nature as the purpose of human life. And they all want to replace the present rulers of the world with their gang! Thus, they are nothing but rationalizers of the general European mania— Bossism!

Africans who participate in those battles—those European civil wars—entertain fantasies much wilder than the myths of the European oracles. The Europeans often make their myths prevail in reality but the African's Eurocentric fantasy remains a figment of his/her imagination. Let us abandon these myth makers and start studying the enemy on our own terms and in our interests.

Christopher Marlowe, in his drama *Tamburlaine The Great*, captured the eternal ethos of the European worldview. He put these words in the mouth of the great Aryan conqueror Tamburlaine, who lusted for only one thing, to rule through conquest.

> Tamb. The thirst of reign and sweetness of a crown
> That caused the eldest son of heavenly Ops,
> To thrust his doting father from his chair,
> And place himself in the empyreal Heaven,
> Moved me to manage arms against thy state.
> What better precedent than mighty Jove?
> Nature that framed us of four elements,
> Warring within our breasts for regiment,
> Doth teach us all to have aspiring minds:
> Our soul, whose faculties can comprehend
> The wondrous architecture of the world,
> And measure every wandering planet's course,
> Still climbing after knowledge infinite,
> And always moving as the restless spheres.
> Will us to wear ourselves, and never rest.

Until we reach the ripest fruit of all,
That perfect bliss and some felicity,
The sweet fruition of an earthly crown. (p. 27)

R E F E R E N C E S

Aeschylus. 1975. *Prometheus Bound.* Translated by James Sculley and C. J. Herrington. London: Oxford University Press.

Avestas. 1977. *The Sacred Books of the East.* Parts II and III, vols. 4, 23, 31. Ed. by F. Max Müller. New Delhi: Asian Educational Services.

Bacon, Francis. 1955. *Novum Organum. Selected Writings of Francis Bacon.* Ed. by Hugh G. Dich. New York: Modern Library.

Baldwin, Joseph. 1979. "Education and Oppression in the American Context." *Journal of Inner City Studies*, vol. 1.

Blyden, Edward Wilmot. 1971. *Black Spokesman: Selected Published Writings of Edward Wilmot Blyden.* London: Frank Cass and Co.

Clark, Cedric, et al. 1975. "Voodoo or I.Q." *Journal of Black Psychology.*

Carruthers, Jacob H. 1975. "The Capitalistic Roots of Karl Marx's Communistic Theory." *Afrocentric World Review*, vol. 1, no. 3.

—. 1972. *Science and Oppression.* Chicago: Kemetic Institute.

Cruse, Harold. 1967. *The Crisis of the Negro Intellectual.* New York: William Morrow.

Diop, Cheikh Anta. 1974. *The African Origin of Civilization: Myth or Reality.* Westport: Lawrence Hill.

—. 1978. *The Cultural Unity of Black Africa.* Chicago: Third World Press.

Du Bois, W.E.B. 1968. *Black Reconstruction in America 1860–1880.* New York: The World Publishing Company.

Easton, Hosea. "A Treatise on the Intellectual Character and Civil and Political Condition of the Colored People of the United States." *Negro Protest Pamphlets*, ed. Dorothy Porter. New York: Ayer.

Freud, Sigmund. 1991. *New Introductory Lectures in Psychoanalysis.* Translated and edited by James Strachey, assisted by Angela Richards. London: Penguin Books.

Forsythe, Dennis. 1973. "Radical Sociology and Blacks" in *The Death of White Sociology.* Ed. by Joyce A. Ladner. New York: Vintage Books Random House.

Franklin, John Hope. 1971. *From Slavery to Freedom.* New York: Alfred A. Knopf.

Frazier, E. Franklin. 1973. "The Failure of the Negro Intellectual" in *The Death of White Sociology.* Ed. by Joyce A. Ladner. New York: Vintage Books Random House.

Gerber, H. A. 1923. *Myths of Northern Lands.* New York: American Book Company.

Hesiod. 1973. "Theogony" and "Works and Days" in *Hesiod and Theognis.* Translated and with introductions by Dorothea Wender. Middlesex: Penguin Books.

Hobbes, Thomas. 1958. *The Leviathan.* Parts I and II. New York: Bobbs-Merrill.

James, George G. M. 1954. *Stolen Legacy.* New York: Philosophical Library.

Locke, John. 1952. *The Second Treatise on Government.* New York: Bobbs-Merrill.

Mabona, Mongameli. "Towards an African Philosophy." *Presence Africaine,* vol. unknown.

Marlowe, Christopher. *Tamburlaine in Five Plays.* 3rd printing. Ed. by Havelok Ellis. New York: Hill and Wang.

Marx, Karl and Capitol. 1959. *The Communist Manifesto and Other Writings.* Edited and with an introduction by Max Eastman. New York: The Hudson Library.

McWorther, Gerald. 1973. "The Ideology of Black Social Science" in *The Death of White Sociology.* Ed. Joyce A. Ladner. New York: Vintage Books Random House.

Moore, Carlos. 1972. *Were Marx and Engles White Racists?* Chicago: Third World Press.

Plato. 1949. *The Timaeus.* New York: The Liberal Arts Press.

Rainsford, Marcus. 1805. *An Historical Account of the Black Empire of Haiti.* London: Albion Press.

Saint-Simon, Henri de. 1964. *The New Christianity in Social Argougateola. The Science of Man and Other Writings.* New York: Harper.

Tacitus. 1970. *The Apricola and The Germainia.* Middlesex: Penguin Books.

Thompson, Anderson. 1975. "Developing an African Historiography." *Black Books Bulletin,* vol. 3: 4–13.

Thucydides. 1943. *The Peloponnesian War.* London: Oxford University Press.

Veblen, Thorstein. 1969. *Veblen on Marx, Race, Science, and Economics.* New York: Capricorn Books.

Vedas. 1972. *Hindu Scriptures.* Translated by Zaehner. London: Dent.

Venidad. 1977. *The Sacred Books of the East. The Zend Avestas,* Vol. 4. Ed. by F. Max Müller. New Delhi: Asian Educational Services.

Weber, Max. 1958. *The Protestant Ethic and the Spirit of Capitalism.* New York: Charles Scribner and Sons.

Wright, Bobby E. 1984. *The Psychopathic Racial Personality and other Essays.* Chicago: Third World Press.

Yasna. 1977. *The Sacred Books of the East. The Zend Avestas.* Vol. 31. Ed. by F. Max Müller. New Delhi: Asian Educational Services.

—. 1977. *The Sacred Books of the East. The Zend Avestas.* Vol. 23. Ed. by F. Max Müller. New Delhi: Asian Educational Services.

4

Africa and Western Education

Problems and Prospects

Come back to the Black Land
Come back to the place
where you were born
Kiss the ground at the great gate
Mingle with the officials.

—Senwosret

When we examine the place of Africa in Western intellectual history, we discover two almost diametrically opposed traditions. One I will call the ancient tradition and the other, the new orthodoxy. The ancient tradition can be traced to early Greek thinkers like Homer and Hesiod. This tradition was reinforced throughout the Greco-Roman Era and was basically unchallenged throughout the Middle Ages and early modernity, holding sway until the end of the eighteenth century. The rise of the modern tradition is symbolized by the Napoleonic invasion of Egypt in 1798.

The earlier tradition is based upon belief that Greeks generally held what is now called Africa in high regard and considered the African nations of Egypt and Ethiopia as the oldest nations on earth. There was no apparent disagreement with Herodotus' assertion that both the Egyptians and Ethiopians were black (*Ethiopian* meant "burnt skin" and included those who are now called Africans). There was also evidently widespread agreement that there was cultural kinship between the Egyptians and Ethiopians. In fact, Diodorus, during the Roman period, opined that the Egyptians were originally a colony of the

Ethiopians.

In order to bring the ancient tradition into clearer focus, let us consider the masters of ancient Western thought, Aristotle and Plato, who are considered the fountainheads of Western wisdom. Aristotle, who is considered by contemporary scholars as the first political scientist, said:

> It is no new or even recent discovery of political science that the state should be divided into classes....To this date it is the case in Egypt....In Egypt the system is believed to have been introduced by the legislation of Sesostris....The division into classes originated in Egypt....(Necessity...has always been the mother of invention.) Egypt bears witness to the antiquity of political institutions. Her people are recognized as the most ancient of all races; and from time out of mind they have had a legal code and a regular system of government. We ought therefore, to make good use of what has come down to us from the past, and merely try to supplement its defects. (*Politics*, p. 243)

Aristotle, in his reference to Egyptian history, was undoubtedly referring to what Plato referred to as the "things depicted or graven there [in Egypt] ten thousand years ago" (Plato, p. 101). In the *Timaeus*, Plato put these words in the mouth of an Egyptian priest who was giving a lesson to Solon the founder of the Athenian Constitution, and the epitome of Greek wisdom:

> Now this has the form of myth, but really signifies...a great conflagration of things upon earth which recur after long intervals; at such times those who live upon the mountain and in the dry lofty places are more liable to destruction than those who dwell by rivers or on the seashore, and from this calamity the Nile, who is our ever-failing savior, delivers and preserves us. When on the other hand, the gods purge the earth with a deluge of water (i.e., a flood), the survivors in your country are herders and shepherds who dwell on the mountains, but those who like you, live in cities are carried by the rivers into the sea. Whereas in this land, neither then nor at any other time, does water

62

come down from above on the fields having always a
tendency to come up from below; for which reason the
traditions preserved here are the most ancient. Whatever
happened either in your country or our own or any of the
regions of which we are informed,—if there were any
actions noble or great or in any other way remarkable, they
have all been written down by us of old and are preserved in
our temples. Whereas just when you and other nations are
beginning to be provided with letters and the other
requisites of civilized life, after the usual interval, the stream
from heaven, like a pestilence, comes pouring down and
leaving only those of you who are destitute of letters and
education; and so you begin all over again like children, and
know nothing of what happened in ancient times. (pp. 6–7)

The focus on Plato's philosophy, which consisted of attacks on
Greek poets and other carriers of Greek tradition, can be understood
better in the context of his knowledge of Egypt, the oldest continuous
civilization with which he was acquainted. Plato finally answered the
problem of the embarrassing Greek tradition by suggesting that it was
due to the shallow foundations of Greek society, which was relatively
young because it had been wiped out many times, thus causing the
Hellenes to frequently start from scratch. The passage reveals that
Plato thought this cyclic and catastrophic historical process was true for
all nations except the Egyptians, who managed to escape the
destructive floods and fires (and wars?) that other nations suffered
periodically. That is why the ancient Greeks, who probably never
knew about Sumer, thought Egypt was the most ancient nation on
earth.

In *The Laws*, Plato's praise of Egyptian culture was more specific.
As is well known, Plato's political philosophy is founded on education.
In fact, the possibility of creating the ideal state, as per *The Republic,* is
dependent not only on the emergence of a Philosopher King but on the
removal of all people over the age of ten years so that the proper
education will produce a generation capable of attaining the good life.
Plato found the model for his education program in the laws and
pedagogy of ancient Egypt. One need but consider the crucial role of
music and mathematical education in Plato's philosophy to appreciate

his high regard for Egyptian wisdom and education. Concerning music education he said:

> The law...in Egypt...is marvelous, even in the telling....[This state of things is] worthy in the highest degree of a statesman and legislator....To effect this would be the task of a god or a godlike man. (Plato, p. 101)

In regard to education in mathematics, Plato asserted: "One ought to declare, then, that [our] children should learn as much of these subjects as the innumerable crowd of children in Egypt learn along with their letters" (p. 107).

This praise of Egyptian pedagogy ends with another indictment of the Greek tradition: "When I was told...of our conditions in regard to this matter. I was ashamed, not only of myself, but of all Greek world" (p. 109).

As previously mentioned, the ancient traditions held sway from eighth century B.C. to the end of 1700 A.D., a period of about twenty-five hundred years. The Greek scholars traveled to Egypt for generations in search of wisdom. Even the Hebrew tradition in the Old Testament concurred with the notion that Egypt was a place of high civilization, sometimes a friendly haven and at other times a hostile oppressor. Abraham, Jacob, and Joseph sought refuge in Egypt. Even Francis Bacon in the seventeenth century praised the ancient Egyptian attitude about science (Bacon 1955, pp. 491, 492, 537). In his 1789 publication, *Ruins of Nations*, Count Constantine Francis Volney, a French Orientalist on the eve of the modern tradition asserted:

> A people, now forgotten, discovered while others were yet barbarians, the elements of the arts and sciences. A race of men now rejected from society for their sable skin and frizzled hair, founded...those civil and religious systems which still govern the universe. (pp. 16, 17)

In contrast, the New Orthodoxy tradition reinforced mostly negative views of Africa. This persuasion did not begin all at once. Indeed, one could point to certain adverse criticisms of Africa and even

Egypt among the ancients. The chattel slave system and the rationalization for the system, based on racial characteristics by great philosophers like Montesquieu, had significantly lowered the prestige of the African race (*The Spirit of the Laws*, 1949). In short, the New Orthodoxy maintains that black Africans never developed civilization and that those civilizations that were on the continent were brought in by foreign invaders. Furthermore, this modern position significantly lowered the quality of Egyptian contributions to world civilization. Perhaps the most devastating aspect of this position is the attempt to culturally and racially alienate Egypt from the rest of Africa.

The invasion of Egypt by Napoleon ushered in a new era of Egyptology. Napoleon took with his army a second army of intellectuals charged with the responsibility of exhaustively investigating the ancient Nile Valley civilization. The potential of this commitment to scientific survey and research has been realized through the establishment of the international discipline of Egyptology and such research centers as the Oriental Institute in Chicago. Unfortunately, that initiative was tarnished by the infection of the European intellectual world with the poison of white supremacy. This infusion accompanied the establishment or reestablishment of all of the intellectual disciplines of the modern world that emerged in the nineteenth century. Political science, sociology, psychology, economics, for example, were similarly tarnished.

The epitome of this intellectual corruption is the *Philosophy of History* by Georg Wilhelm Freidrich Hegel. I will focus only on what Hegel put forth concerning Africa and Egypt, since his larger framework, while relevant, would divert us too much from our present purpose. Hegel (1956) asserted that the "Negro" in his African environment:

> Exhibits the natural man in his completely wild and untamed state...there is nothing harmonious with humanity to be found in this type of character. (p. 93)

He further concluded that the condition of Africans "is capable of no development or culture" and that enslavement to more advanced Europeans is necessary to the "increase of human feeling among the

Negroes" and is an advance toward "becoming participants in a higher morality...a phase of their education" (p. 98).

Hegel's discussion of Africa occurs in his introduction, before he begins the philosophy of history proper. Furthermore, he discusses African life under the heading "Geography," which symbolizes his contempt for African society. In ending his discussion on Africa, Hegel asserts:

> At this point we leave Africa not to mention it again. [He does however manage to mention it again]. For it is not a historical part of the world; it has no movements or development to exhibit. Historical movements in it—that is in its northern part—belong to the Asiatic or European world. Carthage displayed there an important transitionary phase of civilization; but, as a Phoenician colony, it belongs to Asia. Egypt will be considered in reference to its western phase, but it does not belong to the African Spirit. What we properly understand by Africa is the unhistorical, undeveloped spirit, still involved in the conditions of mere nature, and which had to be presented here only as on the threshold of the world's history. (p. 99)

When Hegel discusses Egypt, he remarks:

> It...surprises to find among them, in the vicinity of African stupidity reflective intelligence, a thoroughly rational organization characterizing all institutions and the most astonishing works of art. (p. 199)

But the Egyptian civilization is hampered by the African influence which surrounds it. Hegel continues:

> We have here...a spirit entirely different, one of stirring and urgent impulses. We have here the African element in combination with oriental massiveness....It is that African imprisonment of ideas combined with the infinite impulse of the spirit [which] has still...an iron band around its forehead, so that it cannot attain to the free consciousness of its existence. (p. 207)

I am stirring up these "old memories" only because the ideas expressed by Hegel, consciously or unconsciously, guided many of the founders of modern academic disciplines that deal with the history and sociology of the various peoples of the world, including archeology and Egyptology. Because of this widely shared negative and unscientific attitude toward Africa and African people, we have a massive problem of distortion and falsification in Western education concerning Africa, which in turn is the basis of the endemic alienation of black children throughout the educational process.

For example, the Hegelian racial attitude led Breasted (1937), one of the most brilliant Egyptologists, to divert his attention from his scientific work to pursue an argument that only European peoples were responsible for the initiation of civilization. Concerning the Africans he asserted:

> The conclusion maintained by some historians that the Egyptian was of African Negro origin is now refuted...at best he may have been slightly tinctured with Negro blood. (p. 26)

The separation of Egypt from African people was devastating, but the process of debasement did not end there. Some Egyptologists under this anti-black persuasion began to emphasize the poor quality of ancient Egyptian achievements in comparison with other civilizations of antiquity. For example, one leader of modern archaeology queried:

> Did ancient Egypt contribute any significant elements to the continuing philosophy, ethics or world-consciousness of later time? No, not directly in fields which one may specify, as is the case of Babylonian science, Hebrew theology, or Greek or Chinese rationalism. One might critically say...that her intellectual and spiritual contributions were not up to her length of years and her physical memorial, and that she herself was unable to realize on her promising beginnings in many fields. (Wilson, 1977, p. 131)

Many of these quoted works are nonetheless useful because they are generally scientific in many respects. However, opinions regarding

Africa have adversely affected the minds of many students and educators. Now that the younger generation of scholars is abandoning the attempt to give Europeans credit for all significant achievements in antiquity and admitting that it does not know the races of the ancients, the stage has been set for correction.

Before we turn to prospects for improvement, let us suppose that an instructor was given the task of "teaching about Europe" under the following conditions and rules:

1. Mali had invaded Europe in the fifteenth century and, with other African states, had ultimately colonized the entire continent.

2. Millions of Europeans had been taken to another continent as the slaves of African people.

3. The leading African intellectuals, who controlled the educational system, asserted that Europeans had never made any contributions to world civilization.

4. Greece and Rome were not established by Europeans. The founders of those civilizations were light colored Africans.

5. Christianity was a foreign import into Europe.

6. The only sources for European antiquity were the life patterns of the Tutonic tribes: the Vikings, Pikes, Jutes, Goths, Franks, and the like.

One would surmise that courses in world history and Western civilization would be significantly different from the courses which presently exist.

The Prospects:
A Reconstruction in Thinking About Africa

In an effort to correct the modern educational approach to Africa, we must focus on both aspects of the problem. One problem is, of course, that most students are taught little or nothing about Africa. The remedy would be to teach about Africa more often and in more places throughout the curricula. But if we merely increase the quantity of what is generally taught, we probably will make the situation worse.

Lyndon B. Johnson, in a speech at Howard University to a predominantly black audience, asserted that black people would never be equal to white people until they had equal history. Some black people were offended by that statement but he made a good point. Teaching about Africa must begin with the equalization of African history.

The first step in that equalization is the putting back of ancient Egypt into Africa where it belongs. Once that is done, Africa begins to take shape. The relationship between Ancient Egypt and inner Africa is somewhat similar to the relationship between Greece/Rome and inner Europe. If anything, the Egyptian-inner African connection was more sustained, widespread, and reciprocal. The literature of the ancient Greeks, Hebrews, and Egyptians themselves amply support this construction.

Egypt was the connection between the international community of antiquity and inner Africa, as were Greece and Rome *vis-`a-vis* inner Europe. Islam, which came into Africa through Egypt, has the same kind of relationship with much of inner Africa as has Christianity, which came into Europe via Greece and Rome, with inner Europe. Just as European history often focuses on successive power centers, that is, Greece, Rome, the Holy Roman Empire, Spain, France, Britain, and so on, so African history can be unfolded by treating Egypt, Kush, Axum, Ghana, Ngola, Monamatopa, and so on. In other words, if Africa is taught from a historical perspective rather than an anthropological perspective, equality begins to emerge. It should be noted that ancient Romans, that is, Caesar and Tacitus, did study the German and British tribes similar to the way in which present day

69

anthropologists study Africans.

Teaching about Africa must go further, beyond history and social science. When the engineering in books about construction projects of ancient Egypt and Kush is treated with the same respect as the Greek projects in engineering books; when the architectural styles and techniques of Timbuktu and Axum are afforded parity in the books of architecture; when Egyptian and Yoruba medicine are given a place of import in the history of science, we will be on the road to recovery.

✳ How many elementary, high school, or college students have the opportunity to read Egyptian literature or to compare the Egyptian concept of good speech (what they called *Medew Nefer*) with the Greek concept of logos? Where in the general educational process is Egyptian poetry studied? No attention is generally given to Dogan cosmology or Egyptian ethics in philosophy courses. There is a great deal of material, but the problem is that there is no conceptualization of how to use it and all too often no determination to use it at all.

✳✳ *African Glory* by John C. deGraft-Johnson, a Ghanian scholar, would make an excellent high school text. *Introduction to African Civilization* by John G. Jackson can also be used with guidance. Other useful sources include *Precolonial Black Africa* by C.A. Diop, *The Destruction of Black Civilization* by Chancellor Williams, and *When Egypt Ruled the East* by George Steindorff and Keith C. Seele. In addition, *The Journal of African Civilizations* is an excellent source for scholarly articles on Africa and its achievements. An excellent collection of Egyptian literature, which is available in paperback, is Miriam Lichtheim's *Ancient Egyptian Literature* in three volumes. Some of this material will have to be reworked to use at various levels, but such reworking can be done by groups of teachers who are themselves willing to learn. ✳✳

If we use the same historical framework to study African exploration of and forced migration to the Western Hemisphere, then the focus will shift from what happened to Africans, to what Africans did when they found themselves enslaved. One thing many did all over the hemisphere was escape from the plantations and establish independent African communities. From these bases they attacked the plantations and, in one case, established an independent republic, that is, Palmares, which technically was the first independent republic in the

Western Hemisphere, established in 1595. In another significant case, that is significantly underreported in mainstream history, the black slaves in Haiti freed themselves by defeating Napoleon's army, which was the most powerful military force in Europe at the time.

This chapter on Africa and Western Education opened with an epigraph that begins: "Come Back to the Black Land." This is a story which you can in turn share with your students and colleagues. The protagonist, the young man Sinuhe, was an official on an expedition in the company of Prince Senwosret when the prince received notice that the Pharaoh Amenenhat I had just been assassinated. The prince raced back to the capitol to take charge and become the new pharaoh, but Sinuhe, fearing trouble, fled from the country and after awhile settled in a foreign country where he was well received. The reason for Sinuhe's fear and motivation for leaving is never completely explained in the story.

Sinuhe, however, settles in his adopted land, becomes prosperous and famous, marries, has a family, and seems to become established as a naturalized citizen. He participates in civic duties and military campaigns in his new land and is rewarded for his outstanding service. However, Sinuhe does not completely lose touch with his native Egypt. In the first place, he becomes a confidant and advisor concerning Egypt to the ruler of his adopted land. In the second place, he becomes the contact person and host of all Egyptians who travel to this Asiatic country. All in all, Sinuhe seems to have it made in this "good land."

At the height of his popularity and prosperity, Sinuhe is threatened by a native bully who evidently resents his success. This bully forces Sinuhe into a duel to the death. Sinuhe appeals to his supporters, including the ruler who seems sympathetic, but powerless to stop the wrongdoer. And so Sinuhe has to duel against this giant. (Here the story is reminiscent of David and Goliath or rather vice versa).

Against the apparent odds, Sinuhe wins. However, this experience convinces Sinuhe that he is an alien and cannot be completely at home and content unless he returns to Egypt. Sinuhe, who by now is an old man, therefore, sends a petition to Pharaoh Senwosret I, begging to be permitted to return home so he can die in

71

peace. Surprisingly and without hesitation, the pharaoh sends him the invitation with which I started this talk:

Come back to the Black Land
Come back to the place where you were born
Kiss the ground at the great gate
and mingle with the officials.

And so Sinuhe returned home where he was received with great joy and honor. Just as Sinuhe returned to Egypt for contentment, so the people of antiquity sought comfort and wisdom in Africa. Hebrews like the father, Abraham, Jacob, father of the twelve tribes, and his son Joseph, sought refuge and wisdom in Egypt, as did the family of Jesus after them. The disciples of the prophet Mohammed fled to Ethiopia when they were hounded in Arabia; and so in our struggle to create order out of the present curriculum disorder, let us accept Senwosret's invitation as did Aristotle and other ancient Greeks: Let us "Come back to the Black Land."

REFERENCES

Aristotle. 1962. *Politics.* Translated with an introduction by T. A. Sinclair. Baltimore: Penguin Books.

Bacon, Frances. 1955. *Novum Organum. Selected Writings of Francis Bacon.* Ed. by Hugh G. Dich. New York: Modern Library.

Breasted, James Henry. 1937. *A History of Egypt: From the Earliest Times to the Persian Conquest.* New York: Charles Scribner and Sons.

deGraft-Johnson, John C. 1954. *African Glory: A Story of Vanished Negro Civilizations.* New York: Walden and Company.

Diop, Cheikh Anta. 1987. *Precolonial Black Africa.* Westport: Lawrence Hill.

Hegel, Georg Wilhelm Friedrich. 1956. *The Philosophy of History.* New York: Dover.

Lichtheim, Miriam. 1973. *Ancient Egyptian Literature,* vol. I Berkeley: University of California, Berkeley Press.

Montesquieu, Charles. 1949. *The Spirit of the Laws.* New York: Hafner.

Plato. 1949. *The Timeaus.* New York: The Liberal Arts Press.

—. 1960. *The Laws.* London: J. M. Dent and Sons.

Volney, C. F. 1890. *Ruins of Nations.* New York: Peter Eckler.

Wilson, John A., et. al. 1946. "Egypt on values of life" in *The Intellectual Adventure of Ancient Man.* Chicago: University of Chicago Press.

5

An Alternative to Political Science

L et us begin this inquiry by focusing on two statements made by a group of black political scientists. The first statement reads as follows: "In the leading study of the profession [political science] by Somit and Tanenhaus, the role and status of Black academics is ignored completely." The other statement reads:

> With W.E.B. Du Bois leading the way successive generations of Black scholars and literati fashioned their research and composed their verse from the raw materials of Black degradation in America.

Both of these statements were made in a study by Paul L. Puryear, Maurice Woodard, and Vernon Gray entitled "The Comparative Status of Black and White Political Scientists," completed in September 1977 and published in Maurice Woodard's (ed.) *Blacks and Political Science* (pp. 24–102). This study is food for thought in its own right, but I will not directly discuss the status of black political scientists which has probably changed very little from the lowly condition described in that work. The Somit and Tanenhaus study and the last chapter of one of Du Bois' works have something in common which is the point of departure for this essay. Somit and Tanenhaus and Du Bois focus on John W. Burgess, albeit for different reasons.

W.E.B. Du Bois, who is often thought of as the father of black social scientists, raised a significant question for black political scientists to consider in his *Black Reconstruction* (1968, p. 726): "Subtract from Burgess his belief that only white people can rule, and he is in essential agreement with me." Albert Somit and Joseph Tanenhaus (1964), in their study *The Development of American Political Science from Burges to Behavioralism,* accuse this same John W. Burgess of the paternity of

American Political Science (pp. 16–21). According to their historical sketch, the Columbia School of Political Science, which Burgess founded:

> was the formative institution in the development of the discipline, since its program was the one that other universities consciously emulated or deliberately deviated from in setting up their own graduate work in political science. It was the one early program, furthermore, that displayed anything like the range of interests and emphasis encountered in contemporary departments.(p. 21)

Du Bois' conclusion about Burgess was based upon his criticism of Burgess as an "ex-confederate soldier." (Somit and Tanenhaus merely indicated that Burgess served in the Civil War, not mentioning which side.) Burgess, who according to Du Bois went to college with "a box of books, a box of tallow candles and a 'Negro Boy,'" explicitly expounded 'Nordic supremacy' which colored all his political theories" (p. 718). In fact, as Du Bois (1968) pointed out, Burgess had asserted: "A black skin means membership in a race of men which has never of itself succeeded in subjecting passion to reason...never...created any civilization of any kind" (pp. 718–719).

Since for Burgess "history is the chief preparation for the study of...political science," his view of history would be the foundation of any political science established by him. Thus, Du Bois, who saw only a problem of racism with Burgess' theory, which was otherwise in agreement with Du Bois' own theories, epitomizes the dilemma of contemporary black political scientists who, if Somit and Tanenhaus are correct, are guided by the "range of interest and emphasis" established by Burgess.

The key to the Du Bois' dilemma is clearly indicated by him:

> As a Negro, I cannot do this writing without believing in the essential humanity of Negroes....I cannot for a moment subscribe to that bizarre doctrine of race that makes most men inferior to the few. But too as a student of science, I want to be fair, objective and judicial. (p. 725)

His dilemma was quite simply a conflict between his loyalty to his race on the one hand and his loyalty to his chosen discipline on the other.

Surely, a political science which was founded by Burgess and whose branches still come from the founding tree, and whose roots lie in Hegelian Germany (it was Hegel who asserted that the African state was the antithesis to true constitutional development) deserves to be challenged.

I do not, however, wish to pursue the argument from the standpoint that the founding fathers of political science were racists, nor do I wish to belabor the fact that institutional racism still places black political scientists at a disadvantage. Du Bois in his study and Puryear, Woodard, and Gray in their work have covered those problems sufficiently for present purposes.

What I would like to examine is the more fundamental problem of the usefulness of political science for black people. In this regard, I would like to return to the foundation of political science among the Greeks. Sheldon Wolin's criticism of Plato can get us started. Wolin asserted that Plato's formulation of the polity resulted in a community "devoid of politics" (Wolin 1949, p. 75). Wolin also argued that "Aristotle came closer to the practice of Athenian democracy," and that "Aristotle wisely noted that Plato's community would cease to be a political association" (p. 63).

I will focus on the conflict between Plato's philosophy (and to a lesser extent, Aristotle's) and the actual Greek political association. This conflict resulted from the introduction of Egyptian wisdom concerning governance into Greece. George G. M. James asserts that the basis of Greek philosophy was the Egyptian Mystery system and that philosophy was alien to Greek life. Thus, Socrates was executed and Plato and Aristotle had to run for their lives because of their "criminal" activities *vis-`a-vis* the introduction of foreign ideas into Hellenic life. Similarly, Cheikh Anta Diop demonstrates the devastating practical impact of the Egyptian ideas of governance on the development of territorial states among the early Europeans. The evidence for this Egyptian influence on Greek political philosophy can be seen in Plato's *Laws* (pp. 656, 659, 747, 799) and in *Timeaus* (pp. 21–26).

As Wolin suggests, Plato tried to introduce a philosophy of

governance which was at odds with the practice of politics. Plato wanted to remove politics from governance (*The Republic* provides the archetype for this theme) and to, among other things, control poets, artists and musicians (*Laws*, pp. 656–57). Both of these themes were fundamental to the concept of governance in ancient Egypt. (see "The Instruction of Ptahhotep," "The Instruction for Merikare," and "The Philosophy of Neferti" in Miriam Lichtheim's *Ancient Egyptian Literature*, 1973.)

Plato's motivation, however, was in reality quite Greek because what he actually wanted was the imposition of a veneer of morality and ethics on the discussion of governance *vis-`a-vis* the facts of the clash of naked interests that characterized Greek life in the polis. Plato, who as Diop asserted in *The Cultural Unity of Black Africa* (1978), could not rise above the narrow confines of the Greek city-state, was he still as Greek as his less philosophic contemporaries because he merely wanted to establish the claim of this group as the rightful rulers along with their interests. Put another way, the Sophists (who were the enemies of Plato i.e., the main competitors of the philosophers) were for the most part foreigners and pursued their interests in teaching others how to rule. The philosophers, on the other hand, pursued their interests by attempting to rule (directly when possible and indirectly when not) and pacifying all other interests.

The character of Greek life in the polis was fundamentally different from life in ancient Egypt and thus required a different conception of governance. To begin with, there is no equivalence to the word *politics* or any of its derivatives in the ancient Egyptian language. To explain this, I will quote at length from a recent essay I wrote:

> The explanation for this variance is historical and may be attributed to the retarded development of the Greek and European world. There are two characteristics of Eurasian culture that produced politics and its hand maiden political science. First, as Cheikh Anta Diop points out, the Greeks never developed a higher form of government than the polis, which until nearly the end of Hellenistic civilization never attained the characteristics of a real city. The Greek polis was at its inception an armed fort and exhibited that

characteristic throughout Greek civilization. As Diop put it 'Even Plato in his *Republic* could not rise above the idea of a city-state.' Thus, the affairs of the city were the highest form of public commitment. One needs to remember that the political science of this area is the foundation of all subsequent political thought among the Europeans and others.

A second and perhaps more significant feature of Greek politics is the basic concept of the city itself and how the good life is pursued therein. The *Republic* focuses on Thrasymacus' definition of justice as the *interest* of the stronger party. This means that each city is hopelessly divided between the few and the many, the rich and poor, the haves and have nots, the oligarches and the demos. What is advantageous to one group is disadvantageous to the other. Thus, each city is two nations and the perennial problem of actual politics and theoretical politics (political science) is the resolution of that conflict. As it was in the beginning so it is at the end. This is the European context from Plato thru Machiavelli, Locke, Madison, and Marx to the present day.

In contrast, the (Egyptian) civilization was based upon a true territorial state. The wisdom appropriate for the governance of a (large united) country is of course qualitively different from that required for one's party to gain ascendency through running the affairs of *polis*. However, great were Memphis and Thebes, the capitols of ancient Egypt at different times. Egypt with its forty-two administrative districts and hundreds of cities and towns, necessarily required a cosmopolitan ethos unknown to Greek civilization. This is not to say that some of the people of Egypt did not vie for influence through public affairs—many did. They did not all possess the same amount of property. But *interest* was never considered the foundation of the juridical order. As stated above, the Greek dialogue attempted to cover the interest perspective but the veil was always thin and never determinate in a positive sense. This is one of the arguments made by St. Augustine when he contrasted the worth of *prophesy* with

79

the worthlessness of philosophy in the *City of God*. Of course Machiavelli finally put the pretense to rest with *The Prince*. The fact is that in ancient Egypt there was governance of a relatively large territory with local dignitaries and many occupational specialities. They emphasized building and great projects and subordinated the individual's quest for advancement while at the same time provided adequate scope for the talented to raise to positions which they merited through good works.

The Greek concept of freedom is the prime value characteristic of the European political system. The Chief god (Zeus or Wodin) is completely free to do as he wants, e.g., to rape any goddess or woman, to exploit and destroy any god or man according to his whim. Thus, only one can be free, all others must be in bondage. This idea caused the Greek political philosophers to de-emphasize freedom, although the freedom from drudgery and work was a *sine qua non* for political life. Thus, the body of free citizens, like Zeus, had to have a body of slaves to do the work. Freedom in this sense is still a great deal among Europeans.

I am by no means romanticizing the culture of ancient Egypt. There were many instances of wrongdoing and petty hustling but these were never elevated to a level of dignity as serious contenders for the ethics of the society as is true in Greece and Rome and Europe. Thus, "Politics" in the historical and common sense traditions of Europe never developed in Egypt, and the "Republic" as a form of interest accommodation never arose among the Egyptians, nor any other African people as Diop (*The African Origin of Civilization*) pointed out. (Jacob Carruthers, "Tawi: The United Two Lands")

I have discussed the Greek foundations of political science because every political scientist who is considered truly profound explores these roots. Plato and Aristotle are considered the founders of political science. But are Greek foundations appropriate for Africans, as Ali Mazrui suggested when he proclaimed: "Africa has to establish that she can be as 'Greek' as the next person," and that Africans must claim their "share of the Hellenic heritage of man"? Is it sufficient to proclaim Aristotle as "the master who knows" as Kwame Nkrumah put it in his "Motion of Destiny" speech in 1953? Since the foundations and structure of political science are alien to African culture, it would appear that Diop was correct in 1978 when he said:

> Egyptian culture enjoys a position *vis-`a-vis* present day African culture analogous to the role which Greco-Latin culture plays in regard to contemporary western culture… as long as we ignore ancient Egyptian culture, the oldest evidence of an African civilization we will be unable to create anything in the domain of the social sciences that could be considered as scientific. (Diop, p. 31)

At this point, one may ask if understanding the Egyptian and African historical foundations are relevant to the current problems faced by Africans and more specifically, African-Americans. Why can't black political scientists fashion research "from the raw materials of Black degradation in America?"

First of all, we must point out that there is no essential difference in the problems confronting African political scientists on the African continent and African political scientists in America. Both groups are essentially working with the "raw materials of Black degradation" and are guided by the basic European political science foundations. As long as they are shackled to that framework, black political scientists are more or less victims of the vicissitudes of that discipline. Thus, in 1935, during the period when the white supremacist system of segregation was being put together, Du Bois (who was not a political scientist proper; there was only one black with a Ph.D. in political science when *Black Reconstruction* was written) protested against the overt racism that emerged along with political science. In 1977 Puryear, Woodard, and Gray were exposing institutional racism (by then there were a few hundred black political scientists). Black scholars who are interested in the politics of Europeans and what sometimes goes under the name of black politics should certainly have a radically different view of the Europeans who are targeting on the same areas of scholarly pursuit. For the European and white American political scientists, political science and its focus, politics, are the natural extensions of their historical way of life. To them "African politics" in Africa and black politics in America are, although sometimes quite significant, subdivisions which are not fully mature and developed. For them the end of African politics is integration into the world as organized by Europeans.

Political science and politics were exported by Arabs and Europeans to Africa and were superimposed on African life. For us, African politics is defined by a struggle to regain and maintain our national freedom. The question that remains is whether political science can be used in that regard and, if so, in what sense? Political science, which is nothing more than the study of the dominion of one group and its interests over other groups must be studied by Africans. The study of political science is one way of studying the worldwide system of dominion that must be overcome. It is therefore useful to have black scholars study political science just as it is useful to study any pathology. However, such study in itself cannot provide the guidance necessary for formulating answers, or even questions, concerning the ultimate world organization for which we should strive. Nor is it capable of recommending actions in which black people should engage. These functions can only be provided when black scholars develop a foundation for national life. Such a foundation is provided by a return to the wisdom of governance in African life.

This wisdom begins with the elevation of governance itself above the clash of interests of national life. Interests are essentially private conflicts which are mediated by government, but which do not enter government itself. Party politics, even "one party politics," is inconsistent with African life and may well account for the present condition of national life in Africa and black America. This idea will require a lot of debate because black people have been entrenched in Machiavellianism and Madisonianism; it is difficult for us to even imagine that a society can be substantially free from the contest for governmental office, or, that if such a society could exist, it would be desirable and not, by definition, despotic. However, we need frank and open study and discourse on the possibility of the wisdom of African governance as an alternative to political science.

R E F E R E N C E S

Carruthers, Jacob H. 1979. "Tawi: The United Two Lands." Unpublished paper.

Diop, Cheikh Anta. 1978. *The Cultural Unity of Black Africa*. Chicago: Third World Press.

Du Bois, W.E.B. 1968. *Black Reconstruction in America 1860–1880*. New York: The World Publishing Company.

James, George G. M. 1976. *Stolen Legacy*. San Francisco: Julian Richardson Associates.

Lichtheim, Miriam. 1973. *Ancient Egyptian Literature*, vol. 1. Berkeley: University of California, Berkely Press.

Madhubuti, Haki R., ed. 1976. "BBB Interviews Dr. Cheikh Anta Diop." *Black Books Bulletin* 4:4 (winter). 30–37.

Mazrui, Ali. 1967. *Ancient Greece in African Political Thought*. Nairobi: Kenya East African Publishing House.

Nkrumah, Kwame. 1973. *Revolutionary Path*. New York: International Publishers.

Plato. 1949. *The Timaeus*. New York: The Liberal Arts Press.

—. 1960. *The Laws*. London: J. M. Dent and Sons.

Puryear, Paul L., Maurice Woodard, and Vernon Gray, eds. 1977. "The Comparative Status of Black and White Political Scientists," in *Blacks, and Political Science*. American Political Science Association.

Somit, Albert and Joseph Tanenhaus. 1964. *The Development of American Political Science from Burgers to Behaviorism.* New York: Atherton Press.

Wolin, Sheldon. 1949. *Politics and Vision.* Boston: Little, Brown and Company.

PART II

DEFENDERS OF
WESTERN CIVILIZATION

The Battle Over the Multicultural Curriculum

Advocates of an African-centered curriculum and similar approaches to multiculturalism have been engaged in intellectual and academic warfare with the defenders of Western civilization who rightly see the proposals as threats to the supremacy of "Western" ways of thinking about and explaining what has happened and is happening in the world. This paper is intended to bring some clarity to the position of those who advocate the African-centered curriculum and similar approaches by responding to the arguments which one group of defenders have made in an attempt to undermine the soundness of the challenges to orthodoxy.

The proposal for an African-centered curriculum is only one aspect of the fully defined project that recommends a massive infusion into the curriculum of correct and relevant information and materials about Africa. Such inclusion must occur in all disciplines and grade levels of the curriculum and in the development of basic skills and cognitive thinking. Some of the advocates of such a program also emphasize the need to adopt an African-centered curriculum strategy for schools with predominately African-American school enrollments. This aspect of the proposal is based upon the belief that even the most carefully developed multicultural curriculum will be unavoidably centered in the culture of the community by or in which the program is developed and taught. That means that if nothing else is done in the United States, the educational curriculum will have a Eurocentric focus. This in itself is not inconsistent with the idea of a multicultural curriculum, provided the planners adhere to the principle of multiculturalism. Due, however, to the history of cultural oppression, suppression, and repression especially *vis-`a-vis* Africans, an African-centered curriculum should be developed and established in predominately African-American schools to assist in correcting the cultural distortion inherent in the Eurocentric focused curriculum and to exert pressure on the Eurocentric curriculum to remain faithful to the commitment of multiculturalism. Such interdependent curricular power bases are consistent with the historical reality of the country and the requirements for equal opportunity *vis-`a-vis* cultural education.

Defenders of Western civilization fit in either of the following camps: hard-liners and soft-liners. The hard-liners are represented by Alan Bloom, Mortimer Adler, William Bennet, and perhaps E.D. Hirsch, Jr. They advocate the return to a core curriculum of the values of Western civilization as it is defined in the tradition of the "great books." They see Western culture as the only relevant culture. For them the best way to help peoples of non-Western heritage is to give them extra support in acquiring the skills and orientation which will make them culturally literate in this tradition. Africans will, therefore, be able to benefit from the expanding equality of opportunity produced by the march toward the full achievement of the ideals of Western civilization. Hard-liners fear that any concentrated focus on the "exotic" and nostalgic cultures of past eras is a waste of valuable time.

Many of the European-American defenders of Western civilization have abandoned this position and belong to the soft-liner camp. Soft-liners advocate a multicultural curriculum. Their leading spokesperson, Diane Ravitch, calls their position pluralistic multiculturalism, which she contrasts with particularistic multiculturalism. The views of Professor Ravitch are expressed in the following articles, all published in 1990: "Democracy and Diversity: Multicultural Education in America," "Multiculturalism E. Pluribus Plures," and "Multiculturalism Yes, Particularism No." Pluralism, a concept used to characterize the basic structural characteristic of modern democracy, has been around for a while. However, it has never successfully refuted the charge by scholars such as C. Wright Mills and Ferdinan Lundberg that there is a power monopoly in the United States and that pluralism is nothing more than propaganda. Pluralism requires several relatively equal power bases for controlling the target phenomenon, whether that phenomenon be politics, economics, or culture. This certainly is not, and never has been, the case in the United States. One must therefore be careful with Diane Ravitch's terminology.

The Soft-liner Arguments

The soft-liner argument against programs like the African-centered curriculum is divided into four general objections:

1. the purpose of multicultural education,
2. the standards of sound scholarship,
3. the unity of the pluralistic American culture, and
4. the best interests and needs of both European-American and African-American children.

Soft-liners argue that the attack on the cultural aspect of the curriculum and the advocacy of alternatives such as the African-centered perspective really promote reverse ethnocentrism. This is what Ravitch calls particularistic multiculturalism, which, in her view, is antithetical to no multiculturalism. Her thesis assumes that there is a true balance that can be achieved in the construction of the multicultural curriculum. Such balance should portray the actual contributions from all of the cultural groups in a society. She also assumes that a culturally neutral framework can be developed which will automatically assign cultural contributions to the respective groups "whenever historically appropriate." Furthermore, Professor Ravitch seems to believe that the multicultural curriculum already exists because as she states in her essay "Diversity and Democracy":

> In recent years, history and literature textbooks for elementary and secondary students have been revised to incorporate [a] broader perspective of the American past [which includes "the history of women, blacks and various ethnic minorities"]. (p. 18)

To her credit, Ravitch does admit that "in all too many cases, the additions remain merely add-ons and sidebars to the main story." She hastens to encourage "elementary and secondary texts" to tell the "story in which people of many different backgrounds have joined together to become one nation, all Americans."

The above statements by Ravitch bring her position into sharper focus. She believes that the United States is a multicultural society. Therefore, if one teaches about this society, one is teaching multiculturally. This position, coupled with her insistence that the curriculum emphasizes the "common culture" which "has been formed by the interaction of its subsidiary cultures" reflects the basic flaw in her line of reasoning. The multicultural character of the United States, a la Ravitch, is one "that has been influenced by immigrants, American Indians, African slaves, and their descendants." The fact that the European immigrants and their descendants made, and continue to make, the rules and the choices about cultural inclusion seems to be totally ignored. Disenfranchised "American Indians" and "African slaves," and their descendants were at the mercy of European immigrants who decided which Indian and African cultural features would be included and which would be suppressed. In some cases the immigrants and their descendants invented Indian and African cultural features such as the broken-English speaking red-skin Brave and the grinning, shuffling, happy-go-lucky Negro.

In order to understand this problem let us examine the ideal multicultural curriculum which Diane Ravitch helped to draft in California:

> World history was increased to three required years, providing enough time to examine the civilizations that developed in Africa, the Near East, China, India, and elsewhere, the civilizations of the Maya, Incas, and Aztecs; the growth of Western civilization in Europe; and the problems of the twentieth century world. Teachers of these courses are encouraged to use the literature and art of diverse cultures, their myths, legends, religious literature, poems, novels, biographies, and so on. ("Democracy and Diversity," p. 19)

What did world history include before the increase to "three required years"? Was it a world history that did not provide "enough time" to examine the civilization of Africa; was it world history in name only? The logical conclusion is that the world history that had been established by European academics was modified (perhaps reformed) to include more attention to the history of Africa, and so on. We may note here that Diane Ravitch included in this expanded world history more time to examine the growth of Western civilization. In other words, the reformed curriculum is merely an expanded version of the unreformed one because surely African civilization and others were examined to some extent.

Although more time should be devoted to all world cultures, the major problem in teaching world history is not that too little time is devoted to non-Western cultures, but that what is taught, whether a little or a great deal, is basically wrong. Diane Ravitch does not really discuss this very important issue except to assert that:

> a generation of scholarship...has enriched our knowledge about the historical experiences of women, blacks, and members of other minority groups in various societies. As a result of the new scholarship, our schools and our institutions of learning have in recent years begun to embrace..."cultural democracy," a recognition that we must listen to a "diversity of voices" to understand our culture, past and present. ("Multiculturalism Yes," p. A44)

While such a proclamation is certainly a welcomed step away from the hard-line defenders of Western civilization, there is little evidence that cultural democracy has been seriously embraced. Cultural democracy cannot be achieved as long as the curriculum is enthralled in Western historiography and the broader modern European philosophy from which it is derived.

It is not enough to "examine the civilizations that developed in Africa, the Near East, China, India (or) the civilizations of the Mayas, Incas, and Aztecs," one must also retell the story of the world so that the basic tale of history as the "Greek miracle" and its reverberations through time can be overturned and replaced with the truth. In other words, the present story of civilization must be exposed as essentially false and replaced by one that is more accurate. Otherwise, students might come away with an even stronger impression that the way of living under Western civilization is naturally superior to all other ways of life. Indeed, without explaining the intellectual crimes of major European historians and philosophers, one cannot possibly understand even the necessity of an emphasis on African-centered multiculturalism. Nor can one understand why intellectuals such as Alan Bloom, Mortimer Adler, and E. D. Hirsch Jr., and psuedo intellectuals such as William Bennet, vigorously argue for the continued triumph of Western civilization. Nor can one understand why Diane Ravitch reacts so indignantly to the critique of the current curriculum philosophy which is an indispensable part of the African-centered position.

More specifically, in order for a truly multicultural curriculum to develop, ancient Egypt must be unequivocally addressed as an African civilization. Such an orientation must include the repudiation of the claims that the civilization came from outside Africa and that either the masses or conquering classes were white. The ancient Egyptians should be accepted as black and as related to inner Africa as the ancient Greeks are accepted as white and related to inner Europe. The influence of ancient Egypt and Ethiopia on the other civilizations of tricontinental antiquity and the high regard that the Hebrew authors of the Old Testament and Greeks like Herodotus, Isocrates, Plato, Aristotle and Plutarch had for ancient Egypt must be related as a moral aspect of world history. The influence of ancient Mesopotamia on ancient Hebrew and Greek culture must also be explained. The origin of history as we know it from these two river valley civilizations are proportionately much more deserving of indepth treatment than the brief period of Greek civilization. The issue of appropriate inclusion in both quantitative and qualitative terms is a revolutionary problem, not one to be answered by a "let's put something about them in the course" attitude. What is demanded is a different theory of history and a different historiography.

Furthermore, the basic framework for world history still follows the milestones of European history: ancient history ends with the fall of Rome, while modern history begins with the European Renaissance. As long as such structural elements remain a part of the curriculum, the resulting history is unacceptably Eurocentric.

Let us look at another aspect of the pluralistic multicultural curriculum offered by Diane Ravitch:

> In the teaching of American history, racial and ethnic minorities are woven into the central story, not represented as mere footnotes. For example, major attention is paid to slavery in American history; to the abolition movement; to the rise of Jim Crow laws and segregation after the Civil War; and a full unit is devoted to the Civil Rights movement of the twentieth century. Wherever historically appropriate, the curriculum recognizes the importance of ethnic groups in the building of the nation. Students learn about the Hispanic roots of the Southwest, the cultures of Native American tribes, and Asian and Chicano immigrants to California. And the internment of Japanese-Americans during World War II is confronted and honestly treated as a violation of basic human rights. ("Democracy and Diversity," p. 19)

Again, the reform of the American history course follows the format of the old curriculum. The European–American story has been spiced up with some interesting sidelights into what was happening in the meantime to and among the African-Americans, Indians, Mexicans, and so on. African–Americans are expected to take solace in the fact that "a full unit was devoted to the Civil Rights movement."

The events selected by Professor Ravitch to demonstrate appropriate inclusion of the historical cultural significance of African Americans clearly expose the problem. She selected those events that do not challenge the orthodox interpretation of American history. For example, she did not mention rebellions by expatriated Africans in the Western Hemisphere as deserving a "full unit." This could mean that she just omitted the reference in her articles or it could mean that such events were not significantly included in the reformed curriculum. In either case, what we have is a selection process based upon a theory of American history which Ravitch not only promotes, but which dictates her concept of multiculturalism.

In another instance Diane Ravitch proclaims:

> The movie *Glory* is a fine example of pluralistic education at its best. This depiction of the most famous

> black Civil War regiment demonstrates the courage and determination of the black soldiers; it shows whites who were vicious racists, and whites who gave their lives to the cause of black freedom. Everyone who sees the movie leaves with a greater understanding of the black contribution to the building of America and can identify with the heroism of the Massachusetts 54th. ("Democracy and Diversity," p. 18)

Ravitch does not suspect that many African-Americans were not among the "everyone" who left the movie "with a greater understanding of the black contribution to the building of America." Indeed some African-Americans view *Glory* as an idolization of a courageous white Northerner who led a group of black people who were not allowed to have African-American officers direct their participation in a war for their own liberation. Many view *Glory* as the Northern states of America's *Gone With The Wind*. Each movie contained images of European-Americans and Africans in the United States during the Civil War; featured African-American actors who won Academy Awards for supporting roles; and were applauded as examples of American multiculturalism. Indeed, each movie is an outstanding example of the kind of multiculturalism advocated by soft-liners.

Diane Ravitch's view of history is evidently oblivious to the existence of a military unit trained and led by African-Americans which was isolated and kept out of combat for political reasons. However good-intentioned the "whites who gave their lives to the cause of black freedom," they showed no resolve to reject the doctrine and practice of white supremacy.

Ravitch fails to recognize that American culture is the product of the European invasion, conquest, colonization, settlement, and exploitation of the Western Hemisphere. The most appropriate summary of that culture is expressed in names used to designate various geographical areas which celebrate the project: New England, New York, Hispaniola, and so on. In fact, the historiography of the Western Hemisphere is even more Eurocentric than the Western framework for world history.

This leads to the real target of Ravitch, the consultants who advocate what she terms "particularism." She rejects their criticism of the New York curriculum guides. She denounces them for asserting that the guides project dominant European-American values that belittle the contributions of American minorities and non-Western civilizations for its "hidden assumptions of white supremacy" and "white nationalism." To the contrary she asserts that "the charges have little merit" (p. 20). In fact, according to her, an example of "bias," (her emphasis) by the African-American consultant is the charge that "Egypt is studied as a part of the Middle East instead of as a part of African Civilization." Diane Ravitch goes on to counter: "As it happens, scholars disagree about whether Egypt should be considered part of Africa or part of the Middle East; choosing one alternative rather than the other is not evidence of bias." ("Democracy and Diversity," p. 19) The fact that some European and Europeanized scholars deny the Africanness of ancient Egypt is not a trivial issue. The taking of ancient Egypt out of Africa and Africans out of ancient Egypt is at the heart of the doctrine of white supremacy. This feat of intellectual falsification must be repudiated before any true multicultural curriculum can be developed.

Her solution to the "controversy is to let students investigate the question." We agree, but insist that this investigation be based upon a full review of the context of the intellectual conspiracy to erase the idea of African humanity and civilization from historical memory. This conspiracy was advocated by European intellectuals such as David Hume, Charles Montesquieu, Georg Hegel, and Arnold Toynbee. Only then will students and teachers begin to understand why the issue is so vital.

The claim that ancient Egypt and Egyptians were not Africans was first made in 1839, by Champollian-Figeac, brother of the scholar credited with deciphering heiroglyphs. Responding to Count Volney's statement that the highly civilized ancient Egyptians were a "race of blacks," Champollian-Figeac issued this statement:

> The two physical traits of black skin and kinky hair are not enough to stamp a race as negro and Volney's conclusion as to the negro origin of the ancient population of Egypt is glaringly false and inadmissible. (pp. 26–7)

This idea was reproclaimed in 1910 by another Egyptologist,

95

James Breasted, the founder of University of Chicago's Oriental Institute: "The conclusion maintained by some historians that the Egyptian was of African Negro origin is now refuted...at best he may have been slightly tinctured with negro blood" (p. 26).

Because ancient thinkers generally thought that the Egyptians were black, this fact had to be expressly and repeatedly refuted. After these repetitions by such influential scholars as Champollian and Breasted, many thinkers began to reject the traditional views expressed by Herodotus and Aristotle that the ancient Egyptians, like the ancient Ethiopians, had black skin and wooly hair. Even the evidence on the walls of the tombs and temples which clearly depicted the Egyptians as brown and black-skinned, in comparison to the olive-skinned western Asians and southern Europeans and the fair or white skin of one group of ancient Libyans, was ignored. Students would need access to a representative sampling of the iconography, not just of Egyptian Royalty. They could then compare these pictures and status with pictures of present-day Africans in the various parts of Africa. Students would then become aware that the African populations of all parts of Africa contain a wide variety of complexions, from light brown to very dark brown or black. This was also the color range of ancient Egyptians.

Scholars can be and have been biased and worse. The disagreement among scholars over the culture and race of the ancient Egyptians is a product of unsound scholarship and downright dishonesty. It is ironic that some of the scholars who are trying to correct these distortions and fabrications are now accused of revisionism and unsound scholarship.

Implicit in the essays by Ravitch is the idea that great progress has been made since the 1960s regarding multiculturalism. She states that "since the 60s there has been a great deal of new scholarship about the history of women, blacks and various ethnic minorities." However, she does not mention that the "new scholarship" was directly inspired by the revolt of the African-American college students who, while protesting against the policy of white supremacy in its blatant form of segregation, began demanding what was then called "Black Studies." The critique of American curriculum philosophy, which was a part of the movement, was exploited by white women, Chicanos, Native

Americans, and various non-Anglo-Saxon European ethnic groups. Black Studies programs, however, were quickly relegated to second class academic status and prevented from completing the revolution in curriculum philosophy and practice.

A final problem with Ravitch's position is her suggestion that multicultural education has no concern with science and mathematics. Today, science education ignores the fact that the ancient Egyptians were considered by individuals such as Aristotle and Francis Bacon to be the founders of mathematics and certain sciences. Ignoring the Egyptian mathematical and medical texts, while still explaining the impact of Euclid and Pythagoras on geometry, is a clear case of unacceptable Eurocentrism. Highlighting the Hypocratic Oath, while ignoring the medicine and surgery of the ancient Egyptians, is yet another example. In fact, one can take science and mathematics from elementary school through the Ph.D. degree and never learn that a single African contributed one idea to either science or mathematics.

The Ravitch reaction to the critique of the consultants is related to her fundamental concept of how education in the areas of social science, history, and literature ought to function in the multicultural agenda. She seems to be committed to the idea that multiculturalism ought to be directed toward explicating the unity which is inherent in American pluralism. She honestly feels that the proponents of what she calls particularism undermine the unity because they emphasize the differences and the conflicts, and thus divide the various ethnic groups into camps of oppressors and victims. She does not seem to care whether or not such emphasis is a reflection of reality or not. This implicitly ideological objective tends to undermine Ravitch's argument for sound scholarship. Although her ideas on this matter are not clearly explained, she seems to suggest that the cultural configuration which exists is the one that the curriculum must support or rationalize. Ravitch explains this in relation to the curriculum which she helped design for the state of California:

> Multiculturalism is treated as a dynamic aspect of American culture, not as an alternative to it. A major strand of the curriculum is called 'National Identity.' This is described as follows: Students must: recognize that American society is now and always has been pluralistic and multicultural.

From the first encounter between indigenous peoples and exploring Europeans, the inhabitants of the North American continent have represented a variety of races, religions, languages, and ethnic and cultural groups. With the passage of time, the United States has grown increasingly diverse in its social and cultural composition. Yet, even as our people have become increasingly diverse, there is broad recognition that we are one people. Whatever our origins, we are all Americans. ("Democracy and Diversity," p. 19)

We agree that the United States always has been multicultural (pluralistic is another matter because it connotes power). The problem, however, is that there has not been what Ravitch refers to as "Cultural democracy." She, however, does not deny the dominance of European-American culture. According to her, such dominance is not due to racism. She argues about:

> ...the matter-of-fact consequences of European influence and European immigration. Nearly 80 percent of the population of the United States today is of European descent; the political and economic institutions of the United States were deeply influenced by European ideas. Europe's legacy to us is the set of moral and political values that we Americans subsequently refined and reshaped to enable us, in all our diversity, to live together in freedom and peace. ("Democracy and Diversity," p. 20)

We may point out that the racial oppression and cultural debasement of African peoples that are endemic to the United States political society are also the result of European ideas. The "multiculturalism" that characterizes that condition must be accepted in order for us to "live together in freedom and peace," according to Ravitch. But what has been pursued and largely achieved on the cultural as well as political front is "pacification" not peace, "repression" not freedom.

In searching for the cause of the critique of American curriculum policy, Diane Ravitch zeroes in on the self-esteem issue. According to her, the African-centered position is based upon:

> a pedagogical theory, a conviction that changes in the
> curriculum will raise the self-esteem of children from racial
> and ethnic minorities and will lead to improved academic
> performance. According to the theory, minority children
> who presently perform poorly will have higher self-esteem
> and higher performance if their teachers feature the
> achievements of minority cultures instead of the
> achievements of Europeans and white Americans.
> ("Democracy and Diversity," p. 46)

Indeed, this is a point raised by many proponents of the African-centered curriculum, although not well explained by most of them. It seems obvious that if the truth is taught about African peoples, African culture, and African history that more African students will have higher esteem for the African race than is the case where the distorted image of Africa is taught. However, adopting an African-centered curriculum will not in itself improve individual self-esteem or academic performance. Raising the image of the group is an objective of the African-centered curriculum, but not the main objective.

This issue detracts from the major and central objective of the African-centered curriculum. The objective is to restore the truth about Africa to the world, a result which is good for everybody. Once ancient Egypt is placed back in Africa, we can then begin to examine the reciprocal cultural connections among the people of tricontinental antiquity (Africa-Asia-Europe). We can compare their literature, cosmologies, and languages and examine their influences on their respective continental neighbors.

While the soft-liners have pursued a policy of giving up a little in order to gain much more, the hard-liners continue their rigid position as defenders of Western civilization. For example, sixty new authors were recently admitted to the exclusive *Great Books of the Western World* club. Not one of the initiates was African or African-American. It seems as though a grandfather clause was adopted, as the club consists only of authors who died before 1950. The editors evidently made no attempt to include selections from the many African authors who wrote in Western languages and discoursed the issues included in the Western great conversation.

The soft-liner position seems to enjoy rather wide appeal among journalists and mainstream academia. Nonetheless, the position has failed to win over those African thinkers who are advocating the African-centered curriculum and similar proposals.

The defenders, both hard-liners and soft-liners, are stunned by the large number of highly intelligent, educated African scholars, Africans in scientific professional and business careers, and rank and file members of the African community in the United States who are committed to the success of the project for African-centeredness in the curriculum. The lack of understanding of the defenders tells us that the battle is far from over. It also tells us that a genuine multicultural program is not presently possible in the United States.

Perhaps a time will come when the various ethnocultural, racial groups which constitute the population of the United States can live together as cultural, social, and political equals, and thus refute the prediction made by the European-American founding father Thomas Jefferson. Let us, however take care of first things first. We must start by showing a mutual respect for the intellectual positions being argued.

R E F E R E N C E S

Breasted, James Henry. 1937. *A History of Egypt: From the Earliest Times to the Persian Conquest.* New York: Charles Scribner and Sons.

Champollian-Figeac, Jacques-Joseph. 1839. *Egypte Ancien.* Paris: Fermin Didot.

Du Bois, W.E.B. 1968. *Black Reconstruction in America 1860–1880.* New York: The World Publishing Company.

——. 1975. *The World and Africa.* New York: International Publishers.

Hegel, Georg Wilhelm Friedrich. 1956. *The Philosophy of History.* New York: Dover.

Ravitch, Diane. 1990. "Democracy and Diversity: Multicultural Education in America." *American Educator* (Spring).

——. 1990. "Multiculturalism and E Pluribus Plures." *American Scholar* (Summer).

——. 1990. "Multiculturalism Yes, Particularism No." *The Chronicle of Higher Education* (October).

7

A Critique of Eurocentric Comparisons of the Cultures of Tricontinental Antiquity

While the construction of frameworks for cultural comparisons does not appear to be a major object of either Henri Frankfort et al's *The Intellectual Adventure of Ancient Man* (1977) or Martin Bernal's *Black Athena* (1987), they nonetheless utilize such frameworks as essential foundations for their projects. The two works, which focus on the civilizations of tricontinental antiquity,* not only attempt to analyze certain significant aspects of the cultures, but also address the cross cultural connections and comparisons.

The comparative framework is perhaps easier to identify in Bernal's work because he explicitly builds several models to facilitate his argument. The models in the work by Frankfort, while perhaps less explicit, are necessary to the arguments put forth in the introduction and conclusion, and are less obviously germane to the cultural analysis of the three substantive sections of the work.

Before consideration of these comparative frameworks, some

---

*Tricontinental antiquity is a term that I use to include the civilizations of Northeastern Africa, Western Asia and Southern Europe from 3100 B.C.E. to 400 A.C.E. Such a term is more descriptive of the composition of the "Ancient World" than is the Eurocentric convention, Mediterranean civilization. This conclusion is based on the fact that the oldest known civilizations of antiquity (Egypt and Mesopotamia) were not oriented toward the Mediterranean Sea, but toward these respective subcontinents.

preliminary explanations are in order, especially as they relate to the foci of this essay. Frankfort's work specifically analyzed Egypt, Mesopotamia, and the Hebrews, however, in its conclusion, it includes a penetrating comparison of Greek culture with the three afore-mentioned civilizations. Bernal focused on Egypt, the Levant, and Greece, yet, in a less systematic way, Bernal treats Mesopotamia at various points (pp. 364–66). Thus, both projects dealt with ancient African, Asian, and European cultures. In that sense we can attempt to explicate their comparative frameworks.

The Frankfort Model

Henri Frankfort and his wife began the development and use of their comparative framework in the introduction to the volume entitled "Myth and Reality." The title "Myth and Reality" expresses the essence of the comparison; it describes the speculative thought of the "Ancients" as mythopoeic and compares it with modern scientific thought. The chronological dimension is implicit in the formulation by the inclusion of "modern savages" in the same category with the Ancients. In the conclusion, entitled "The Emancipation of Thought from Myth," the Ancients are separated into the following two camps: those still entrapped in mythopoeic thought and those who largely broke with the primitive mode of speculative thought. According to the Frankforts, the latter camp is composed of two unique cases, the Hebrews and Greeks, each rejecting important dimensions of the primitive pattern. The chronological implications are lessened by the assertion that, outside the two exceptions, antiquity remained in the primitive mode.

It is in the context of this tripartite framework that the Frankforts compare the four "civilizations." Within the first category of mythopoeic thought they place Mesopotamia, Egypt, and "primitive" cultures including modern savages. The Frankforts (1977) note that "a great variety of attitudes and outlooks are possible" (p. 364) among cultures characterized by mythopoeic thought. They point to "a thorough contrast between the Egyptian and Mesopotamian views as to the nature of the universe in which man lives" (p. 366). The result is that the Mesopotamians "express a haunting fear that the unaccountable and turbulent powers (i.e. gods) may at anytime bring disaster to human society" (p. 366). Thus "man was at the mercy of decisions he could neither influence or gauge." But the Egyptians believed that nature presented itself as an established order in which changes are superficial. The Frankforts hold that for the Egyptians a harmonious integration of nature and society existed at all times. While the Frankforts view these differences as "very far-reaching" they conclude that the two peoples agreed in the "fundamental assumptions that the individual is a part of society, that society is embedded in nature, and that nature is but the manifestation of the divine" (pp. 366–67). In addition the, Frankforts contend that the gods of the Egyptians and Mesopotamians were "immanent" (p. 363).

The second category in the Frankforts' scheme concerns the Hebrews and Greeks. Each group "broke with the mode of speculation which...prevailed up to their time" (p. 363). According to the Frankforts, "the dominant tenet of Hebrew Thought is the absolute transcendence of God" (p. 367). This means that the Hebrews with their "infinite moral courage" (p. 373) transcended the ancient myth of immanent godhead and "created...the new myth of the will of God." For the Frankforts this doctrine, which enabled the Hebrews to leave the realm of mythopoeic thought, represents "a high degree of abstraction" (p. 369). This reading also claims that man is "not merely the servant of god as...in Mesopotamia; nor was he placed as in Egypt at a preordained station in a static universe which...could not be questioned." On the contrary "man...was the interpreter and the servant of God...with the task of bringing about the realization of God's will." Thus assert the Frankforts, "not cosmic phenomena but history itself (became) pregnant with meaning; history had become a revelation of the dynamic will of God" (p. 370). This characteristic led the Frankforts to conclude that although "it is possible to detect the episodes of Egyptian and Mesopotamian beliefs in many episodes of the Old Testament...the overwhelming impression...is one, not of derivations, but of originality" (p. 367).

The Frankforts turn to the characterization of the Greeks by asserting that "it remained for the Greeks with their peculiar intellectual courage to discover a form of speculative thought in which myth was entirely overcome" (p. 373). The comparison begins with the observation that the Greeks recognized that "man contains a divine and immortal spark" and thus they "placed man closer to the gods than the Egyptians or Babylonians had ever done" (p. 374). From this posture the Greeks produced a number of secular or private thinkers who, according to the Frankforts, were freed from the responsibility of concern with "spiritual matters" (p. 376). This freedom allowed them to search for an origin of the universe which was not based upon myth. In other words, "the (Greeks) asked for an immanent and lasting ground of existence" which "transfers the problems of man in nature from the realm of faith and poetic intuition to the intellectual sphere" (p. 376). The Greeks "hold that the universe is an intelligible whole" (p. 377). Thus adhering to this analysis the "Greeks presumed that a single order underlies the chaos of our perception and, furthermore, that we are able to comprehend that order" (p. 377). The resulting search for the *Arche* (first principle or cause) of all things led to a variety of answers such as (water) *Thales*, (air) *Anaximenes*, (the boundless) *Anaximander,* (and fire) *Heraclitus*. These answers were unique in that they were asserted without resorting to divine personification, thus they demonstrated the "power of abstraction" (p. 380) beyond anything then known.

The Frankforts point out that this type of speculative thought was called "logos" by Heraclitus. They suggest that "Reason" is the best translation of "logos." Completing their analysis, the Frankforts proclaim that "it is this tacit or outspoken appeal to reason (and) the independence from the prescriptive sanctities of religion which places early Greek philosophy in the sharpest contrast with the thought of the ancient Near East" (p. 386). While the Frankforts admit that Greek contact with the "leading centers" of the ancient world, such as "Egypt and Babylon," was in some way related to their "meteoric (cultural) development," they hasten to assert that "what the Greeks borrowed, they transmuted" (p. 373). Thus, the meteoric developments of the Greeks, like that of the Hebrews, is original.

The emancipated thought of the Greeks and Hebrews appears to lead directly to the third category—modern scientific thought. This mode of speculative thought, like the Greek, claims to "reduce the chaos of perceptions to an order in which typical events take place according to universal laws" (p. 15). Modern scientific thought objectifies the target of inquiry and, again like the Greeks, shuns personification and deification of the qualities and processes of nature. In other words, it "is emotionally indifferent and articulate" (p. 5). Modern science, for the Frankforts appears to be even more emancipated than mythopoeic thought.

B e r n a l ' s   M o d e l s

Martin Bernal might classify the Frankfort analytical model as an example of the "Broad Aryan Model." Bernal's project is a penetrating critique of modern historiography. He attacks the "Aryan Model," which he asserts replaced the superior "Ancient Model." Both models address the relationship between Greek culture and the cultures of African and Asian antiquity. Bernal (1987) succinctly defined the Ancient Model as the "conventional view among Greeks in the Classical and Helinistic ages," according to which "Greek culture had arisen as a result of colonization, around 1500 B.C., by Egyptians and Pheonicians who had civilized the native inhabitants" and from whom the "Greeks had continued to borrow heavily" (p. 1).

Bernal's Aryan Model asserted that Greek civilization is "the result of the mixture of the Indo-European-speaking Helenes" (p. 2) who invaded from the north and their indigenous European subjects. According to Bernal, this latter model which denied the Egyptian connection and questioned the Phoenician one developed not because of new information, but because of a number of external factors including the rise of racism in the eighteenth century. The late nineteenth century expansion of this model to deny the semetic connection is called the Extreme Aryan Model by Bernal, while the older is referred to as the Broad Aryan Model. These models are the foci of Volume I of *Black Athena* which is subtitled the *History of Ancient Greece*. The subtitle summarizes Bernal's major point that the Aryan Model is at odds with the truth about antiquity.

Bernal evidently believes that the Ancient Model, with an appropriate modification, explains the essential cultural connections among the civilizations of antiquity. This model emphasizes "the striking similarities found among populations all around the Mediterranean" (p. 14). Although considerable attention is devoted to "linguistic divisions among the peoples of its (Mediterranean) south and north coasts," (p. 14) the cultural differences among the targeted civilizations are not significantly treated in Volume I of *Black Athena*. This is perhaps because Bernal's major thrust is to show the Afro-Asiatic foundations of Greek culture. While such treatment is consistent with his political objective which is "to lessen European cultural arrogance," (p. 73) the usefulness of the model to explain the differences is extremely limited.

In the context of his Ancient Model, Bernal emphasizes the extent to which various Greek writers attribute Egyptian (and to a lesser extent Phonecian) origins to various Greek ideas and customs especially in the areas of politics and religion. Again the overwhelming concern is with similarities and supports the position that Greek culture was derivative, a position minimized by the Frankforts.

Bernal's Ancient Model is also used to explain the relationship between ancient and modern culture. What is significant in this regard is that Bernal points out the high regard early modern scholars had for the ancient Egyptian legacy. In fact, according to Bernal, throughout the development of Western intellectual history until the end of the eighteenth century, Egyptian influence was paramount. During the Renaissance "the Egyptians were seen as the origin of all wisdom and arts" (p. 153). Bernal asserts that one of the pioneers of modern science, Sir Isaac Newton, "was convinced that atomic theory, heliocentricity and gravitation" had been known by the ancient Egyptians (p. 167). Bernal adds that "This enthusiasm (for Egypt) soared in the century from 1680 to 1780," pointing out that even Montesquieu agreed that "the Egyptians were the best philosophers in the world" (p. 170). This view of the speculative thought of ancient Egypt was based upon the reading of their use of mythology as "an allegorical interpretation of historical events or natural phenomena" (p. 181) rather than as "the clumsy telling" of what they considered literal truths" (p. 181). Thus the mythopoeic thought of the Frankforts disappears. The implication *a la* Bernal is that the Aryan Model is an attempt to artificially impose fundamental differences in modes of thought upon the ancients and moderns that do not in fact exist. This implies that the speculative thought of the Ancient Egyptians was the foundation for modern science. Bernal's conclusions about cultural connections are thus the opposite of those advanced by the Frankforts.

Commentary

Bernal's critique of the Aryan Model certainly focuses on the general inadequacy of the comparative framework utilized by the Frankforts. The Frankforts draw a sharp contrast between the thought of the ancient Egyptians and the ancient Greeks and deemphasize the influence of Egyptian culture upon Greek culture. This point was perhaps put more clearly by John Wilson, author of the chapters on Egypt in *The Intellectual Adventure of Ancient Man* (Frankfort, 1977). Wilson queried: "Did ancient Egypt contribute any significant element to the continuing philosophy, ethics, or world consciousness of later times?" His answer summarizes the position not only of the Frankforts, but also Bernal's Broad Ancient Model:

> No, not directly in fields which one may specify, as in the case of Babylonian science, Hebrew theology, or Greek or Chinese rationalism. One might critically say that the weight of ancient Egypt was not consonant with her size, that her intellectual and spiritual contributions were not up to her length of years and her physical memorial, and that she herself was unable to realize on her promising beginnings in many fields...that culture had reached her intellectual and spiritual heights too early to develop any philosophy which could be transmitted in cultural heritage to the ages. Like Moses, she had had a distant glimpse of the Promised Land, but it was left to others to cross the Jordan and begin the Conquest. (p. 119)

This appraisal is at such odds with the opinion of ancient Greek thinkers like Herodotus, Plato, and Aristotle that one can reasonably attribute the conclusions to the cultural arrogance and racism which Bernal asserts are major reasons for the rejection of the Ancient Model and its replacement by the Aryan Model. For example, Aristotle, in *Politics*, wrote:

> It is no new or even recent discovery of political science that the state should be divided into classes...to this day it is the case in Egypt...in Egypt the system is believed to have been introduced by the legislation of Sesostris...the division into classes originated in Egypt...Egypt bears witness to the antiquity of political institutions. Her people are recognized as the most ancient of all races; and from time out of mind they have had a legal code and a regular system of government. We ought therefore, to make good use of what has come down to us from the past, and merely try to supplement its defects. (*Politics*, Book VIII, 1329, p. 243)

This statement is important because it indicates that Aristotle accepted the notion that Greek philosophy was an extension of a more ancient Egyptian wisdom. This same idea had been advanced by Plato, Aristotle's teacher, in the *Timaeus*.

> In the first place, there is the caste of priests, which is separated from all the others; next there are the artificers, who ply their several crafts by themselves and do not intermix; and also there is the class of shepherds and of hunters, as well as that of husbandmen; and you will observe, too, that the warriors in Egypt are distinct from all the other classes, and are commanded by law to devote themselves solely to military pursuits. (*Timaeus*, p. 13)

While such statements support a suggestion that the Greek thinkers clothed their ideas with the aura of antiquity for purposes of legitimacy, they also support the reading that the Greek thinkers actually believed that the statements represented the truth of the matter. Both readings are equally possible and probable, especially since social class was so vital to Plato's concept of a just society.

Statements made by Plato in *The Laws* support this latter reading. These statements are concerned with the very critical matter of proper education as the foundation of a well-regulated state. Concerning music and art education, he said:

> The law...in Egypt...is marvelous, even in the telling...this state of things (is) worthy in the highest degree of a

statesman and legislator...to effect this would be the task of
a God or a God-like man. (*Laws*, I, p. 101)

In regard to education in mathematics Plato asserted: "One ought to
declare then that [our] children should learn as much of these subjects
as the innumerable crowd of children in Egypt learn along with their
letters" (*Laws*, II, p. 107). This praise of Egyptian pedagogy by Plato
ended with another indictment of the Greek educational tradition:
"When I was told...of our conditions in regard to this matter...I was
ashamed, not only of myself, but of all Greek world" (*Laws*, p. 109).

The upshot is that not only did the Greek thinkers invoke the
reputed authority of Egyptian antiquity (an Egypt conceived of as more
ancient *vis-`a-vis* classical Greece than is ancient Greece *vis-`a-vis*
present day Europe), they also consciously adopted Egyptian ideas into
their works. While this does not conclusively prove that all of the
major Greek philosophical ideas were "stolen" from the Egyptians, it
certainly does bring into question the assertion that all of the ideas
originated with the Greeks themselves.

While the Frankfort Model is flawed from one standpoint, it does
focus on some fundamental differences between the Greek way and the
Egyptian way which Bernal evidently ignores. The distinction between
the mode of thought which attributes personality to the object of
inquiry and one that insists on the thingification of the target of
investigation is fundamental. Even more critical is the contrast
between the alienation inherent in the Greek mode of thought and the
harmony which characterizes the ancient Egyptian mode. The contrast
can best be seen in the cosmogonies of the two cultures. Cosmic
conflicts characterize the Greek cosmogony. The implicit conflict
between the progeny of chaos and the children of earth is followed by
the warfare between the first patriarch sky and the progeny of his
spouse. This warfare is coupled with a basic conflict between the first
divine couple, sky and earth. The latter conflict leads to the
generational cycle of hostilities between father and son that result in the
emasculation of the fathers of two generations. The general warfare
between two camps of divinities ends in the organization of the
universe as it now exists. Human beings were evidently created for the
sport of the gods, or, perhaps, to serve them through sacrifice (see

Hesiod *Theogony*, pp. 17–36).

The worldview of fundamental alienation characterizes the literature of Greece from the age of Homer through the classical period. Alienation is the dominant theme of the dramas and the philosophies. Greek philosophy itself begins with an attack on the Greek tradition. In this sense, Greek philosophy is truly revolutionary, as is Greek political life. Greek philosopy's general critique of tradition is joined by attacks against fellow philosophers. This is especially true in the case of Aristotle and his teacher Plato.

If one pursues the theme of fundamental alienation, it becomes evident that, at the level of cosmogony, Hesiod's *Theogony* and the Mesopotamian *Enuma Elish* have more in common with one another that than they do the cosmogony of Egypt. In the Mesopotamian myth, the general motif is generational and sexual alienation. In fact, the literature of Mesopotamia, like Greek literature, is generally pessimistic. Most of the Egyptian stories on the other hand have a happy ending and there is a generally admitted optimism which characterizes Egyptian civilization.

In this regard, modern science is much more akin to the Mesopotamian and Greek worldviews than to the Egyptian one. The matter-of-fact objectivity of modern science shares the same pessimistic orientation found in the Eurasian cultures. Furthermore, the alienation between divinity and humanity is a necessary condition for the scientific persuasion, a fact that the Frankfort Model seems to ignore.

Because he does not analyze the profound cultural differences between the cultures of antiquity, Martin Bernal's criticism of modern historiography fails to explain the rejection of the Ancient Model. While Bernal's charge that the rejection of the Ancient Model and the fabrication of the Aryan Model is generally sound, he overlooks the possibility that one of the reasons for the rejection of the Ancient Model may have been the recognition of a profound difference. In other words the Ancient Model, even as revised by Bernal, fails to provide a useful account of the cultural connections among the cultures of antiquity. An appropriate model would account for both the cultural differences and the "striking cultural similarities," while assuming a remote unity between two main divisions of humanity.

A n o t h e r   V i e w

In order to eliminate the inadequacies of the Frankfort and Bernal schema, we may need to adopt an approach which I call the "Old Tradition" (see Chapter 4). This is presented as a bare outline and is not intended to be exhaustive; much more work is required to fully develop this framework. An appropriate model would assume a remote unity between two main divisions of humanity. This approach is based upon a significant modification of Cheikh Anta Diop's "Two Cradle Theory," which posits a fundamental factual juxtaposition between African and Eurasian cultures (see Diop, *African Origin of Civilization,* 1974, pp. 111–115; Diop, *Cultural Unity of Black Africa* 1959, passim). Such an approach would account for similarities, such as primeval water, between the Egyptian and Mesopotamian creation myths. It would also account for the "mythopoeic" elements embedded in Mesopotamian, Greek, and Hebrew cultures.

The basic division would be between African and Eurasian worldviews, and each major division would contain chronological subdivisions. In the case of the Eurasian category, the civilization could be divided into four chronological subcategories: (1) the most ancient, including Sumerian, Akkadian, Babylonian, Hittite, and Ugarith; (2) late antiquity, including Phoenician, Hebrew, Persian, and Greek; (3) early religious cultures, especially Christianity and Islam; and (4) Modern Western civilization.

The African category would be divided as follows:(1) the most ancient, including the Kushitic—Egyptian Civilization;(2) late antiquity, including post-Egyptian Pharaonic Kush and pre-Christian Axum; (3) the third period, including the Christian and Islamic religions in relationship to the indigenous African forms of spirituality and the African-based Hermetic tradition; and (4) the fourth period, including the cultural reactions of African societies to European conquests of Africa.

The suggested approach could also account for the legends and other evidence of colonization of Greece by Egyptians and Western Asians which were noted by Bernal. Bernal's implicit concept of colonization in the modern political sense of aggressive imperialism is not required by the Ancient Model. If colonization is considered in its ancient, rather than modern, context then it is likely that colonies of settlers from Egypt and Phoenicia resided in Greek territory. It is logical to suggest that Egyptian colonies existed in Greece and these settlements facilitated economic and cultural exchanges, similar to the way in which later Greek colonies existed in Asia and Africa. Phoenician colonies existed in Africa, and Egyptian colonies existed in Western Asia. The Egyptian settlements in Greece were possibly so small that they received no documentary notice in Egypt, although they probably became a part of Greek legend.

This position, first stated at the Oriental Institute in 1986, was rejected by the "New Orthodoxy." The new orthodoxy began with the advent of the doctrine of white supremacy put forth by such "giants" of mid-eighteenth century philosophy as David Hume and Charles Montesquieu. In addition to invidious racial comparisons, which they held in common, Montesquieu (1974) put forth a tripartite sociology of cultural evolution that placed African societies at the bottom of the development scale (pp. 238–239, 276, 332). He asserted that "Africans on the coast were . . . barbarians and savages" (p. 332) and separated Africans from Egyptians, whom he stated were the "best philosophers in the world" (p. 239).

Hume (1912) not only suspected "the Negroes to be naturally inferior to the whites," (p. 208) he also saw Egypt as inferior to Greece. He noted :

> It has been observed by the ancients, that all arts and sciences arose among free nations; and, that the...Egyptians, notwithstanding their ease, opulence, and luxury, made but faint efforts toward a relish in those finer pleasures, which were carried to such perfections by the Greeks. (p. 89)

The resemblance between the intellectual tyranny of the new orthodoxy and the military and biological tyranny imposed on peoples of the African continent cannot be overlooked. The ancient worldview of alienation facilitated the physical onslaught which, in turn, produced a need for the emergence of a philosophical doctrine of white supremacy.

Unlike Bernal's Ancient Model, the Old Tradition as a

comparative framework is not static and like traditions in all societies, it evolves and adjusts to changing circumstances. This framework accounts for all of the cultural similarities which Bernal emphasized, as well as the cultural differences stressed by the Frankforts and associates. It also accounts for the rejection of the Old Tradition by modern European thinkers.

R E F E R E N C E S

Bernal, Martin. 1987. *Black Athena: The Afroasiatc Roots of Classical Civilization.* Vol. I The Fabrication of Ancient Greece, 1785–1985. New Brunswick: Rutgers University Press.

Diop, Cheikh Anta. 1959. *The Cultural Unity of Black Africa.* Paris: Presence Africaine.

—. 1974. *The African Origin of Civilization: Myth or Reality.* Westport: Lawrence Hill.

Frankfort, Henri., et al. 1977. *The Intellectual Adventure of Ancient Man.* Chicago: University of Chicago Press.

Heidel, Alexander 1951. *The Babylonian Genesis: The Story of Creation.* Chicago: University of Chicago Press.

Hesiod. 1953. *Theogony.* Translated by Norman O. Brown. Indianapolis: Bobbs-Merrill.

Hume, David. 1912. *Essays: Moral, Political and Literary.* New York: Liberty Classics.

Montesquieu, Charles. 1974. *The Spirit of the Laws.* New York: Hafner.

8

Reflections on the Question of the Race of the Ancient Egyptians

In an article entitled "Were the Ancient Egyptians Black or White?" Frank Yurco argues that the ancient Egyptians were neither black nor white, but "heterogeneous" (Yurco 1989, *Biblical Archeology Review*, p. 24). He further suggests that the ancient Egyptians should neither be shackled with "our cultural baggage" nor "our primitive contemporary racial labels" because, as he asserts, the ancient Egyptian "didn't think in those terms." While the spirit of Yurco's petition is commendable, the racial cultural baggage ought to be removed from an analysis of the ancient Egyptians by, first of all, admitting that they were black.

To prove that the ancient Egyptians were black, one needs to consider the evidence on which Yurco based his conclusions. An examination of selected pharaohic mummies reveals that "Seqenen-Re...had tightly curled, wooly hair...and strongly Nubian features" and that "Thutmose IV...had wavy hair and Egypto-Nubian facial features." Both of these were ancestors of Nefertiti, whom Yurco describes as a "light Mediterranean type." Consider also a conclusion that Yurco made concerning the Twelfth Dynasty royal personages who had "strong Nubian features and dark coloring" as seen in their sculpture and relief work." An accompanying photograph of a relief of Senwosret I "displays" the pharaoh with "such Nubian traits as thick lips and a broad nose with flaring nostrils."

Describing the ancient Egyptians as black by no means ignores the conclusion made by Yurco that the mummies of Yuya, his daughter Queen Tiy, and Ramses II were all probably light-skinned with non-Nubian traits. However, the terms which Yurco inadvertently uses ("Semitic" to depict Ramses and "Syro-Palestinians;" "negroid" to characterize "Nubians, Kushites, and central Africans;" and "caucasoid" to indicate blond-haired, blue-eyed "Mitanni") are very nonscientific when applied to ethnicity. In fact, Semitic is more appropriately used as a linguistic term. Each of these types, as well as the statutes of Prince Rahotep and his wife Nofret, can be described as black when placed in the context of the population of ancient Egypt.

Regarding the general depiction of the ancient Egyptian population, Frank Yurco points out that the "Egyptian painters and sculptors were careful observers" who depicted themselves, and the foreigners with whom they had contact, quite realistically, especially after the beginning of the Middle Kingdom. "Not surprisingly," Yurco points out "most tomb owners in the Thebian new kingdom Necropolis are depicted with brown complexions, as we see among their modern-day descendants." Summarizing the color range of the ancient Egyptians, Frank Yurco concludes that "the peoples of the Nile Valley present a continuum, from the lighter Northern Egyptians, to the browner Upper Egyptian, to the still browner Nubians and Kushites, to the ultra-dark brown Nilotic peoples." "Among the foreigners" he continues, "the Nubians were closest ethnically to the Egyptians." Another fact he points out is that "in the late pre-dynastic period...the Nubians shared the same culture as the Egyptians and even evolved the same pharaonic structure." In fact, the first known occurrence of pharaonic culture was in Nubia (p. 26).

It is in this context that we should consider Frank Yurco's comparison of the ancient Egyptians with modern day Egyptians.

> The ancient Egyptians, like their modern descendants, were of varying complexions of color, from the light Mediterranean type...to the light brown of Middle Egypt, to the darker brown of Upper Egypt to the darkest shade round Aswan...where even today, the population shifts to Nubian....In short ancient Egypt, like modern Egypt,

consisted of a very heterogeneous population. (pp. 24, 25)

Although I agree with the statement regarding the similarity of color range, populations of the modern day Egyptian cities such as Alexandria, Cairo, Abydos, and even Luxor are lighter in complexion than were the ancient Egyptian populations. The color range of the cross section of ancient Egyptians is more similar to the present-day population of Aswan than to Cairo or Luxor; Aswan is not unlike the populations of Khartoum, Sudan; Addis Abba, Ethiopia; and the southside of Chicago. Regarding what he calls "modern Afro-Americans," Professor Yurco allows, that some Afro-Americans, "particularly those of mixed racial ancestry, will find they look like some ancient (and modern Egyptians)." In point of fact, the cross section of African-Americans, including those who are not of "mixed racial ancestry," will find they look like the cross section of ancient Egyptians (p. 25).

Frank Yurco's article was a response to a letter to the editor that was printed in *Biblical Archaeology Review*. According to the review's editors, the author of the letter, Mrs. Joan P. Wilson, "asserted that the Egyptian Queen Nefertiti was Black, and indeed, that the Egyptians are a Black race of people." This letter does not place the "cultural baggage from our society" on the ancient Egyptians, rather it protests against the cultural baggage which has suffocated the ancient Egyptian civilization for more than two centuries. This "cultural baggage" was dumped on ancient Egypt during the process of establishing the doctrine of "white supremacy" (p. 18).

The emerging doctrine of white supremacy could not gain credibility among those who were familiar with the traditional wisdom among educated Europeans that the ancient Africans of Egypt had achieved a very high level of civilization and had transmitted to the ancient Greeks many of the major ideas considered a part of Greek civilization. Georg Wilhelm Friedrich Hegel (1956) supplied the solution to this latter difficulty when, at the beginning of the nineteenth century, he asserted that Africa was "not a historical part of the world. Historical movement in it—that is in its northern part— belong to the Asiatic or European world...Egypt will be considered in reference to its western phase, but it does not belong to the African spirit" (p. 99). Thus Hegel removed Africans from history, and took Egypt out of Africa and Africans out of Egypt.

Hegel's position was soon adopted by some of the newly emerging modern Egyptologists.

Though never totally accepted by all European writers, the Hegelian solution was dominant during the nineteenth century and enabled some of the leading Egyptologists to assert with James H. Breasted, founder of the University of Chicago's Oriental Institute, that: "the conclusion maintained by some historians that the Egyptian was of African Negro origin is now refuted" (Breasted 1937, p. 26). In the same vein, the Egyptologist Herman Junker concluded that even the ancient Nubians were not "Negro" (Junker 1921, pp. 121–132).

Egyptologists have been debating the race of ancient Egyptians for almost two hundred years. Many still cling to the doctrine put forth by Champollian and Breasted; others assert that the ancient Egyptians were racially similar to the Berbers of North Africa; some believe that the Nile Valley dwellers were of Western Asian or Semitic stock, while many younger Egyptologists argue that the race of the ancient Egyptian is unknown, unknowable, and irrelevant. Martin Bernal (1987) put forth a position that is similar to Yurco's. Bernal stated:

> At least for the last seven thousand years, the population of Egypt has contained African, South-West Asian and Mediterranean types. It is also clear that the further south, or up the Nile, one goes, the Blacker and more Negroid the population becomes, and that this has been the case for the same length of time. As I stated in the Introduction, I believe that Egyptian civilization was fundamentally African and that the African element was stronger in the Old and Middle Kingdoms, before the Hyksos invasion, than it later became. Furthermore, I am convinced that many of the most powerful Egyptian dynasties which were based in Upper Egypt—the 1st, 11th 12th and 18th—were made up of pharaohs whom one can usefully call Black (p. 242)

Yet another group of scholars of African descent, including the late Cheikh Anta Diop of Senegal and Théophile Obenga of the Republic of the Congo, argue that the ancient Egyptians were black in the same sense that Africans south of the Sahara are considered black.

In 1974, at the insistence of Professor Diop, the United Nations Educational Scientific and Cultural Organization (UNESCO) convened an international conference of Egyptologists to discuss the issue. At the conference, after hearing the arguments of Drs. Diop and Obenga, the European and American Egyptologists agreed that the language and culture of the ancient Egyptians originated in Africa. However, the scholars refused to conclude that the population was black.

While the ancient Egyptians were neither black supremacists nor guilty of color discrimination in the sense of modern white supremacy, the argument that the Nile Valley dwellers were black is extremely important. The intellectual crimes and errors of the past must be corrected. Modern scholars who use contemporary views about race to deny the Africanness of the ancient Egyptians are employing a nonscientific concept of race which was handed to them by white supremacist intellectuals. Scholars have drawn, and continue to draw, conclusions based upon their own racial attitudes. Those who would solve the problem as Yurco suggests have the best of intentions, however their integration position is no more *scientific* than the position taken by Diop. On the other hand, the position taken by Breasted and others is somewhat dishonest.

Herodotus and Aristotle used the word *melagchroes* to refer to the skin color of the Egyptians and Ethiopians. When used to designate the phenotype associated with the continent of Africa, the term includes a variety of skin colors ranging from light brown to black. This range could be found in Southern Africa during the nineteenth century among groups such as the yellowish brown Khoi and the chocolate brown Zulus. Such a range is depicted in the iconography of Kemet from the Fifth through the Twentieth Dynasties.

The ancient Greeks sometimes used the term *melagchroes* to refer to skin color differences among what we would today call white people. This is also true today. Even today southern Italians, individual southern Europeans, and Western Asians are sometimes called black. Nonetheless most people are able to distinguish between the two uses. Why black scholars such as Frank Snowden, who would be nonblack by the standards he uses *vis-`a-vis* the ancient Egyptians, cannot make those distinctions is somewhat curious (Snowden 1989, pp. 83–93).

The Kemites were as black as the Greeks were white. Like other southern Europeans, many Greeks had a dark olive or bronze complexion and curly, dark brunette hair. The populations tended to become progressively lighter the further north one traveled. The claim concerning the blackness of the Kemites is no more outrageous than the claim concerning the whiteness of the Greeks. It is pointless to quibble about what Herodotus meant when he stated that the Kemites were black with kinky hair or to debate what percentage of which dynasties were black or whether true Africans had inverted lips. How inverted were the lips of the average ancient Greek; how Caucasoid were their features? The irony is scholars who call the Kemites black are now on the defensive and attacked as revisionists. If white supremacists had not lied about Egyptians and Africans in the first place, we would not be presently arguing about this matter.

Concerning the color of present-day Egyptians in relation to those of antiquity, Frank Yurco cites studies which indicate that in regard to blood and skeletal types contemporary Egyptians are the same as the ancient ones. He then incorrectly indicates that massive migrations from Europe or Asia did not occur. To the contrary, there were certainly significant influxes to various parts of Egypt by Moslems and Turks. One would need a thorough study of the historical population of Egypt before coming to the conclusions reached by Yurco. On the contrary, the belief that contemporary Egyptians are lighter than the ancient Egyptians is supported by the iconography of antiquity.

Finally, regarding the assertion that the ancient Egyptians were more Mediterranean in type than inner African, the iconography of ancient Egypt clearly distinguishes between the color of the Western Asians, Libyans, and Egyptians. The evidence from the walls of the tombs and temples clearly depicts the Egyptians as brown-and black-skinned in comparison to the olive-skinned Western Asians and southern Europeans and the fair-skinned groups of ancient Libyans.

Indeed, the visual evidence suggests that the population of ancient Egypt, like the African populations of all parts of Africa, contained a wide variety of complexions from light brown to very dark brown or black. This is true of West Africa as well as South and East

Africa. This was also the color range of ancient Egyptians.

The cultural baggage of "primitive racial labels" will not be removed from ancient Egypt until it is removed from the modern world. Scholars can alleviate the problem of cultural white supremacy by admitting that the ancient Egyptians were black in the sense that the term is used to describe contemporary African peoples in North America, the Caribbean, and much of Africa. When Herodotus referred to the ancient Egyptians and Ethiopians as black with wooly hair, he was not placing the racial cultural baggage of modern society upon them. He was merely describing them in conventional terms and in relation to people who lived in Europe, parts of Asia, and even perhaps, other parts of Africa. That is the sense in which the ancient Egyptians should be considered black.

White supremacy is a misguided and criminal doctrine which should be abandoned. When the scholars admit, and the reading public accepts, that the ancient Egyptian civilization was authored by people who would be called black or Negro by contemporary criteria, then we can begin to correctly identify the civilizations of antiquity. We can then say that the Greek civilization and its (mixed) people were European, the Mesopotamian and Phoenician civilizations and their (mixed) people were Asian, and the Egyptian civilization and its (mixed) people were African. Common sense will do the rest.

REFERENCES

Bernal, Martin. 1987. *Black Athena : The Afroasiatic Roots of Classical Civilization.* Vol. I. The Fabrication of Ancient Greece 1785–1985. New Brunswick: Rutgers University Press.

Biblical Archaeology Review. May/June. "Queries and Comments."

Breasted, James H. 1938. *The Conquest of Civilization,* ed. Edith Williams Ware. New York: Harper Brothers.

—. 1937. *A History of Egypt: From the Earliest Times to the Persian Conquest.* New York: Charles Scribner and Sons.

Diop, Cheikh Anta. 1978. *The Peopling of Ancient Egypt and The Deciphering of Meroetic Script.* UNESCO.

Drake, St. Clair. 1987. *Black Folk Here and There.* Los Angeles: Center for Afro-American Studies, University of California, Los Angeles. Vol. 1.

Hegel, Georg Wilhelm Friedrich. 1956. *The Philosophy of History.* New York: Dover.

Herodotus. 1987. *The History.* Translated by David Grene. Chicago: University of Chicago Press.

Hume, David. 1987. *Essays: Moral, Political, and Literary.* Indianapolis: Liberty Classics.

Junker, Herman. 1921. "The First Appearance of the Negro in History." *Journal of Egyptian Archaeology,* vol. 7.

Montesquieu, Charles. 1949. *The Spirit of the Laws.* New York: Hafner.

Snowden, Frank M. Jr. 1989. "Bernal's 'Blacks', Herodotus and Other Classical Evidence." *Arethusa*, Special Issue (Fall).

Williams, Bruce. 1986. *Excavations Between Abu Simbel and The Sudan Frontier*, Part I: the A-Group Royal Cemetery at Qustul: Cemetery L. Chicago: The Oriental Institute of the University of Chicago.

Yurco, Frank. 1989. "The Ancient Egyptian Marketplace," *Field Museum of Natural History*. Bulletin, February.

—. 1989. "Were the Ancient Egyptians Black or White?" *Biblical Archaeology Review*, (September/October).

9

Neo-Hegelian Multiculturalism
A Critique of Arthur Schlesinger Jr.'s
The Disuniting of America

Francis Fukuyama and Yuji Aida, two scholars of Japanese origin, anticipated the spirit of Arthur Schlesinger Jr.'s essay defending Western civilization. Francis Fukuyama's essay, entitled "The End of History," asserts that Hegel has been vindicated because the whole world has surrendered to the civil society (Western democratic capitalism) which is the core of Western civilization and, thus, the fulfillment of the spirit of history. Yuji Aida, a professor of European renaissance history at the University of Koyto, predicted the disuniting of the United States in the wake of the rise of African-American and Hispanic-American populations,with special emphasis on the growth of their ethnic and racial consciousness. Aida speculated that the rise of African-American and Hispanic-American power would result in the regression of the United States to an agricultural society due to the anticipated inability of Africans and Hispanics to maintain modern industrial and postindustrial society.

In his great dialectical interpretation of world history, Georg Hegel states that the spirit of history proper begins in the Orient—China specifically—and then begins to evolve toward the West, finally reaching its apex in the future German peoples. Hegel proclaimed that all cultures should be examined in the context of their contributions to what he felt was the development of the world spirit. However, in his examination, Africa proper was "not part of the historical process." According to Hegel, the only part of the African continent which was involved in history "was its northern part, which" belongs to either the Orient or to the West.

The present multicultural project revealed by Arthur Schlesinger Jr. and company agrees in spirit with Fukuyama, Aida, and Hegel. While Schlesinger Jr. would probably take issue with Hegel and insist that the Western Hemisphere, or at least the United States of America, is a part of the Western civilization epoch of history and while he would disagree with Aida and argue that African-Americans and Hispanic-Americans will not succeed in taking over the United States, he certainly seems to agree with their assessments of African culture and the role of Africans in world history.

The following critique finds that Schlesinger Jr., who represents himself as a liberal draped in the dappled cloak of cultural pluralism and its ultimate truths, is in fact a hard-line defender of Western civilization. Western civilization, the formal name assigned to the modern European project, has at its core the doctrine and practice of white supremacy.

Schlesinger Jr.'s argument exposes the incompatibility between multiculturalism and African-centered education which is due to the hidden agenda of the designers of the multicultural campaign. This hidden agenda is the continuation of the tradition of Western superiority, Anglo-Saxon dominance, and white supremacy in the educational process.

The irony of the present conflict is revealed in the fact that the current emphasis on multiculturalism was made possible because of the Black Studies revolt of the 1960s. The Black Studies revolt, led by African-American college students, inspired and spawned ethnic and women studies. Multiculturalism, arising in that context, asserts that once the multicultural curriculum is established, there will be no need, nor room, for Black Studies.

In this regard, multiculturalism is an echo of integration; both have been highly promoted as methods of education reform which purport to correct past injustices. Integration, which was advanced as the answer to the inferior education given African-Americans under the system of segregation, has managed to ensure an inferior education for African-Americans. This cultural pluralism advocated by Schlesinger Jr., his intellectual ward, Diane Ravitch, and others, is designed to accomplish the same result which the unrefined Anglo-Saxon European American curriculum accomplished, namely to proclaim European cultural superiority, albeit under a less offensive veneer of white supremacy. No better case can be made for the appropriateness of and necessity for an African-centered curriculum. It is in this context that we turn to an examination of *The Disuniting of America* and its author.

Decomposition of America

Arthur Schlesinger Jr., the epitome of John F. Kennedy's brain trust during the brief era of the "New Frontier," has taken up the cause of defending Western civilization against the African-centered curriculum movement. In his essay, *The Disuniting of America* (1991), Schlesinger Jr.'s. professed aim is a noble one, namely to prevent the decomposition of America. He warns against the tendency toward decomposition which, according to him, is intertwined with the African-centered curriculum and similar programs.

However, readers come nearest to Schlesinger Jr.'s real interest at the beginning of Chapter 3, "The Battle of the School," which reads: "Doctrinaire ethnicity in general and the dogmatic black version in particular raise questions that deserve careful and dispassionate examination" (p. 40). This priority is necessary because: "Generous-hearted people, Black and White, go along with Afrocentrism out of a decent sympathy for the insulted and injured of American society and of a decent concern to bind the wounds" (p. 40). In other words, for Schlesinger Jr., the greatest threat from the African-centered curriculum movement is the guilt trip and intimidation it causes among the "white majority" (p. 79). By exposing the movement as a flawed and evil project, Schlesinger Jr. wants to bring closure to the "debate about the curriculum" which is a "debate about what it means to be an American" (p. 3). For him, an American is one who subscribes to the "melting pot" theory articulated by an eighteenth-century Frankish-American, Hector Crevecoeur.

Before commenting on Professor Schlesinger Jr.'s critique of the attack on the melting pot theory, let us examine the idea of Crevecoeur upon which *The Disuniting of America* relies so heavily. Crevecoeur published his letters in 1782, during the period when the European settlers in the thirteen British colonies were disuniting the British dominion. It must be noted that Schlesinger Jr. does not comment on that act of violent separatism, although there were many who deplored the decomposition of the noble, British historical and political heritage. This begs the following questions: Is the right of Anglo-Saxons to physically and politically separate from other Anglo-Saxons through the use of violence more honorable than the right of African-Americans to advocate cultural autonomy without violence? Or is it a matter of timing?

Returning to Crevecoeur, in his letter which some editors have entitled "What is an American," he states, "He is either a European or the descendant of an European" (p. 2). In 1782, when this letter was written, the population of the thirteen states consisted of about one-half million Africans, two and one-half million Europeans, and an unknown number of original inhabitants. Crevecoeur specifically named "English, Scots, Irish, French, Dutch, Germans and Swedes," while tacitly excluding Africans and the original inhabitants."

The reason why Africans were excluded from "we the people" is partially revealed in *The Federalist #54* by James Madison (1937), who is sometimes identified as the father of the constitution: "the laws have transformed the negroes into subjects of property [and] if the laws were to restore the rights which have been taken away, the negroes could no longer be refused an equal share of representation with the other inhabitants" (p. 355).

Thus, from the outset, "America" was disunited; this established disunity between European-Americans and the Africans in America was in someway endorsed by every president and major political figure during the antebellum era, including Abraham Lincoln, who favored colonization, and Benjamin Franklin, who, though often cited for his relatively liberal views, argued in his earlier years:

> The Number of purely White people in the world is proportionally very small. All Africa is black or tawny. America (exclusive of new comers) wholly so. And in Europe, the Spaniards, Italians, French, Russians and Swedes, are generally of what we call a swarthy Complexion; as are the Germans also, the Saxons only excepted, who with the English make-up the principal Body of White People of the Face of the Earth. I could

wish their Numbers were increased. And while we are, as I may call it, Scouring our Planet, by clearing America of Woods, and so making this Side of our Globe reflect a brighter Light to the Eyes of Inhabitants in Mars or Venus, why should we in the Sight of Superior Beings, darken its People? Why increase the Sons of Africa, by Planting them in America, where we have so fair an Opportunity, by excluding all Blacks and Tawnys, of increasing the lovely White and red? But perhaps I am partial to the Complexion of my Country, for such Kind of Partiality is natural to Mankind (p. 234).

Arthur Schlesinger Jr. (1991) notes the exclusion of Africans, and he viewed it as an aberration which resulted from "America's most conspicuous failure to live up to the creed" (p. 14). He continues by asserting that "noble ideals had been pronounced if for all Americans, yet in practice they applied only to white people" (p. 14). On the contrary, Africans were not considered Americans, as Crevecoeur's letter implied. Alexis de Tocqueville, in his *Democracy in America,* advanced this conclusion. Though he notes de Tocqueville's conclusion, Schlesinger Jr. forgets to mention that de Tocqueville also concluded that separation was the most probable solution.

Furthermore, though recognizing that European-Americans continued to deny freedom to African-Americans after the Civil War, Schlesinger Jr. asserts that African-Americans prevailed after World War II because they held on to the American Creed and "proclaimed their pride and demanded their rights" (p. 15). In reality, Africans had continuously revolted against slavery and oppression, long before there was an "American Creed." In addition, Schlesinger Jr. fails to see that the Civil Rights movement neither resulted in the melting of the United States African population into the American pot, nor in the equal inclusion of Africans in America in the civil society. He does not seem to understand that Africans and Europeans in this country have been and continue to be in a state of disunity. Suggesting that a future union of white and black races in the United States is a state to which all members of both groups should aspire is one thing. However, assuming a present and a past union is flatly incorrect.

The Schlesingers' Intergenerational Contribution

In an attempt to introduce himself to the reader, Arthur Schlesinger Jr. uses Chapter 3 of *The Disuniting of America* to clarify his belief "in the pluralistic approach to the writing and teaching of history" (p. 41) and to inform readers of his heritage as the son of Schlesinger Sr., who is described as a "great champion of social history, of urban history, and immigration history" (p. 41). Arthur Schlesinger Sr. was also an active member of the executive council for the "Association of the Study of Negro Life and History"; Schlesinger Jr. was himself a member of the executive council of the *Journal of Negro History*. His father was a staunch friend of Carter G. Woodson, Charles Wesley, Rayford Logan, John Hope Franklin, and others. Though Professor Schlesinger Jr. claims to support black history and believe "in the importance of teaching Americans the history of civil rights" (p. 41), many students of African-American and African history do not view the Schlesinger intergenerational contribution to African-American history in a positive fashion. One scholar quoted Schlesinger Sr. as having written, in reference to the chattel slave system in the United States that: "On balance...the bondsmen were better fed, clothed, and sheltered, and led easier and probably healthier lives than if they had remained in Africa" (Jones 1972, "The Schlesingers")

The Schlesingers are of German descent, and their treatment of peoples of African descent is reminiscent of the great German philosopher Georg Wilhelm Friederich Hegel. In his *The Philosophy of History* (1956), Hegel concluded that slavery was an improvement upon the condition of the "Negro." Among Africans, Hegel asserted, "Tyranny is regarded as no wrong" and "justice and morality" are held in "perfect contempt." He continued, "nothing but external force can hold the state together....A ruler stands at the head for sensuous barbarism can only be restrained by despotic power" (p. 98).

It is difficult to ignore the Hegelian echoes in the following assertions of Schlesinger Jr. (1991).

> The West needs no lectures on the superior virtue of those "sun people" (Africans) who sustained slavery until Western *imperialism* abolished it...who still keep women in subjection and cut off their clitorises, who carry out social persecutions...against fellow Africans from the wrong *tribe* who show themselves either incapable of operating a democracy or ideologically hostile to the democratic idea, and who in their *tyrannies* and massacres...have stamped with utmost brutality on human rights...democracy would find it hard...to put down roots in a *tribalist* and patrimonial culture, that long before the West *invaded* Africa, had sacrialized the personal...authority of *chieftains* and ordained the submission of the rest...corruption is regarded through much of Africa as no more than the prerogative of power. (Schlesinger, pp. 76–77)

Schlesinger Jr. seems to have devoted much attention to the role of Africans in America, and never demonstrated any attempt to present the perspectives of African-Americans. Several of the works of Schlesinger Jr. reveal that he is more interested in what liberal whites did for Negroes than what African Americans actually did for themselves. Furthermore, Schlesinger Jr. has devoted most of his energy to lecturing African-American scholars about what he considers to be their "bad history." This was his theme when he criticized African-American scholars who disapproved of William Styron's *The Confessions of Nat Turner,* and this is his basic theme in *The Disuniting of America.*

Needless to say, any cultural pluralism based upon the Schlesinger historical tradition is considered grossly inadequate and blatantly white supremacist, not only by African-centered scholars, but by many black historians in the Eurocentric tradition. It is in these contexts that one must consider both Schlesinger Jr.'s claims to be a cultural pluralist and his argument against the African-centered curriculum. Schlesinger Jr.'s comments on Africans and African-Americans seem to be based neither upon research nor careful perusal of secondary sources. He does not appear to have any expertise in psychology or professional education and, by his own admission, he is not an expert on ancient Egypt. Yet, these are the very matters upon which he focuses in the essay. It is difficult to determine what qualifies Schlesinger to speak on cultural pluralism. His major qualifications seem to be a neo-Hegelian white supremacist attitude and emotional commitment to the defense of Western civilization. The younger Schlesinger's argument begins by positing two theories of population composition of the United States. The melting pot theory is, for Schlesinger, the theory of the "founders" and the one that not only went unchallenged until the twentieth century, but is the ideal toward which the masses of inhabitants, whatever their origin or experience in the country, strive and have striven throughout the history of the country. Schlesinger believes that in the course of history, theory has been somewhat modified to include cultural pluralism, but with the basic thrust that all will adopt a new "American" identity as the ultimate resolution of the temporary tension as embodied in the motto *E Pluribus Unum*.

The second theory, the "Tower of Babel" theory, for Schlesinger Jr., has been evoked by certain spokespersons for the late-coming immigrants and certain non-European ethnics who were originally badly treated and harder to melt than Crevecoeur's northwestern Europeans. The "Tower of Babel" theory has achieved some healthy consequences according to Schlesinger. It has prodded the dominant culture into multicultural inclusion. Most of the ethnic leaders who advocated this approach abandoned it when the ethnic group began to move into the mainstream. Schlesinger cited Irish Americans and Jewish Americans as examples of this tendency.

Schlesinger Jr. warns that the theory if taken too far may lead to disharmonious relations among various groups within the population. He argues that the advocates of African-centeredness have gone too far. As he put it: "The ethnic upsurge...threatens to become a counterrevolution against the original theory of America as 'one people,' a common culture, a single nation" (p. 17).

Bad History

As a preface to his argument that African-centered history is "bad history," Schlesinger Jr. explains that history has two major roles: it is an academic discipline with standards of accuracy and objectivity in the reconstructing of the past (p. 20), and it is the memory of a nation; and, as such it defines national identity which, in turn, becomes a means of shaping history.

> The invocation of history is indispensable to nations and groups in the process of making themselves. How else can people establish the legitimacy of its personality, the continuity of its traditions, the correctness of its course? (p. 21)

Schlesinger Jr. recognizes that, in the second sense, history is used by both the ruling class and the victims of power (p. 22). He does not clarify whether "national (or group) memory" history is, by definition, "bad history."

However, he does imply that history as group memory is a weapon and that using history as a weapon is an abuse of history. Whatever the case, the reader is left with the impression that Anglo-Saxon European, top dog history, if not good history, is at least less bad than African-centered, underdog history. Three subtle themes seem to support this inference. In the first place Anglo-Saxon European history is based in part on "unassailable facts" (p. 24). Second, it is basically honest and since the job of redressing the balance has been splendidly undertaken in recent years (p. 27), it reflects the diversity of the "Nation."

The second theme is based on Schlesinger's conclusion that historically, the new entrants into the country have attempted to assimilate, abandoning their old national identities and invoking the Anglo-Saxon canon. Thus the American Creed has historically prevailed against its competitor. Even the elite spokespersons for the "ethnic cult" have been converted or silenced, eventually. This is also true, Schlesinger asserts, of the masses of African-Americans who Schlesinger believes reject the position of the African-centered advocates.

The third theme which seems to undergird Schlesinger Jr.'s history lesson is that for him, Anglo-Saxon top dog history is a nobler ideal than its adversary. Since it is from the Anglo-Saxon heritage that the basic American creed emerged, it is fitting that the noble lie which it projects is a nobler lie than the ideals put forth by the African-centered historians.

It appears that the only role "history as a discipline" plays for Schlesinger Jr. is as a framework for criticizing underdog history. The fact that American civilization is a myth, a dream concocted by a long string of Anglo-Saxon lovers from the French American Crevecoeur to the German American Schlesinger Jr. does not save it from Schlesinger's own definition of bad history. Thus, what Schlesinger is proposing is that the African-centered historians give up and abandon their bad history and accept white supremacy's bad history. Among many African-centered thinkers, liberal white supremacy is just as unacceptable as conservative white supremacy.

In his critique, Schlesinger questions whether or not the African-centered position is "in fact true" (p. 41). This question, which was put to the argument that black Africa is the birthplace of science, philosophy, religion, medicine, and technology, suggests that Schlesinger is going to judge African-centered history by the standards of history as a discipline. Schlesinger then admits, "I am far from being an expert on Egyptian history" (p. 41), and then he goes on to point out that many scholars regard Mesopotamia as the cradle of civilization. However, such an observation does not settle the matter. Other scholars still support the position held by Herodotus, Plato, Aristotle, Volney, and Breasted that ancient Egypt was the birthplace. The debate will continue because the "facts" are, in themselves, inconclusive.

A second African-centered proposition examined by Schlesinger Jr. is the assertion that "Egypt was essentially a black African country" (p. 41). Since he is not an expert on the subject he defers to an African American classicist, Frank Snowden, and to the Egyptologists Frank Yurco and Miriam Lichtheim, all of whom deny that the ancient Egyptians were black. Lichtheim goes so far as to assert that the Nubians were not black (p. 42). The point is not whether one is an expert on Egyptian history (neither classicist nor Egyptologists are necessarily experts on Egyptian or any other history), but whether there are any experts on race. In view of the inability of the proponents of race theory, after two hundred and fifty years, to develop a clear definition of race and what constitutes racial characteristics or distinct delineation as to what the races are, I would submit that Snowden,

Yurco, and Lichtheim are no more qualified to determine the race of the ancient Egyptians than any other scholar of human affairs. Those who pioneered in the development of white supremacy theory, including Hume and Montesquieu, used the term "Negro" (derived from the Spanish word for black) in the context of complexion or color. Thus, Negro, black, and African came to be synonymous terms. In this sense, "black," in reference to race, has generally included a wide variety of shades of brown-skinned people, presumed to be of African descent. This variety can be observed in all sections of what is often called "Black Africa." A similar variety constituted the basic population of ancient Egypt, as witnessed by the quite distinct iconography still evident in the lower Nile Valley.

I would submit that those of us who have been called Negro, black, and African all our lives, who are various shades of tan, brown, and black, whose mothers and fathers lived their lives as blacks are more entitled to determine what race is than are European scholars and their brainwashed African American dependents. Certainly, if the ancient Greeks, Romans, Arabs, and Jews are entitled to be called whites, the ancient Egyptians and Nubians are entitled to be called blacks. Again, Mr. Schlesinger has not proved that African-centered scholars are wrong on this issue.

The third criticism of the African-centered position results from the way Schlesinger perceives the African-centered treatment of the West African Kingdoms. He reprimands the African scholars because they do not teach "about the tyrannous authority," the African emperors exercised, "the ferocity of their wars," "the tribal massacres," "the squalid lot of the common people," "the captives sold into slavery," "the complicity with the Atlantic slave trade," or "the persistence of slavery in Africa after it was abolished in the west" (p. 42). This alleged fault is of course based upon Schlesinger's negative evaluation of African culture before European colonization. In this regard Schlesinger Jr. seems to rely on outdated European accounts and descriptions of African life. Such assertions are generally rejected by the school of European Africanists who have presented Africa in a more objective light during the last forty years. Evidently, the Hegelian tradition is hard to break among some scholars.

The bad history charge is also directed at the African-centered position's emphasis on the significance of the connection between Africans in America and the historical African heritage. "It is hard to see what living connection exists between American Blacks today and their heterogeneous West African ancestors three centuries ago," ponders Schlesinger (p. 44). He goes on to cite a list of African Americans who he feels rejected the relevancy of the African connection. His list includes David Walker and W.E.B. Du Bois. Such conclusion reveals Schlesinger's ignorance of the intellectual history of African Americans. In the first place, Walker's appeal was *explicitly and expressly aimed at all Africans* "of every nation, language and tongue under heaven." In the second place, Walker directly connects the Africans in America with the ancient Egyptians. He said in that regard: "The Egyptians were Africans...about the same as you see the colored people of the United States at the present day."

As for Du Bois, his keen interest in Africa was a dominant theme of his research and organizational activity over a period of fifty years. Du Bois wrote *The Negro* (1915), *Black Folk Then and Now* (1939), and *The World and Africa* (1945). In the meantime, he helped to organize five Pan African Congresses and was one of the strongest critics of Western historiography for attempting to alienate Pan African linkages. Africa was his home when he died in 1963.

Schlesinger (1991) also ignores the nineteenth and twentieth century debates among African Americans over the issue of emigration. The long history of that dialogue cannot be dismissed by asserting: "From time to time, black leaders, notably Martin Delany in the mid-19th century and Marcus Garvey in the 1920's, excited passing interest in Africa" (p. 45).

In short, Mr. Schlesinger's examination of the position of African Americans on the African connection is bad history whether from purposeful distortion or mere ignorance. Schlesinger Jr. really attempts to hammer the African-centered curriculum on what he considers to be its real focus—the elevation of the self-esteem of African American students. He accuses the proponents of the African-centered curriculum of using "bad history" as "psychological therapy" and asserts that, on the contrary, the African-centered curriculum will achieve the exact opposite (p. 52). In order to "prove" his point, he quotes from *Brown v. Board of Education*. In other words, Schlesinger equates

African-centered education with the white supremacy system of segregation. Segregation can be properly defined as the system of neoslavery, popularly referred to as Jim Crow.

His reading of Dr. Kenneth Clark's theory of the psychological effects of the theory and practice of white supremacy (segregation) is quite defective. Teaching about the African origins of civilization and the historical role of African peoples is the exact opposite of the teachings of the segregationists and Hegelians. How could such diametrically opposite teachings achieve the same result? Some advocates of the African-centered curriculum, including Asa Hilliard, Leonard Jeffries, and Molefi Asante, emphasize that the self-esteem issue is *not* their *primary* argument. The restoration of truth is the priority for many African-centered scholars.

Whether African-centered education elevates the self-esteem of African American children is a proposition which can be scientifically tested. Certainly it is not illogical to assume that improving the historical image of Africa will at least increase the respect which Africans and all other peoples have for African humanity. Does Schlesinger Jr. really believe that teaching African Americans that Western civilization is superior to African culture will improve their self-esteem more than teaching them the truth? Hopefully the thousands of African American parents and teachers who are demanding African content in the classroom, and not Schlesinger, will settle the argument.

Schlesinger makes much about the fact that not all African American scholars have accepted the African-centered position. He proudly asserts that "Serious *Black* scholars...regard Afrocentricity with skepticism" (p. 53). Schlesinger's presumed authority to determine which African scholars are "serious" epitomizes liberal white supremacy.

It was not the "separation of the races" that caused many Africans to feel oppressed (what Schlesinger and others in error call inferior). It was the enforced system of white supremacy which achieved this end. Kenneth Clark's research, when properly read, also supports that point. Is it surprising that people who are oppressed feel oppressed? Schlesinger Jr.'s superiority complex causes him to argue that teaching African American children that they are not a part of the American heritage is bound to damage them. If teaching African American children that African American people are politically, socially, economically, and culturally oppressed damages them any more than the actual oppression, then the African-centered advocates are guilty as charged. Surely, teaching them that they are not oppressed when they actually are will not prepare them to change their situation. The African-centered position is based upon the belief that teaching the oppressed the truth, that is, that the oppression is based upon false, flawed, and arbitrary doctrines, is the best way to lead to liberation.

Cultural Pluralism

The cornerstone of Schlesinger's cultural pluralism is his argument that, although the United States is a culturally pluralistic country, its foundation and dominant cultural theme is not only European, but also white Anglo-Saxon Protestant. That, for Schlesinger Jr., is an unassailable fact and to teach otherwise "is to falsify history" (p. 24). Over the years the Anglo-Saxon dominance has been duly toned down for Schlesinger: "The American synthesis has an inevitable Anglo-Saxon coloration, but is no longer an exercise in Anglo-Saxon domination. The republic embodies ideals that transcend ethnic, religious, and political lines" (p. 67).

Schlesinger also insists that: "For generations blacks have grown up in an American culture, on which they have had significant influence and to which they have made significant contributions" (p. 59).

But Schlesinger explains neither what Africans in America influence nor what those contributions were. Apparently, they did not contribute the political ideals that represent the creed. Indeed, as Schlesinger asserts, Europe was the birthplace of the republic and eighty percent of Americans are of European descent. Therefore, as he asserts when he quotes Irving Howe, "The Bible, Homer, Plato, Sophocles and Shakespeare are central to our culture."

With the exception of his inability to define or articulate the "black" influence, most African-centered scholars probably agree with the factual components of Schlesinger Jr.'s argument. Many African scholars would emphasize that there is, however, a counter culture shared by many African Americans. But most importantly for many

African-centered scholars, the American culture is seen as a culture of tyranny which admits only certain elements from non-Anglo-Saxon culture and eliminates practically all true human elements from the non-European populations, especially the African inhabitants. Much of what is included from these powerless populations is either fabricated or mutilated by the dominant culture.

We must consider Schlesinger Jr.'s criticism of "Even the best historians who write about African slaves as childlike and improvident Sambo on the old plantation" (p. 27). Included are Charles and Mary Beard, Henry Steele Comminger, and Frederick Jackson Turner to whom he refers as the "Great" (p. 9). Two questions are pertinent. First, how can these historians be considered the "best" or the "Great" when they so unprofessionally treated the history of such a significant aspect of U.S. history and demeaned such a significant group of "Americans?" Second, how does the expressed attitudes of these "best" historians differ from Schlesinger the elder and Schlesinger the younger's attitudes about "tribal Africa?" His answer would seem to be summed up by his assertion that "historians are human" (p. 20).

One of the major reasons for the dominance of this culture of the Bible, Plato, and Shakespeare is that it has enjoyed a monopoly in teaching content. Much of this culture is the culture of the curriculum. Certainly Plato, Homer, and Shakespeare are not taught in the average home or on the streetcorners. This taught culture is a weapon to shape the minds of the students. It is, however, by no means self-evident that the Bible is superior to the literature of ancient Egypt or that *The Odessey* is superior to the *Epic of Sundiata* or Plato's *Republic* is superior to the teachings of Ptahhotep. Thus, if Ptahhotep had been taught instead of Plato, then the culture might very well be African-centered. The teaching of Plato to peoples of African descent is no more natural or historic than teaching Ptahhotep.

Schlesinger questioned the logic of connecting African Americans with an African heritage after three hundred years of disconnection. Yet there is no questioning the logic that through the survival of the classical tradition that is inextricably wedded to the academic process, all Europeans are connected to the ancient Greek and Roman worlds which existed and declined thousands of years ago. Schlesinger Jr.'s justification emphasized two points. First, the classical Greek to modern Anglo-Saxon heritage is what survived and thus is the ideal which should dominate the curriculum. Second, he infers that African Americans (and other non-European Americans) now have equal opportunity to share that Greco-Anglo-Saxon heritage. Besides, he might add the Greco-Anglo-Saxon (and biblical) heritage has been suitably modified to include relevant contributions from the African American heritage, such as jazz (p. 72).

Those of us who are attempting to serve the cultural and academic needs of the school children want more. We point out that the Biblical-Greco-Romano-Anglo-Saxon tradition is disseminated through the educational process; the home is not equipped to pass it on. It is therefore not appropriate to suggest that teaching ethnic heritage which differs from the mainstream should be the responsibility of the private sector. This reflects and maintains a flawed bias in the cultural domain. Besides the perpetuation of lies for all students, it places African Americans, Asian Americans, Hispanic Americans, and some non-Anglo-Saxon Europeans at varying degrees of disadvantagement.

Schlesinger Jr. caps this point by emphasizing his conclusion that the rank and file of African Americans consider themselves black Americans, with stress on *Americans*. This is demonstrated in his essay by bits of evidence—the skepticism he sees in those he calls "serious" and "respected" black scholars (p. 53); and the assertion of African American leaders of the nineteenth and twentieth centuries (pp. 44–45). He also cites his black friends who "laughed and said that American Blacks could not care less about Africa" in 1956 when he was trying to drum up support for the presidential candidacy of Adlai Stevenson, who lost to Eisenhower (p. 45). He finally points to certain opinion polls which found a preference among the Africans in America for being referred to as black rather than African American (p. 79). I suppose a similar poll would indicate that Europeans in America would prefer being called white to European American. It must also be pointed out that fifty years ago my generation militantly insisted we should be called Negro rather than colored, and many Africans in America one hundred and fifty years ago rejected being called black and insisted on being called colored. Things change in time and change has to begin somewhere.

Schlesinger's argument is undergirded by his characterizations of

African-centered scholars. He parades them and their images in the pages of his essay to the targeted readers of "The Larger Agenda Series."

Several points about the publication itself are in order before resuming the discussion of Schlesinger's *ad hominem* attack on the African-centered scholars. In the first place, the publication is directed primarily to a non-academic audience. According to its self-definition, the series of which it is a part explores "subjects of importance to managers and policy makers in business and the public sector."

Perhaps, the targeting of such a clientele explains the second point, which questions the inclusion of advertisements with such a "serious" essay. Eighteen of the pamphlet's ninety-one pages are filled with Federal Express ads, slickly crafted to suggest the ethnic variety of Federal Express employees.

A third feature of the publication is the way in which the photographs of various individuals are included. The photographs of all of the imaged African-centered scholars are printed one after the other in Chapter Two, which is entitled "History as a Weapon." Whereas, the African Americans who apparently do not support such a view are included in Chapter Three entitled "The Battle of the Schools." Furthermore, all of the photographs of both African Americans and European Americans are snapshots placed in the margins of the various pages, except the one of Dr. Leonard Jeffries which, along with the caption, takes up a half page and looms as something of a mug shot. This appears to be a publication of photos of Africans to be on the look out for.

Turning to the characterization of the African scholars by Schlesinger Jr, with the exception of Dr. Maulana Karenga, he selects only those statements he considers the most objectionable and ignores the context. He also quotes from negative reports of their public address which themselves are distortions of what really occurred. He labels Dr. Jeffries as "The irrepressible Leonard Jeffries of CCNY" (p. 63). What does irrepressible mean for Arthur Schlesinger Jr.? According to *Webster's Collegiate Dictionary*, irrepressible means "impossible to repress, restrain, or control" (p. 640). Apparently Schlesinger can't get away from Hegelian opinions of Africans and the liberal white supremacist temptation to control Africans.

Schlesinger (1991) makes no attempt to analyze the positions of the African-centered scholars in any serious sense; the several works of Molefi Asante are considered only superficially. Nor does Schlesinger indicate any awareness of the essays of Asa Hilliard.

Schlesinger also questions the credentials, psychological condition and motives of the advocates of African-centered education. Concerning the committee which approved the curriculum of inclusion recommended by Leonard Jeffries and others, he emphasized that there was "not one historian among its 17 members" (p. 33). Again admitting that he was not an expert on Egyptian history, he went on to assert "but neither are the educators and psychologists who push Afrocentrism." (p. 41). If, however, scholars were limited to the narrow definition of their degree disciplines it is difficult to determine on what basis Schlesinger is qualified to write anything concerning the African-centered curriculum. He is not an educator in the narrow sense. Nor is he a psychologist, although he makes judgements about psychological hypothesis. Nor is he evidently well versed on African American history, African history, or, by his own admission, Egyptian history.

Many of the scholars criticized by Schlesinger have devoted a considerable part of their lives to the study of that which was withheld and mutilated by Western historiography. They are well-trained scholars who have applied the general standards of research and scholarship to their work. As Thomas Kuhn and Martin Bernal pointed out, most of the truly significant progressive changes in the content and methodology of the production of knowledge came from talented "outsiders."

Schlesinger subtly suggests that the African-centered advocates suffer from both paranoia (p. 63) and a "persecution complex" (p. 63). His evasive and subtle handling of these innuendos seem designed to alert the reader to what Schlesinger feels is the basic irrationality and ingratitude of the African-centered intellectuals.

Schlesinger's final thrust is aimed at totally discrediting the African-centered scholars because of bad motives. He accuses those who take advantage of "white guilt" of "cynical black exploitation and manipulation" (p. 36). He also indicts the African-centered thinkers for their political "motives" (p. 53). He considers the campaign nothing "more than the pastime of a few angry, ambitious, and perhaps despairing zealots and hustlers" (p. 47), and finally, in this regard, asserts that "academia has its Al Sharpton's" (p. 53). Schlesinger's total lack of respect for men and women, including the reverend Al Sharpton, who have committed and in some cases risked their lives trying to dismantle white supremacy oppression disqualifies him from addressing anybody as a scholar on these matters. Schlesinger resigned from a pro-bono voluntary appointment to a committee to evaluate proposed revisions to the "Curriculum of Inclusion" to become a paid consultant. He then wrote a manuscript which was published in a format that is largely an advertising brochure for Federal Express. He therefore is in no position to comment on the motives of scholars and activists in the African American community, especially since he harbors neo-Hegelian white supremacy attitudes.

Before concluding, let us consider two final issues embedded in Schlesinger's essay. One is the duplicitous treatment of what he calls the "serious" and "respected" black scholars, such as Henry Louis Gates, who regard "Afrocentricity with skepticism" (p. 53). Thus he exploits the debate among African thinkers in order to create the aura of African "tribalism" that he feels is indigenous to African culture. This is quite similar to the policy of the white supremacist regime in South Africa which tries to create tribalism by creating a violent Zulu versus Xosha conflict.

Yet, lest the "serious black scholars" become complacent in their apparent acceptance by such an eminent German American scholar-historian, let us point out his subtle ridicule of the very issues which they employ in their moderate attempt to assert an Afro-American ethnic component of the Anglo-European dominated cultural pluralism of Schlesinger and the defenders of Western civilization. Those who explore the deconstruction and postconstruction avenues of literary critique, as well as those who confront the canon of "American literature," are cleverly satirized by Schlesinger Jr. because they use analytical weapons developed in the tradition of the canon (p. 72-73). The give-away, however, is Schlesinger's proud support of the canon which includes a number of "rebels" such as Emerson, Thoreau, and O'Neil (p. 73). Not only, however, does he not mention any African Americans or Hispanic Americans in this regard, he does not even indicate that there is anything deficient about such a canon. What the "serious" and "respected" black scholars should bear in mind is that if and when the intellectual army of Western civilization demolishes the African-centered scholars, the Afro-American scholars are next in line. Remember what happened to Martin Luther King, Jr. after Malcolm X was assassinated.

Another issue woven into Schlesinger's work is his defense of Diane Ravitch, who is a soft-liner defender of Western civilization. He suggests that "ethnic chauvinists" think they can bully her "because she is a woman" (p. 66). He further asserts that her "unpardonable offense seems to be her concern about the *unum* as well as about *pluribus*" (p. 66). He ignores the fact that Ravitch, whom he praises as "an enlightened advocate of school reform," (p. 66) initiated a vicious campaign against the advocacy of the African-centered curriculum. For Schlesinger, she may well represent "a first-class historian of American education...and a steadfast champion of cultural pluralism," but to some African-centered scholars she is a good example of a poorly informed advocate of the curriculum of white supremacy. Schlesinger's patronizing statements on behalf of the honor of a white woman are reminiscent of the bitter days of blatant Bilboism. (Theodore G. Bilbo was a U.S. Senator from Mississippi who expressly and openly espoused white supremacy.)

Arthur Schlesinger's statement *The Disuniting of America* is one of the best that African-centered scholars can use to demonstrate the necessity of an African-centered curriculum. The fact that a European American historian boldly advocates a neo-Hegelian view of Africa and slavery with a Tocquevillian picture of Africans in America as a vital component of an acceptable multicultural curriculum reveals the real impact of the so-called cultural pluralists who promote the multicultural curriculum as the best alternative to African-centeredness.

In fact, Schlesinger's diatribe gives white liberalism a serious bruise. Asserting that he is going to examine the issues dispassionately in the tradition of "honest history," he is overtaken by his emotions, loses his composure, and begins to attack African culture in terms (i.e., "tribalism") that most serious and respected European and European American scholars abandoned decades ago. Both Schlesinger Jr. and his father, from whom he received his liberal tradition, are on record as holding Hegelian positions about Africans and Africans in America.

Schlesinger's position on African intellectuals seems to coincide with the general colonist's attitude regarding the "natives." He divides African American thinkers into good and bad camps and completely vilifies the bad ones whose only crime seems to be that they reject Schlesinger's questionable and mythological picture of pluralistic America. His treatment of the African-centered perspective completely ignores its basic assertion, which is that a great lie underlies the doctrine of Western civilization and the historiography that underpins it. He also ignores the argument that the Eurocentric curriculum continues to perpetuate the falsification of history and prevents the establishment of cultural equality in this country.

Schlesinger Jr. does not give recognition to the fact that the precursor of the African-centered curriculum project, the Black Studies movement of the 1960s and 1970s, was the cause of the emergence of multiculturalism. Multiculturalism was in turn employed as a weapon against the underlying basis, the Black Studies curriculum. Thus, in the real world we are faced with a choice between multiculturalism, which is a facade for the white supremacy curriculum, or African-centered education which is based upon a quest for the truth in history and cultural equality.

Although Schlesinger has tried to argue that the movement toward African-centered education is rejected by the masses of Africans in America and is serious only because European Americans sympathize with the plight of Africans in America, his diatribe belies a fear that the doctrine of Western civilization may be demolished. Such a fear is well-founded.

To the contrary, what has really frightened Schlesinger and a considerable segment of the intellectual establishment, including college professors and journalists, is the depth of the movement. Although they continually refer to an extreme fringe of disgruntled intellectuals, what they actually find is a rather wide spectrum of Africans in America, from middle-class business and professional persons through working peoples to rap-oriented teenagers, who are demanding the African-centered perspective. The demand by millions of African American parents for an African-based curriculum has truly stunned many of the defenders of Western civilization. In much the same way, white supremacist were shocked at the depth of the Civil Rights movement of the 1950s and 1960s.

Inherent in the African-centered position is the necessity of cultural revolution. The success of the revolution will render the Schlesingers of the world obsolete. The large number of intellectuals and educators will have to be retrained. Textbooks will be replaced. A new intellectual leadership will emerge and the African children will be given an inspiring, rather than depressing, course of instruction. In fact, the world will be liberated from a myth which was hopelessly flawed from its inception—the myth of white supremacy.

R E F E R E N C E S

Aida, Yuji. 1991. "Melting Pot Meltdown in the U.S." *Chicago Tribune* (16 April).

Bernal, Martin. 1987. *Black Athena: The Afroasiatic Roots of Classical Civilization.* Vol. I The Fabrication of Ancient Greece 1785–1985. New Brunswick: Rutgers University Press

Carruthers, Jacob H. 1992. *Critical Commentaries.* Los Angeles: Association for the Study of Classical African Civilizations.

Clarke, John Henrik, ed. *1968. William Styron's Nat Turner: Ten Black Writers Respond.* Westport: Greenwood Press.

Crevecoeur, J. Hector St. John. [1782] 1990. *Letters from An American Farmer.* no press. Reprint.

Douglass, Frederick. 1893. Address Dedicating the Haitian Pavillion at the Chicago Exposition.

Dutty, Bookman. "Bookman's Prayer" in Pauleus Sannon, *Historie de Toussaint L'Ouverture.*

Franklin, Benjamin. "Observation Concerning the Increase of Mankind." *Papers of Benjamin Franklin.* Vol. 4. July 1750–June 1753 (225–234).

Fukuyama, Francis. 1989. "The End of History." *The National Interest.* (Summer).

Hegel, Georg Wilhelm Friedrich. 1956. *The Philosophy of History.* New York: Dover.

Jefferson, Thomas and John Dickinson. 1927. "Declaration of the Causes and Necessity of Taking Up Arms." *Documents Illustrative of the Formation of the Union of the American States.* Washington: Government Printing Office, 10–17.

Jones, Stuart M. 1972. "The Schlesingers on Black History." *Phylon*, 33:2.

Kuhn, Thomas. 1970. *The Structure of Scientific Revolution.* Berkeley: University of California Press.

Madison, James. 1937. *The Federalist 54.* New York: The Modern Library.

Ravitch, Diane. 1990. "Multiculturalism E Pluribus Plures." *American Scholar* (Summer).

Schlesinger, Arthur Jr. 1991. *The Disuniting of America.* Knoxville: Whittle Press.

Styron, William. 1967. *The Confessions of Nat Turner.* New York: Random House.

PART III

INTELLECTUAL CIVIL WAR

10

Black Talk and the White Question
Reflections on Afro-American Critiques of African-Centered Thought

> We have no philosophers or thinkers who command the respect of the intellectual community at large. I am not talking about the few teachers of philosophy who have read Hegel or Kant or James and memorized their thoughts, I am talking about men who have reflected upon the fundamental problems which have always concerned philosophers such as the nature of human knowledge and the meaning or lack of meaning of human existence.
> —E. Franklin Frazier

This chapter is concerned with the speeches of Africans in the long, frigid winter of the European-imposed diaspora. As such, its broader context is the intergenerational conversation among the Africans who have communicated about how to get out of the mess in which we (people of African ancestry) have found ourselves, in what is called the modern world. The primary focus of this commentary is to respond to some statements made by Cornel West and others in reference to the African-centered school of discourse and some of its advocates. Dr. West recently has been singled out as the preeminent African American philosopher (See for example "Philosophers with a Mission" *Time*, June 7, 1993). In order to properly respond to his remarks, however, a review of the wider context is necessary.

Black Talk

The current commentary is part of a continuous dialogue which surfaced in the 1960s, especially in the wake of the Black Studies movement. It is appropriate to begin with a statement issued by E. Franklin Frazier in a talk which was published in 1962, a little before the Black Studies eruption, but after the Black Student movement proper began. Frazier's discourse was entitled "The Failure of the Negro Intellectual." In that speech, he argued that "Negro intellectuals," with exceptions, had failed to address the "Negro" tradition because they were obsessed with integration and the approval of white intellectuals: "American Negro intellectuals...imbued with an integrationist point of view were...unconscious of the important question of the relation of culture and personality and human destiny" (p. 55).

Speaking of this persuasion Frazier continued: "In its hope to achieve acceptance in American life, it would slough off everything that is reminiscent of its Negro origin and its Negro folk background" (p. 56).

Thus, according to Frazier, in their condition of enslavement to the white intelligentsia, these "Negro" scholars had contributed no philosophy or theory to aid their people toward liberation (p. 60). The few exceptions he cited included W. E. B. Du Bois, Paul Robeson and Langston Hughes (p. 64). However, Frazier ignored Marcus Garvey, perhaps because Garvey was dead when he wrote the essay. His rather fleeting mention of the growth of black Muslim movement, however, implies that Frazier did not consider such thinking a viable intellectual alternative (p. 62).

In fact, Frazier seemed to limit his definitions of Negro intellectuals to twentieth-century college-trained scholars and creative literati. The limitations Frazier imposed on his exploration of the productions of Negro intellectuals resulted in a basically ahistorical analysis. He lamented the fact that the intellectuals had not focused on Denmark Vesey and Harriet Tubman, and others, but he made no attempt to address nineteenth-century intellectual positions of Africans in the United States. Nor did he clearly define the thrust of those few who were exceptions to the integrationist intellectuals.

Five years after the publication of "Failure," Harold Cruse echoed the theme with his book *The Crisis of the Negro Intellectual* (1967). Cruse significantly expanded and clarified Frazier's argument. Not only did he connect the problem to its historical context, he identified the stream of discourse opposite to the integrationist's phantom of assimilation as the "nationality strain" (p. 5). Throughout the nineteenth century and much of the twentieth century, the dialogue among Africans in the United States has pitted the proponents of these two schools of thought against one another. Both proclaim liberation of Africans in the Western Hemispheric diaspora as their objective. Although this debate is essentially "Black Talk," it has been noticed and commented on by European American intellectuals and indeed many white thinkers have waded into he the arena and taken sides. This brings us to the issue that is more or less explicitly raised by both Frazier and Cruse, that is, the "White Question." One must examine the "White Question" because as Frazier pointed out in 1973, concerning the integrationist-prone intellectuals: "This class emerged as the result of white American philanthropy. Although the situation has changed and the Negro intellectuals are supported through other means, they are still dependent upon the white community" (p. 59).

Therefore, according to Frazier, "educated Negroes or Negro intellectuals have failed to achieve any intellectual freedom" (p. 58). He continued, asserting they "simply repeat the propaganda which is put out by people who have large economic and political interests to protect" (p. 59). He concluded: "They have been so imbued with the prospect of integration and eventual assimilation that they have thought that they could prove themselves true Americans by not studying the Negro" (p. 60).

A cursory glance at history reveals that what may be called the integration strain has not always avoided mention or study of peoples of African ancestry. Their treatment of the African heritage, however, has been generally significantly different from the Nationalist school. Let us preface our consideration of the historical context of the diasporian dialogue with a reflection on the "White Question."

The White Question

During the *Two Thousand Seasons* (Armah 1973) of our misery, no issue has obstructed the Pan African project of liberation more than the "White Question." The term "White Question" is not intended as the reverse of "The Negro Question" which my colleague, Anderson Thompson, has so adequately defined as the recurring white query, "What is to be done with the Negro?" It is rather an attempt to summarize the most historically divisive controversy among African leadership groups in the United States over the last two centuries. On the other hand, debate among whites about the "Negro Question" has not substantially impeded articulation of the doctrine or practice of "white supremacy."

Nothing better illustrates the problem than the history of the Haitian Revolution, which began a little more than two hundred years ago. Throughout the struggle, various group leaders argued among themselves over ways to deal with the whites. Indeed, the revolution was delayed more than once by the bitter conflict. The argument resurfaced after the victory of the Africans and has blighted Haiti's future ever since.

The various leadership groups feuded over such issues as whether to exterminate all whites; whether to form alliances with whites; whether to treat the white enemy troops as "gentlemen" or to return "tit for tat"; whether to negotiate with whites; whether to aspire for inclusion in a greater French (white) civilization. After the Civil War, which followed the victory over Europe, the prevailing faction traded Haiti's future for the prize of recognition by France at a cost of a $25,000,000 indemnity.

Perhaps, the most conspicuous example of the problem today (200 years later) is the agonizing situation in South Africa. Many observers believe that South Africa would be free of white supremacy immediately if only the Africans would stop fighting among themselves, and adopt a unified stance. A close inspection of the disunity among them would reveal that the "White Question" is the fuel that feeds the debilitating strife. One group seems to favor a continuation of a modified and benign white supremacy; another advocates white inclusion as equals in a multiracial society; another appears to insist on white removal.

The question is not so much whether to deal with whites or not. Indeed, it is virtually impossible not to deal with whites, since the mess has been caused by the white oppression of Africans for the last five centuries or so. (That is, we would not be engaging in this discussion had the whites not messed with us.) Thus, the general question breaks down into several subquestions relating to various aspects of the general problem. One such historically based question is: How should the condition of the African population in the United States be conceptualized? Are we a "nation within a nation" as Martin Delany asserted (1960, p. 209)? If so, should we attempt to separate and become independent? Or, should we attempt to integrate or unite our nation with the oppressor's nation?

Another important and equally historically based question is whether friendly whites should be invited or welcomed into the liberation struggle and/or the debate on methodology. If so, in what way should they be involved? Indeed, this question has been with us a long time as attested by Martin Delany writing in 1852 in his review of the history of the antebellum National Negro Conventions. Delany pointed out that in 1831:

> White gentlemen were introduced to...the Convention, and after gaining permission to speak, expressed their...surprise at the qualifications and talents (of the) members of the Convention (and) expressed (their) determination (to) espouse the cause of elevation of the colored people. (p. 23)

These "white gentlemen" persuaded most members of the Convention to abandon their consideration of emigration from the United States because these "white gentlemen," admitting that since "they, (the whites) had been our oppressors...they (the white gentlemen) would now elevate" the oppressed Africans (p. 24). A few of the members of the convention, however, still favored emigration, a position which Delany himself thought more appropriate. The two aspects of the "White Question" raised in this sketch while by no means exhaustive, do epitomize the perennial issue. Let us now briefly review that historical context.

The Eve of the Great Debate

The two strands or streams of thought that Cruse identified in *The Crisis of the Negro Intellectual* (1967), emerged from a debate which in part was recorded throughout the nineteenth century. The controversy concerned the most appropriate method of dealing with the "mess" in which all people of African ancestry found themselves. The anticipation of the great debate can be inferred from certain events in the last quarter of the eighteenth century. Let us consider the possible development of that anticipation.

Anderson Thompson (1975) raises the question, "What do you think the Africans who arrived in chains fresh from Africa and found themselves in a strange and hostile place called America wanted?" If we may assume the obvious answer, the next question is, how did some Africans come to want to stay in America and become Americans? On the eve of the settler war for independence, one petition of enslaved Africans asserted, "We have no property! We have no wives! No children! We have no city! No country!" (Aptheker 1951, p. 6). In that same year another petition (perhaps by the same African) proposed that the Africans "leave the province (Massachusetts) as soon as we can, from our joint labors procure money to transport ourselves to some part of the coast of *Africa*" (p. 8). It is quite likely that not all participants in the debates signed the petitions or even agreed that such petitions should be directed toward the European settlers. During the era before the Haitian Revolution, petitions were one of three types of recorded communication which reflected various positions taken by the Africans.

The petitions, on the whole, were quite moderate in tone and content. On each side of the petition mode were covert messages. Illustrating what may be called the uncompromising side was the letter accidentally dropped on a street in a Virginia town in 1793. The letter from an African rebel to a fellow freedom fighter referred to a planned military strategy to take "full possession of the whole country." The sender, identified as "Secret Keeper Richmond," offered these words of encouragement to his/her cohort: "Don't be feared, have a good heart, fight brave and we will be free" (p. 28). In this same spirit, one of the members of Gabriel Prosser's revolutionary group asserted to another

158

member, "We have as much right to fight for our liberty as any men" (p. 48). Another made the following statement:

> I have nothing more to offer than what General Washington would have had to offer had he been taken by the British officers and put to trial by them. I have ventured my life in endeavoring to obtain the liberty of my countrymen, and am a willing sacrifice to their cause...I beg as a favor that I may be immediately led to execution. Why, then, all this mockery of a trial? (Bennett 1987, p. 126)

On the conservative side of the petition mode was the collaborator or informer. In 1802, one wrote a letter warning of an impending slave rebellion in Virginia. The letter in part read:

> White people be-ware of your lives, their is a plan now forming and intend to put in execution...if you do not look out...many of you will be put to death, the scam is to kill all...men, women and children...watch they conduct of your Negroes and you will see an alteration...I am a greater friend to some of the whites, and wish to preserve their lives. I am a favorite servant of my master and misses and love them dearly (Aptheker 1951, p. 51).

Nine years earlier, another African informer identified himself/herself as "one of those too unpopular characters...a free Black" (p. 29). He/she explained "tis my love to a people among whom I have been all my life." Thus, the African collaborator was impelled to warn the governor of the danger of a slave insurrection.

The speeches of these informers give us a clue to the question of how some Africans wanted to stay in the country and become Americans. Their love for their masters because of their "favorite" status led them to want to live among their oppressors after becoming free blacks.

The Africans involved in petitioning fall somewhere between those who advocated separation through rebellion and those who sought inclusion in the European American community through demonstrating complete loyalty by betraying other Africans. Some of the petitioners were perhaps ambivalent about the matter. This review of the petition mode of African response to oppression is focused on petitions which address the African population in general, rather than petitions for individual manumission. The main objective was to persuade the oppressors to abolish slavery which was in the express interest of most Africans.

These petitions were embellished with appeals to the political and religious principles of these oppressors, such as, "the natural rights to our freedom" (p. 8), "the Laws of Nature", "The Cause of Liberty", and "the Christian Religion" (p. 11). They also referred to the innocent and idyllic life in a "Populous Pleasant and plentiful country" from which they had been cruelly and "unjustly dragged" (p. 9). The appeals and references to abstract ideals have frequently been incorporated into the struggles of Africans to get out of the mess of oppression in the Western Hemisphere, and do not necessarily mean that those principles inspired them to seek freedom. Africans did not have to wait until they read or heard recitals of the Declaration of Independence to begin their quest to get out of slavery. The free and independent African communities (called Maroon settlements by Europeans) and other self-emancipation processes, such as the Underground Railroad, are ample proofs of this reality.

Let us end this probe with a reference to action. When European settlers revolted against the British, five thousand African men are reported as having served as soldiers for the American settler rebels (Franklin 1947, p. 136). "Tens of thousands," however, defected to the British and when the war was over, at least fourteen thousand were evacuated by the British army (Quarles 1964, pp. 55–56). In other words, of those Africans who are recorded as having made a choice, the overwhelming majority decided not to become Americans. Thus, at least until the formal establishment of the United States of America as a white republic, there is no indication that the African population as a whole wanted to be anything other than free Africans.

After the War, the Africans who remained found that the mess was getting worse. In the 1780s, the European project of philosophical white supremacy reached the emerging white republic full force, announced through the publication of Thomas Jefferson's *Notes on Virginia*. This intellectual atrocity attempted to commit historicide against Africa, to destroy the idea of African civilization, and to mandate the reduction of African peoples to the level of subhuman. It was at this moment of apparently absolute darkness that a new light began to emerge.

The Nineteenth-Century African Dialogue

The nineteenth-century dialogue developed in the wake of the Haitian Revolution. In 1793, Reverend Richard Allen and Absalom Jones responded to a vicious slander against the African people of Philadelphia and spoke militantly against slavery. In their written speech, they made an implicit reference to the Haitian Revolution, then in progress; "the dreadful insurrections they have made...is enough to convince a reasonable man, that great uneasiness and not contentment, is the inhabitant of their hearts" (Aptheker 1951, p. 37). They ended their lecture by referring to the biblical passage "Princes shall come out of Egypt; Ethiopia shall soon stretch out her hands unto God" (p. 38; Psalms 68:31).

A few years later Prince Hall, in an address to the African Lodge which he had founded ten years earlier, was more explicit in his reference to the "French West-Indies" (i.e. Haiti). By 1797 African victory appeared certain and Prince Hall set the tone for the nineteenth century struggle by asserting that "the darkest hour is just before the break of day" (49). He then pointed out that the revolution was an example of Ethiopia beginning "to stretch forth her hand from a sink of slavery to freedom and equality (Frazier 1970, p. 49).

By the beginning of the nineteenth century some of the African leaders in the white republic of the United States were convinced that Africans had no future in the country. Among those were Paul Cuffe. As one of his contemporary admirers said:

> He saw...the force of prejudice operating so powerfully against them (his African brethren), as to give but little...hope that they could ever rise...unless it were in a state...more favorable...than would probably ever be afforded them where the bulk of the population are white. (Fishel 1967, p. 76)

Cuffe therefore spent the last decade of his life organizing and transporting Africans in the United States to repatriate to Africa.

Cuffe's plan was not accepted by all African leaders in the United States and it is in such opposition that we see the beginning of a rationale for staying in the country and perhaps trying to become "American." In 1817, James Forten, who like Cuffe was an African of wealth, chaired a meeting protesting the European-American Colonization Society's scheme to transport free Africans to Africa. The resolution adopted at the meeting read in part:

> Whereas our ancestors (not of choice) were the first successful cultivators of the wilds of America, we their descendants feel ourselves entitled to participate in the blessings of her luxuriant soil, which their blood and sweat manured; and that any measure or system of measures, having a tendency to banish us from her bosom, would not only be cruel, but in direct violation of those principles, which have been the boast of this republic.

> Resolved, that we view with deep abhorrence the unmerited stigma attempted to be cast upon the reputation of the free people of color, by the promoters of this measure, "that they are a dangerous and useless part of the community," when in the state of disfranchisement in which they live, in the hour of danger they ceased to remember their wrongs, and rallied around the standard of their country. (Aptheker, p. 71)

In a letter to Paul Cuffe, doubtless explaining the published resolution which was directed to European Americans, Forten stated a somewhat contrary position:

> My opinion is that they will never become a people until they come out from amongst the white people, but as the majority (who attended the meeting) is decidedly against me I am determined to remain silent, except as to my opinion which I freely give when asked. (Bracey 1970, p. 46)

162

It should be noted that the resolution indicated that the main reason for free Africans staying in the country was not the desire to become American but:

> We will never separate ourselves voluntarily from the slave population in this country, they are our brethren by ties of consanguinity, of suffering, and of wrong; and we feel that there is more virtue in suffering privations with them, than fancied advantages for a reason. (Aptheker 1951, p. 71)

This principle of African unity in the diaspora was coupled with a negative and apprehensive view of contemporary Africa. The resolution explained:

> That without arts, without science, without a proper knowledge of government, to cast into the savage wilds of Africa the free people of color, seems to us the circuitous route through which they must return to perpetual bondage. (p. 71)

This rejection of Africa was largely based on the European-created negative image of "primitive" Africa and not necessarily a rejection of the African heritage.

The early emigration movement was a significant part of the context in which African speakers debated strategies for destroying white supremacy oppression. Hundreds went to Liberia. Many of those who refused to go continued to believe that eventually emigration was the solution. Prince Sanders, who had earlier joined in Paul Cuffe's repatriation plan, finally emigrated to Haiti, became a citizen there, and recommended that other Africans do the same (Bracey 1970, p. 22; Woodson 1925, pp. 59–63). David Walker in his famous *Appeal* unquestionably made a distinction between the "colored people" (African) and the wicked and cruel "Americans," asserting: "We are a people (the Africans), notwithstanding many of you doubt it" (Walker 1965, p. 42). He further asserted, "O Americans!...your destruction is at hand, and will be speedily consummated unless you REPENT (p. 43, Walker's emphasis). Walker started his appeal by contrasting the ancient African (Egyptian) worldview with the ancient European

(Greek) worldview. He concluded that not only were the American Christians of the nineteenth century the most cruel oppressors in history, but that their ancient cultural ancestors were also much more wicked than the ancient Africans (pp. 8–17). Thus, while there was no consensus about returning to Africa, neither was there a consensus among the leaders that Africans ought to be Americans, not at least in the antebellum period.

If James Forten was ambivalent on whether Africans could become Americans, his son James Forten, Jr., a leading abolitionist, was clear. In 1836 the younger Forten asserted, "I love America…I love the stars and stripes" (Quarles 1964, p. 191). Thus, we had finally arrived at the point where some Africans had made a firm decision to stay and fight, for not only abolition of slavery but inclusion in the white republic.

Sometimes such decisions followed a careful review of the historical context. Hosea Easton is an example. In a well-developed speech which he published in 1837, Easton provided a brilliant historical analysis. He followed the dichotomization of Africans and Europeans pioneered by David Walker, anticipated Cheikh Anta Diop's Two Cradle Theory more than a century later. After convincingly arguing that the European way had unjustly conflicted with the African way throughout history, Easton abruptly asserted "circumstances have established as much difference between (contemporary Africans in the United States and his historical continental ancestors) as exists between them and any other race or nation…the colored people who are born in this country, are American in every sense of the word" (Easton 1969, p. 21). This conclusion anticipates the position taken a century later by E. Franklin Frazier (see "Failure" example).

Let us close this historical sketch of the nineteenth-century dialogue or debate among Africans with the speakers who most articulately represented the contrasting views, Martin R. Delany and Frederick Douglass. In their early careers they had worked together as co-editors of the *North Star*. One scholar quotes Douglass as follows , "I thank God for making me a man simply, but Delany always thanks Him for making him a Black man" (Quarles, introduction in Delany 1969, *Condition*).

In 1852, Delany stated the case for nationalism:

Every people should be the originators of their own designs, the projector of their own schemes, and creators of the events that lead to their destiny—the consummation of their desires.

Situated as we are, in the United States, many and almost insurmountable obstacles present themselves. We are four-and-a-half millions in numbers, free and bond; six hundred thousand free, and three-and-a-half millions bond.

We have native hearts and virtues, just as other nations; which in their pristine purity are noble, potent, and worthy of example. We are a nation within a nation;—as the Poles in Russia, the Hungarians in Austria, the Welsh, Irish, and Scotch in the British dominions.

But we have been, by our oppressors, despoiled of our purity, and corrupted in our native characteristics, so that we have inherited their vices, and but few of their virtues, leaving us in character, really a broken people.

Being distinguished by complexion, we are still singled out—although having merged in the habits and customs of our oppressors—as a distinct nation of people.(Quarles 1964, p. 209)

Delany's conclusion about what he considered a self-evident fact, was that Africans in the United States should indeed develop their nation and become a liberating force against slavery. He devised a plan for the establishment of a nation of Africans from the diaspora on the African continent. His plan was interrupted by the Civil War and Reconstruction, but he returned to his project in the last years of his life. He developed the most comprehensive political theory of African Nationalism in the late nineteenth century (Rollin 1868). In his report on his expedition to West Africa where he negotiated a great land deal with African leaders he proclaimed: "Africa for the African race and Black men to rule them. By Black men I mean, men of African descent who claim an identity with the race" (Delany and Campbell 1969, p. 121). He also developed a theoretical framework connecting ancient

Egypt, the Niger River area and Africans of the diaspora (Delany). In short, Delany's position was Pan African Nationalism—i.e. Africans uniting spatially and historically.

Frederick Douglass, who was recognized by European Americans as "the leader" of the Africans in the United States for many years, was committed to the African population becoming a part of the U.S. civil society in the fullest sense. In an 1849 speech to whites he asserted:

> I feel that the Black man in this land has as much right to stay in this land as the white man...in the same year that Pilgrims were landing, slaves were landing on the James River in Virginia. We feel on this score...that we have as much right here as any other class of people...some of our number have fought and bled for this country, and we only ask to be treated as well as those who have fought against it. We are lovers of this country....For my part, I mean, for one, to stay in this country, I have made up my mind to live among you. (Woodson 1925, pp. 185–186)

Although he made a defense of the African claim to the ancient Nile Valley civilization, there is no indication that he ever wavered from his identification with "America." There is nothing in his speeches, however, which I have read that suggest that his regard for the principles of American government or indeed Christianity caused his dedication to fight against slavery and white supremacy oppression; to the contrary, his commitment seems to lie outside his love of America. Two years before he died, in a speech delivered at the Chicago Columbus Exposition of 1893, he proclaimed: "Speaking for the Negro, I can say, we owe much to Walker for his Appeal....But we owe incomparable more to Haiti than to them all. I regard her as the original pioneer emancipator of the nineteenth century" (Easton 1969, p. 113).

In their speeches, these thinkers discussed various aspects of the African cultural revival which emerged during the antebellum period. The connection of the liberation project with the ancient Nile Valley foundations of African civilizations was a significant reference point cultivated primarily by the Nationalists. The Haitian Revolution connection was also emphasized by the Nationalists. From time to time, however, the assimilationists utilized these themes (as the references to Frederick Douglass indicated). The differences between the two groups in regard to these matters were significant. The nationalists considered the ancient Kemetic (Egyptian) civilization and the Haitian Revolution as the foundation pillars for a restoration of African civilization. Thus, the temporary culture of the slavery era would be dismantled and Africans would resume their brutally interrupted heritage.

The Americanists (assimilationists), on the other hand, used these vital moments in two different ways. Firstly, as criticism of the white societies' exclusion of them from full participation. Secondly, the Americanists from time to time used the pillars as inspiration. These uses were not ignored by the Africanists (Nationalists), but were subordinate to the more fundamental incorporation into a comprehensive nationalist "good speech."

As far as my readings indicate, most of the thinkers were connected to the Christian churches that were a part of the African communities in the United States. These churches were the hub of the intergenerational social processes because they were the only bases for such activities allowed by the oppressive European American policy. Birth, adulthood, marriage, and death rites of passage were performed in the churches and, therefore, the members of the community of necessity were also members of the churches. Obviously, some aspects of the American Christian culture were incorporated into these communities. But there is no indication that any particular brand of Euro-American Christianity could be considered a cause of the protest activity of the Americanists or the nation building of the Africanists. In other words, the readings indicate that these activities were probably in opposition to the advice of the majority of the church leaders. Certainly, the focus on ancient Egypt and the Haitian Revolution were outside those cultural limits. Indeed, the Bible was often used to embellish these pillars rather than the reverse.

Let us now simply call the roll on these thinkers. Among the troops in the two armies were those who did not clearly conceptualize their tendencies because the discourses were in their pioneering stages. Some of them changed camps and others established projects that changed direction. With these qualifications, I will name some of the outstanding nationalists: Paul Cuffe, Prince Sanders, John Russwurm, Daniel Coker, David Walker, Martin Delany, Henry Highland Garnet, Alexander Crumell, James Holley, Mary Ann Shad, Henry McNeal Turner, Edwin McCabe and Marcus Garvey.

The assimilationists include Phyllis Wheatley, James Forten Sr., Hosea Easton, Robert Purvis, James Forten, Jr., Frederick Douglass, Booker T. Washington and W. E. B. Du Bois. I omitted classification of Richard Allen and Prince Hall because their proto nationalists tendencies are capable of fitting either tradition.

The torch carried by Delany passed to Bishop Henry McNeal Turner and others and the one carried by Douglass passed to Booker T. Washington, W.E.B. Du Bois, and others. Thus, the dialogue was taken into the twentieth century. It has continued throughout the present century and will accompany us into the twenty-first century. It has been in existence for at least two hundred years. The debate is an intergenerational conversation that deserves our respect. We should strive to let the traditions speak for themselves instead of trying to force them to respond to clever European paradigms.

As pointed out earlier, this debate is essentially about the "White Question." How shall we relate to the whites? This is a query that has plagued us since the beginning of our "two thousand seasons" of agony. It is in this context that we must respond to the group of African literary critics who have been influenced by the recent European intellectual tendencies such as postmodernism, deconstructionism, Foucaultism, and neo-Marxism.

This excursion into the eighteenth-and nineteenth-century African intellectual traditions was necessary because the proponents of the post-modern "Afro-American" intellectuals and their continental counterparts have virtually ignored those traditions in anything but a superficial reference or example. But fleeting references to David Walker and Martin Delany are not adequate to recover the foundations of African Nationalism in the United States. Nor are severe critiques of Edward Wilmot Blyden and Alexander Crummell out of the context of the debates and projects in which they were involved. Therefore, let us connect these young critics to each other and their predecessors; or as they would say, let us locate them. The most well-known ones are Henry Louis Gates, bell hooks, Manning Marable, Cornel West, and the "emerging" Michael Dyson. Some of the leading "continental" born are Anthony Appiah, Paulin Hountonji, and Valentine Mudimbe. Methodologically, they are influenced by European intellectuals such as Michel Foucault, Louis Althrusser and Antonio Gramsci. Contentwise, the ideas of the African American branch are closely connected to E. Franklin Frazier, Richard Wright, Martin Kilson, Frank Snowden, and, I believe, Harold Cruse.

They often admit these connections and influences, either directly or indirectly. Their foci in intellectual criticism have been largely confined to the twentieth century. There are significant differences among the young intellectuals and some of them have pointed this out. There are also differences in the quality of their work, but they are all bright, well read, and articulate.

While all claim they are not "Afro-centrists," their stated opinions about the African-centered movement vary. Some are less negative than others. They all have in common a denunciation of Leonard Jeffries, Louis Farrakhan, and Al Sharpton, which gets back to the "White Question." Another common feature of this school is their uncompromising insistence on dialogue with some elements of the white society and acceptance of some aspects of European culture. They, therefore, have felt compelled to denounce the one African target of unified white opposition. Even the most progressive European intellectuals demand that their loyal African companions at least denounce Leonard Jeffries.

R E F E R E N C E S

Aptheker, Herbert, ed. 1951. *A Documentary History of the Negro People in the United States.* New York: Citadel Press.

Armah, Ayi Kwei. 1973. *Two Thousand Seasons.* Nairobi: East African Publishing House.

Bennett, Lerone, Jr. 1987. *Before the Mayflower: A History of Black America.* Chicago: Johnson Publishing Co.

Bracey, John H. Jr., et al., eds. 1970. *Black Nationalism in America.* New York: Bobbs–Merrill.

Carruthers, Jacob H. 1985. *Irritated Genie: An Essay on the Haitian Revolution.* Chicago: Kemetic Institute.

—. 1994. "Black Intellectuals and the Crisis in Black Education," in *Too Much Schooling Too Little Education,* ed. Mwalimu J. Shujaa. Trenton: Africa World Press.

Cruse, Harold. 1967. *The Crisis of the Negro Intellectual.* New York: William Morrow.

Delany, Martin R. 1960. *Condition, Elevation, Emigration and Destiny of the Colored People of the United States.* New York: Arno Press.

Delany, Martin R. and Robert Campbell. [1860] 1969. "Niger Valley Report," in *Search For a Place: Black Separatism and Africa.* Ann Arbor: University of Michigan Press.

Douglass, Frederick. 1893. Address Dedicating the Haitian Pavilion at the Chicago Exposition.

Easton, Hosea. 1969. "A Treatise on the Intellectual Character and Civil and Political Condition of the Colored People of the United States," in *Negro Protest Pamphlets*, ed. Dorothy Porter. New York: Arno Press.

Fishel, Leslie H., Jr. and Benjamin Quarles. 1967. *The Negro American: A Documentary History.* Glenview: Scott Foresman.

Foucault, Michel. 1970. *The Order of Things.* New York: Vintage Books Random House.

Franklin, John Hope. 1947. *From Slavery to Freedom.* New York: Alfred A. Knopf.

Frazier, E. Franklin. 1973. "The Failure of the Negro Intellectual" in *The Death of White Sociology.* Ed. Joyce Ladner. New York: Vintage Books Random House.

Frazier, Thomas R. 1970. *Afro-American History: Primary Sources.* New York: Harcourt, Brace and World, Inc.

Quarles, Benjamin. 1964. *The Negro in the Making of America.* London: Collier.

Rollin, Frank A. 1868. "Political Destiny," in *Life and Public Services of Martin R. Delany.* Boston: Lee and Sheppard.

Thompson, Anderson. 1975. "Developing an African Historiography." *Black Books Bulletin*, vol 3 (Spring).

Walker, David. 1965. *David Walker's Appeal.* New York: Hill and Wang.

Woodson, Carter G. 1925. *Negro Orators and their Orations.* New York: Russell and Russell.

11

The Fragmented Prophesy and Hybrid Philosophy of Cornel West

This essay is an attempt to address issues raised by Cornel West concerning African Nationalism in the United States in general and African-centered thought in particular. Dr. West's references to the tradition of African Nationalism in the United States, and his comments concerning various proponents of what is variously called Afrocentrism, Afrocentric thought, and African centeredness forces us to analyze his position on these matters.

Since 1982, when he published *Prophesy Deliverance!: An Afro-American Revolutionary Christianity*, his decade-long written position on the "state of the race" has been consistent.

West's position is reflected both in the titles to some of his major works and in concepts which are central to his thought. Dr. West proclaims a "fragmented prophesy," forwards a "hybrid theory," and "evades" African Nationalism. This is evident in his books *Prophetic Fragments* and *American Evasion of Philosophy*, and in his belief that "black Americans...are...hybrid in blood, colors and cultural creations" (*Prophetic Fragments* 1988, p. 41).

The prophesy is fragmented for several reasons. First of all, Dr. West tears patches from several incompatible and contradictory "eschatological" traditions such as Calvinistic theology, enlightenment philosophy, American pragmatism, and Marxist socialism. The resulting fragments are removed from their philosophical moorings presented as loose, unconnected tatters which float in the wind of wild dreams. The second cause of the fragmentation is West's separation of African speeches from the context of their presentations. At times the Africans in the United States spoke to European American oppressors and at other times their speeches were directed toward fellow African-Americans. They were often debating about how to get out of the mess. As Harold Cruse suggests, these speeches tend to be divided along the lines of Americanist and Africanist. The discussion of the speeches in the artificial context of West's argument results in a "hybrid" theory because he mixes what he calls the "best" of the traditions in order to fabricate an ideal solution to the problems faced by Africans in the United States. The resulting "solution" is a monstrous concoction of African aspirations for liberation under the guidance of the standards of Eurocentric "modernity" which are diametrically opposed to African· traditions and liberation. The term "modernity," is used by Dr. West to disguise both the blatant concept of "Western civilization" and the even more "politically incorrect" term "white supremacy."

West evades African nationalism in the United States by ignoring the Pan African context of the tradition, which is at least two centuries old in this country. He fragments the speeches and practices of proponents of nationalism in order to conceal the existence of intergenerational continuity. He further matches themes of African nationalist thought with antinationalist thinkers, a practice which completely distorts their meaning. However, the most glaring aspect of the evasion is in his ignoring the African connection itself. Not only does West fail to deal with the question of ancient Nile Valley civilization, which is a major theme in the present nationalist discourse, but he virtually ignores African history and culture altogether.

Finally, West's philosophy places him in the camp of slave rebellion researchers; individuals who supply information to the oppressor about the mood and condition of the oppressed African masses. His portrait of the African-American community is the kind of image the oppressor demands, and his attack on "bad" blacks such as Len Jeffries is the loyalty test that the master requires. It is in this context that we must review Cornel West's view of *Race Matters* and how much race matters.

D o e s   R a c e   M a t t e r ?

West proclaims that "Race Matters," but that other things, specifically gender, sexual orientation, and above all, class, are of at least equal importance (*Race Matters* 1993, pp. 4, 104). In his 1982 work, he stated:

> This contrast...raises the age-old question as to whether class position or racial status is the major determinant of black oppression in America. This question should be formulated in the following way: whether class position or racial status contributes most to the fundamental form of powerlessness in America.
>
> Racial status contributes greatly to Black oppression. But middle-class Black people are essentially well-paid, white-or blue-collar workers who have little control over their lives primarily because of their class position, not their racial status.
>
> This is so because the same limited control is held by white middle-class people, despite the fact that a higher percentage of whites are well-paid white and blue-collar workers than blacks. Significant degrees of powerlessness pertain to most Americans and this could be so only if class position determines such powerlessness. Therefore, class position contributes more than racial status to the basic form of powerlessness in America. (*Prophesy Deliverance* 1982, p. 115)

The first problem with this statement is the concept "middle class," which was formerly used to be synonymous with the bourgeoisie, or dominant capitalist class. West fails to clarify his use of the term as well as the possible difference between the position of the white and black middle classes. Though the powerlessness of the white middle classes in the United States is not doubted, the implication that such middle-class oppression is as significant as the oppression of Africans of all classes is by no means proved by Dr. West's conclusion.

The gender issue, while important to many Africans, is not

generally perceived as being of equal significance as race—even by some of the leading women thinkers. For example, Dr. Joyce King explained: "I am not denying that sexism exists, but how do you go about solving that element of the struggle without distracting from the struggle that Blacks face as a whole" (Wiley 1992, p. 15). She continued: "We should...work to eliminate the gender problem but to make that a priority would be a mistake. Besides, African women have always had a more significant role in African communities at home and abroad."

In short, while African women have often been mistreated by some African men, their condition is different from that of white women.

Cornel West himself admits the ambivalence of Africans on the subject of homosexuality. Surely most African-American families love their homosexual sons and daughters and want them to be treated fairly and compassionately, but there is no consensus to accept homosexuality as a normal sexual preference in the African-American community. In other words, the relationship of that issue to the problem of white supremacy is quite remote to many Africans across lines of class and gender.

Let me emphasize that many African-American thinkers support the ideas of equal protection of the laws and fair treatment for all individuals. But we insist that the most critical "matter" facing African people, not only in the United States but throughout the diaspora, is the theory and practice of white supremacy.

On the condition of Africans in the United States, West admits that white supremacy has victimized the African population and that racism was established prior to capitalism (*Prophetic Fragments* 1988, p. 99). Further, he states:

> Racist discourses and actions have multiple power functions (such as domination over non-Europeans) that are neither reducible nor intelligible in terms of class exploitation alone. In short, these practices have a reality of their own and cannot simply be reduced to an economic base. (p. 99)

These "racist discourses and actions" that "have multiple power functions (such as domination over non-Europeans)" are, in reality, the theory and practice of white supremacy. In his explanation of these

"Racist discourses and practices," he traces the roots of the discourses to ancient Greece. In his words:

> Race did matter in classical antiquity [but their] racial differences were justified on cultural grounds…whereas at the inception of modern discourse, racial differences are often grounded in nature, that is, in ontology and later biology. (*Prophesy Deliverance* 1982, p. 64)

Dr. West does not discuss "racist" practices in antiquity, so we may assume he considered them either absent or insignificant. In any case he admits, "Race…mattered much less in classical antiquity than it does in modern times" (p. 64). Works by professors Joseph Harris (*Africans and Their History*, 19) and St. Clair Drake (*Black Folk Here and There*) shed considerable light on "racist" discourses and practices in antiquity. Two observations are in order: 1) the discourses and practices labeled as "racist" in antiquity seem to be directed against African people by Asians and Europeans and 2) the modern "racist" discourse is based on the fabrication that Africans are subhuman and the ancient ones do not seem to make such assertions.

Turning to modernity, West gets to the point when he asserts:

> The Afro-American encounter with the modern world has been shaped first and foremost by the doctrine of White Supremacy, which is embodied in institutional practices and enacted in everyday folkways under varying circumstances and evolving conditions. (p. 47)

The Doctrine and Practice of White Supremacy

After the initial identification of the doctrine of white supremacy in his earlier work, West begins to trace the emergence of the "racist" discourse from "marginal disciplines" that emerged in the eighteenth century (*Prophesy Deliverance* 1982, pp. 53–54 and *Prophetic Fragments* 1988, p. 102). But since these discourses emerged three hundred years after the advent of the European slave industry, let us take a glance at West's understanding of the consequences of this industry as related to

Africans enslaved in the United States. West summarized this condition as follows:

> During the colonial provisional stage of American culture, Africans were worse than slaves, they were also denuded proto Americans, in search of identity, systematically stripped of their African heritage and effectively and intentionally excluded from American culture and its roots in European modernity. (*Prophesy Deliverance*, p. 31)

This condition has continued into the present according to West: "Racist practices directed against black, brown and red people are an integral element of U. S. History, including present-day American culture and society" (*Prophetic Fragments*, p. 107). At first, according to West, Africans: "Focused principally on indigenous African practices, rituals, religious and worldviews they had somehow retained...they had not yet arrived at a synthetic Afro-American identity" (*Prophesy Deliverance*, p. 31).

Thus, West's view of the advent of the oppression of Africans is consistent with the intergenerational consensus among African thinkers on this matter. However, his assertion that the Africans during the colonial period were "denuded Americans" is belied by the fact that most Africans viewed themselves as Africans or Ethiopians, rather than as Americans. It is likely that most Africans during the first two hundred years of captivity did not think of themselves as Americans any more than whites thought of Africans as Americans. Most Africans probably wanted to return to Africa as free people and most likely concurred with David Walker, who decades later identified "Americans" as white oppressors. In other words, if those Africans did not come to the country with the intention of becoming Americans, and desired to go back home and continue African practices, it seems presumptuous to accuse them of being "denuded Americans."

It was during the period of the slave industry that the doctrine of white supremacy was established as a philosophical discourse. While West dates the emergence of this doctrine to the eighteenth-century, he does not explain its relationship to the idea of European superiority in social development, which is a major theme of modern philosophy. These ideas were put forth by seventeenth century thinkers like Francis

Bacon (*Novum Organum*) and John Locke (*Second Treatise on Government*). The notions were expanded into philosophical explanations by eighteenth-century thinkers of the Enlightenment such as Montesquieu and Hume. Such elaboration was necessary not merely to rationalize: "The prevailing mode of production, the political interests of the slaveholding class or the psychological needs of the dominant white racial group" (*Prophesy Deliverance*, p. 47).

The doctrine was a necessary moment in the development of the emerging European concept of Western civilization, which is based upon the assertion that civilization was solely developed by European people. Africans and most Asians were outside this line of cultural progress. Thus, one must look further than Montesquieu's chapter "Of the Slavery of the Negroes" (*Prophesy Deliverance*, p. 238) where he made what West labels "Montesquieu's satirical remarks...about black people" (p. 61) and consider his classifications of cultures into a hierarchy of three levels: savage, barbarian, and civilized. According to his scheme:

> The greatest part of the people on the coast of Africa (the only ones with whom most Europeans were acquainted in the mid-18th century) are *savages* and *barbarians*...They are without industry or arts...They have gold in abundance which they receive immediately from nature. Every *civilized* state is therefore in a condition to traffic with them to advantage, by raising their esteem for things of no value, and receiving a very high price in return. (Montesquieu 1949, p. 332)

Montesquieu's protégé, David Hume, not only exposed his "notorious racism...in his famous footnote," (p. 62) but in the same essay he also reinforced Montesquieu's explanation of the basis of European exploitation of Africans: "You may obtain anything of the Negroes by offering them strong drink; and may easily prevail with them to sell, not only their children, but their wives and mistresses, for a cask of brandy" (Hume 1777, p. 214). Having studied in France prior to the publication of his book of essays on national character, Hume, followed the lead of the French masters Montesquieu and Voltaire and asserted:

All the arts and sciences arose among free nations
...*Egyptians*, notwithstanding their ease, opulence, and
luxury, made but faint efforts towards a relish in those finer
pleasures, which were carried to such perfection by the
Greeks. (p. 89)

Thus, contrary to West's conclusion, Montesquieu and Hume
"put forward their own arguments" to justify the doctrine of white
supremacy which became an assumption of European social, political,
and economic discourse from that point on. In other words, white
supremacy was a consciously developed premise of modern European
philosophy and not merely the indirect product of the modern
scientific and esthetic discourses, as is implied by West (*Prophesy
Deliverance*, pp. 47–53).

A f r i c a n   R e s p o n s e s

It is in the context of the philosophically grounded doctrine of
white supremacy, which is not only married to the long-lived inhuman
practice of enslavement of African people but is also the indispensable
premise of Western civilization, that Africans of the diaspora in the
United States developed theories and practices about how to get out of
the mess.

Cornel West's account of the response begins with the acceptance
of E. Franklin Frazier's conclusion: "The process by which the Negroes
were captured and enslaved in the United States stripped them of their
African culture and destroyed their personality" (Frazier 1973, p. 64).

We now know the theory was stated as a part of the African
dialogue more than one hundred and fifty years ago (*Prophesy
Deliverance*, p. 16). West's acceptance of this "1619" concept of
Africans in the United States is enhanced by his high regard for the way
Orlando Patterson phrased it, "natal alienation" (p. 82). The resulting
"social death" of African people (*Prophetic Fragments*, p. 43) and the
"slow but sure death of African gods," (p. 84) led Africans to eventually
build what Cornel West labels the "black church" or "black Christian
communities" as a practical response to the condition of white
supremacy oppression. This 1619 concept of history is the device by

which West accomplishes the evasion of African Nationalism. But what West does not indicate is that the theory upon which this idea of "natal alienation" was based was a fabrication by European intellectuals first stated by Alexis de Tocqueville in 1835. Thus, this is a Eurocentric version of "Negro history." Let us recall the views of Tocqueville:

> The Negro of the United States has lost even the remembrance of his country; the language which his forefathers spoke is never heard around him: he abjured their religion and forgot their customs when he ceased to belong to Africa, without acquiring any claim to European privileges. But he remains half-way between two communities, isolated between two races; sold by the one, repulsed by the other; finding not a spot in the universe to call by the name of country. (pp. 3–4)

Tocqueville's ideas were garneerd from the many interviews he had with European Americans during his yearlong tour of the United States. His conclusion, thus, reflected the opinions of the oppressors rather than the oppressed.

According to West, the forced abandonment of African traditions did not take effect immediately. "During the first phase of African practice in America," (*Prophesy Deliverance*, p. 31), the "Africans held on to their indigenous practices" (*Prophesy Deliverance*, p. 34). In fact, the big change noted by West did not occur among "second–and third–generation Africans in the USA" (*Prophetic Fragments*, p. 161) until around 1800 (*Prophetic Fragments*, p. 35). It is then that West's distinctly "synthetic Afro-American identity" came into being (*Prophesy Deliverance*, p. 31).

West conceptualizes the establishment of the black church as a historic act of courage and defiance which became the effective African culture in the United State. As West sees it, this choice incorporated the values of "Dissenting Protestant Christianity" (*Prophetic Fragments*, p. 43) and "the ideals of Americanism as enunciated in the Declaration of Independence and the Constitution" (*Prophetic Fragments*, p. 41). West believes these early American values were given a good old African twist and finally produced "the best of Black (American?) culture," that is, the "Prophetic black church" and the musical traditions which include spirituals, blues and jazz (*Prophetic Fragments*, p. 43; *Race Matters*, p. 78). West hastens to assert:

> Black Christianity is not merely a reaction to white exclusion; rather it is a distinct culture which revels in its own uniqueness. (*Prophetic Fragments*, p. 163).

Although the prophetic black Christian culture "did not promote explicitly revolutionary action" (*Prophetic Fragments*, pp. 44), West believes that it has kept and still keeps Africans from mass suicide "in an impossible militant struggle for freedom" (*Prophetic Fragments*, p. 44–45). Nonetheless, he credits the tradition for the "suicidal" projects of Gabriel Prosser, Denmark Vesey, and Nat Turner (*Prophetic Fragments*, p. 44). Indeed, according to Dr. West, if we properly season this tradition with another, Marxism/Socialism, it will get us to the promised land.

West, in one of his most recent works, identifies this community, its culture and institutions as "black civil society" (*Race Matters*, pp. 16, 18), but he rejects the attempt to call it a "nation within a nation." Even though West's black civil society is made up of "black families, neighborhoods, schools, churches and mosques," he eschews any semblance of anything other than American nationalism. In fact, "Black Americans are the most American of all Americans...they are the most hybrid in blood, colors, and cultural creations" (*Prophetic Fragments*, p. 41).

The hybrid condition of the African population is due in large part to the rape of African women, but West glosses over this fact [although he does refer to Africans in the USA as "these dark bastard people" (*Prophesy Deliverance*, p. 22)] and explains the reason for Africans choosing to be Americans thusly:

> Afro-American Christian slaves—despite harsh domination—shared too much in common with Euro-America slaveholders in regard to culture and civilization. (*Prophetic Fragments*, p. 44)

As a result, attempts to identify the African population as a nation are labeled as "an ahistorical racial definition of a nation" (*Prophetic Fragments*, p. 99) and "Zionism" (*Prophetic Fragments*, p. 44), because proponents of nationalism have not been able to authenticate claims that "Afro-Americans and Euro-Americans" inhabit "two distinct and different ways of life" (*Prophetic Fragments*, p. 44).

West seems to ignore the context out of which the concept civil society emerges. In the thought of John Locke, where it was most clearly articulated, civil society was the basis out of which a body politic or state emerged (Locke, *Second Treatise on Government*). In other words, in Enlightenment theory, the next step after the establishing of civil society is what we may call the nation state. Thus, the black civil society that West imagines, seems to be a colony under the domination of a sovereign nation, the United States, although West contends that the church is institutionally autonomous (*Prophetic Fragments*, p. 161). West does not conceive of the colony needing or wanting independence, but rather it longs to be absorbed by its oppressor nation. Such a position is reminiscent of the collaborators of the pre-Haitian Revolutionary period, who, because of their favored slave status, loved their oppressor so much that they only wanted to stay near him, albeit in a subordinate status. This, of course, is one of routes taken by some Africans in their quest to be Americans.

The "Black Christian discourse," according to West's construction, expressed "subversive desires and utopian energies" (*Prophetic Fragments*, p. 44). It also promoted: "A tragic sense of life which affirms the workings of evil forces beyond human control while promoting struggle against particular forms of evil in the world" (*Prophetic Fragments*, p. 164). The discourse also: "Views suffering as a stepping-stone to liberation. Yet liberation does not eradicate the suffering in itself" (*Prophetic Fragments*, p. 164). It is not clear how this discourse fits into the aforementioned speeches about "how to get out of the mess," but West feels that the sermons represent the best of the Afro-American "intellectual tradition" (bell hooks and Cornel West, *Breaking Bread*, p. 136). The speeches, like their counterparts, "the Black musical tradition of musical performance," are "oral, improvisational, and histrionic" (*Breaking Bread*, p. 136).

West is also unclear on how the various "literate intellectual" discourses are related to the "black civil society." He asserts that "these literate intellectuals, however, have not mastered their craft commensurate" with the preachers and musicians. West developed several typologies of African thought or discourse in the United States, the most relevant of which are in *Prophesy Deliverance!* and his essays, "Assessing Black Neoconservatism" (*Prophetic Fragments*, pp. 55–63) and "The Dilemma of the Black Intellectual" (*Breaking Bread*, pp. 131–146). The somewhat overlapping resulting categories are "exceptionalist," "assimilationalist," "marginalist," "humanist," "conservative," "liberal," "socialist," "revolutionary," and "critical organic catalyst." Although he mentions nationalism in several of his works, he does not treat the position as a separate category in any of the schemes. West's attempt to evade African Nationalist thought forces him to separate thinkers who are generally considered nationalists into different classifications. For example, he divided the category "Exceptionalist" into two subunits, "strong exceptionalist" and "weak exceptionalist." He placed W.E.B. Du Bois and Elijah Muhammad into the former, and Marcus Garvey and Martin Luther King, Jr. in the latter. Perhaps because I am not a philosopher, I fail to see the usefulness of a classification that places Marcus Garvey, Elijah Muhammad, W.E.B. Du Bois, and Martin Luther King, Jr. in the same general category, and then subdivides them so that Marcus Garvey has more in common with King than he does with Elijah Muhammad.

The one historical taxonomy of discourse which West develops is put forth under a discussion of "The Evolution of Black Theology" (*Prophesy Deliverance*, p. 101). In this theological typology he places some of the nineteenth-century thinkers and leaders such as David Walker and Gabriel Prosser in the category, "Black Theology of Liberation as Critique of Slavery." West, in citing Walker, passes over the fact that Walker addressed the oppressors as "Americans" and "Christians" in distinction to the colored people whom he identified as Africans (p. 47). Furthermore, West does not discuss Walker's linking of the modern Europeans to the ancient Greeks stating that: "Whites have always been an unjust, jealous, unmerciful, avaricious and blood-thirsty set of beings, always seeking after power and authority" (Walker 1965, p. 56).

He clearly distinguished between them and Africans in the United States, who were historically linked to the ancient Egyptians, who were much less aggressive and much more humane (pp. 47, 56). West also overlooks the fact that Walker constantly referred to the whites as "devils" and criticized Africans who wanted to marry white women, flatly stating that he would not give "a pinch of snuff" for a white woman (p. 48).

Walker's denunciation of the American Colonization Society's project to export free Blacks to Liberia demonstrates the complexity of the problems faced by African leaders. He agreed with the resolution to stay in the United States and fight, emphasizing that Africans had as much right to the country as the Europeans: "America is more our country than it is the whites—we have enriched it with our *blood* and *tears*" (p. 103). Thus, it was the land, not the people, which Walker embraced.

In one sense, West's concept of Walker as a prophet of "American unity" is appropriate. Walker's message to the oppressors included the following offer: "Treat us like men, and we will be your friends. And there is no doubt in my mind but that the whole of the past will be sunk into oblivion, we may yet, under God, become a united happy people" (p. 108). But, Walker followed this proposition with a prophesy spoken to the captive and enslaved African people: "God will dash tyrants, in combination with devils, into atoms, and will bring you out from your wretchedness and miseries under these *Christian people !!!*" (p. 109).

Although Walker's nationalism is not coupled with a "back to Africa" movement, it has the essential ingredients of nationalism and sets a clear precedent for Elijah Muhammad to emerge more than a hundred years later.

Indeed, Walker doubtlessly considered himself a Christian, but he explicitly denied that he had anything in common with the European American Christian oppressors, which brings into question West's depiction of this "Black Christian community" and its theological discourses.

Martin Delany, who is identified by West as a "Black religious leader" (*Prophesy Deliverance*, p. 12), is superficially discussed by West, possibly because Delany's critique of African Christians in the United States during the antebellum period is also at variance with West's assessment. In other words, the various leaders of the African community were, for the most part, considered Christians, but their views were so divergent on matters of African liberation that their Christianity cannot be the cause of such contrasting speeches and notices.

West's model fails to account for the sentiments of emigrationists like Daniel Coker who proclaimed, "my soul clings to Africa," (*Bracey*, p. 47) as he advocated that Africans in the United States join him in Liberia. West's evasion of African Nationalist thought further ignores the great speech of James Theodore Holley who held the Haitian Revolution to be a great model for Africans in the United States (*A Vindication of the Negro Race*, 1857). Holley, like Prince Sanders before him, emigrated to Haiti. These nineteenth-century champions of the African race in the United States rejected the commonality with their oppressors that so fascinates Cornel West.

The second stage in West's theological scheme is called "Black Theology of Liberation as Critique of Institutional Racism" (*Prophesy Deliverance*, p. 102). In this class he placed Bishop Henry McNeal Turner, Marcus Garvey, and Reverend Martin Luther King, Jr. Such categorization confounds the great contrasts between the views of the first two on the one hand and King on the other. To say that all three were Christians who opposed white supremacy in the twentieth century is to say practically nothing of significance about them. For the benefit of Dr. West I should point out that the policy of "emigrating to the Black homeland" advocated in speeches of Turner and Garvey were only a small part of their positions on the condition and liberation of Africans in the United States (see Garvey *Philosophy and Opinions;* Tony Martin, *Race First;* and Redkey, *Black Exodus*).

When viewed from the perspective of these "suppressed" historical moments of African practice and discourse, the projects of Marcus Garvey, Elijah Muhammad, Malcolm X, and Leonard Jeffries do not appear merely as frustrated responses to exclusion from Euro-American modernity. Historical grounding would also reveal some important moments in the path Dr. West chooses to take, an issue to which we will return.

In sum, Cornel West's hybrid philosophy produces an interesting product, marrying the struggle of Africans in America to the ideals of their oppressors, results in a "mulatto culture" which is full of gaps and contradictions. It, indeed, is a fragmented framework for prophesy. He has snatched pieces from authentic African traditions here and there, and stitched them to other fragments from European authentic traditions, and produced a quilt that he believes represents the real "America," but which is as incomprehensible to common sense as the patterns in a kaleidoscope.

The Critique of African-Centered Thought

Cornel West seems to be ambivalent about African-centered thought, which he labels "Afrocentrism." In his words:

> Afrocentrism, a contemporary species of black nationalism, is a gallant yet misguided attempt to define an African identity in a white society perceived to be hostile. It is gallant because it puts black doings and sufferings, not white anxieties and fears, at the center of discussion. It is misguided because—out of fear of cultural hybridization and through silence on the issue of class, retrograde views of black women, gay men, and lesbians, and a reluctance to link race to the common good—it reinforces the narrow discussions about race. (*Race Matters*, p. 4)

Leaving aside, for the moment, the positive part of his evaluation, we may conclude that his critique of African-centered thought is synonymous with his position on African Nationalism in general. His critique of "Black" nationalism in general is summarized thusly:

> Notwithstanding deep dissimilarities, differences were not deep enough to give cultural credence and existential authenticity to claims about Afro-Americans and Euro-Americans inhabiting two distinct and different ways of life. Subsequent black nationalist movements have attempted to authenticate such claims—but usually to no avail in regard to revolutionary action. In fact, most black nationalist movements have been Zionist, as with Chief Sam or Marcus Garvey, or explicitly apolitical as with Elijah

Muhammad's Nation of Islam. Maulana Karenga's US—
owing to his creative leadership and openness to
criticism—is the major black nationalist organization which
serves as exception. (*Prophetic Fragments,* p. 44)

While he exempts the nationalist Maulana Karenga, he includes
almost everyone in the United States who identifies with nationalism,
including Malcolm X, about whom West asserted:

Malcolm X's deep pessimism about the capacity and
possibility of white Americans to shed their racism led him,
ironically, to downplay the past and present bonds between
blacks and whites. (*Race Matters,* p. 102)

In addition, Malcolm X's fear of cultural hybridity was
linked to his own personal hybridity (he was the grandson
of a white man), which blurred the very boundaries so
rigidly policed by white supremacist authorities.(*Race
Matters,* p. 103)

This great prophet of black rage—with all his brilliance,
courage, and conviction—remained blind to basic
structures of domination based on class, gender, and sexual
orientation in the Middle East. (*Race Matters,* pp.
103–104).

By relegating Malcolm X to the "prophet of black rage," West
exposes his own limited reading ability when confronted with the
challenge of African Nationalism. Malcolm was a prophet and
champion of African independence. His teaching was like the
teachings of David Walker and Marcus Garvey. He realized that
enslavement to the oppressor's ideas and ideals was more dangerous to
Africans in the long run than was the physical slavery of the chattel
slave system and its successors, segregation and colonialism. He was
the prophet of the decolonization of the African mind. To reduce
Malcolm X to the "prophet of black rage" is not a reflection on
Malcolm but a reflection on the limited horizons of West's hybrid
philosophy.

West's critique even more negatively berates some contemporary advocates of "Black" nationalism like Minister Louis Farrakhan and Leonard Jeffries. When he states:

> The rhetoric of Farrakhan and Jeffries feeds on an undeniable history of black denigration at the hands of Americans of every ethnic and religious group. The delicate issues of black self-love and black self-contempt are then viewed in terms of white put-down and Jewish conspiracy. The precious quest for black self-esteem is reduced to immature and cathartic gestures that bespeak an excessive obsession with whites and Jews. There can be no healthy conception of black humanity based on such obsessions. (*Race Matters*, p. 78)

West's criticism, in part, is cast not only over "black nationalist" and African-centered thinkers but also over "black liberals" including W. E. B. Du Bois (especially his earlier thinking). In this regard, West accused "Black liberal leadership" of the same narrow concern which he feels characterizes nationalism:

> The notion that racial discrimination is the sole cause of the prevailing predicament of the black working poor and underclass is specious...white racism indeed is pernicious and potent—yet it cannot fully explain the socioeconomic position of the majority of black Americans. (*Prophetic Fragments*, p. 59)

As mentioned above, West classifies W. E. B. Du Bois as a "strong exceptionalist," a tradition which "posits Afro-American superiority, not over all others, but specifically over white Americans" (*Prophesy Deliverance*, p. 73). He cites Du Bois' statement, "Negroes differ from whites in their inherent genius and stages of development" (*Prophesy Deliverance*, p. 73) in order to expose "the hypocrisy of Afro-American exceptionalism" (*Prophesy Deliverance*, p. 78) and assert that it "serves principally as a covert strategy for Afro-American entrance into the mainstream of American society." What is amusing is the argument by West that the basic flaw of "black nationalism" (i.e., separation) is the same as the basic flaw of "black liberalism" (i.e., integration). That flaw for West is what he considers the narrow focus on or the "obsession" with race. Thus, West seems to be instinctively opposed to theories that prioritize white supremacy as *the* major problem for peoples of African descent.

Cornel West faults African-centered thought, which he defines as a contemporary version of nationalism, because of six features which he assigns to the tradition. These West-defined flaws are:

1. fear of the hybrid nature of African Americans;
2. silence on class exploitations;
3. opposition to women and gays;
4. obsession with race;
5. antipathy to coalitions and alliances;
6. failure to link race to the common good.

(*Race Matters*, p. 4)

We may usefully label this critique as the "worst of black nationalism" according to Cornel West, because even in the face of such a negative evaluation he sees some usefulness.

Although we have necessarily responded to most of these criticisms on this list, a few additional comments are in order. First, the idea of biological and cultural hybridity with which West is so fascinated is not so much an object of fear as an act of refusal to submit to rape. Although one cannot recover one's lost virginity, there are alternatives to capitulation. One alternative is suicide, which is rejected by most Africans in the United States. Another choice is to fall in love with the rapist, have his children and teach the children to honor and obey their rapist father. This choice is in keeping with West's hybrid philosophy and fragmented prophesy. A third alternative is to denounce the rapist, persist until he is brought before the bar of justice, and, certainly, avoid his company. The third choice is preferred by many of the African-centered thinkers and many, if not most, Africans in the United States.

In relation to cultural hybridity, let us first of all confess that culture is a human creation. Even though it is intergenerational, each generation can make choices about modifying the culture it inherits. One of the choices each generation faces involves the question of whether to accept the culture of our oppressor. Through the generations, some of us have chosen to reject the culture of our oppressors and recover our disrupted ancestral culture. One such example involves the African children of Soweto who, in 1976, refused to be taught in the language of their white supremacist oppressors.

How can we accept a culture that grants significance only to our music and preaching? As Anderson Thompson would say, must we accept a cultural imperium which accepts us as a Sambo culture? Cheikh Anta Diop pointed out that Africans in the diaspora have cultural citizenship (i.e., full citizenship, as opposed to second-class citizenship) only in Africa. Gaining awareness of that citizenship is not just a matter of dignity, it's a matter of physical, spiritual, and mental health. It is a matter of restoring our African personalities after a long winter of cultural estrangement and, in some cases, cultural amnesia. We may not be able to get our virginity back after the rape, but we do not have to marry the rapist, as is the custom in some European cultures.

The nationalist position on culture also answers West's concern about class and gender. A careful reading of the advocates of nationalism, such as David Walker, Martin Delany, Malcolm X, Cheikh Anta Diop, and Leonard Jeffries, reveals a critique of modern European culture which many of us feel is diametrically opposed to African culture. One only need to revisit Diop's "Two Cradle Theory" to understand that the critique is directed against Western materialism, as well as the Western tradition of female oppression. We do not apologize for ranking those very important issues below white supremacy. Once the theory and practice of worldwide white supremacy is overthrown, African people can begin the process of developing societies based upon African principles that reject obsessive materialism and female oppression.

Professor West's remaining concerns *vis-`a-vis* African-centered thought are linked to his American obsession. He severely knocks the nationalists for not embracing alliances and coalitions with "non-blacks." For him, effective work can be accomplished only through "concrete strategies of principled coalitions and democratic alliances" (*Race Matters*, p. 104). The real "challenge" for him requires:

Close dialogue with European, Asian, African, Latin

American, and Native American intellectuals yet rooted in the best of the Afro-American intellectual past. These new forms of theoretical activity must learn from Marxism (class and imperialist oppression), populism (local peoples' empowerment), civic republicanism (decentralized democratic control), liberalism (individual liberties, due process of law, separation of church and state, and checks and balances), and womanism (women's control of their bodies and destinies), as well as ecologism (communition with rather than domination of nature), and elements of Garveyism (dignity of African peoples). (*Prophetic Fragments*, p. 49)

Thus, there should be an alliance of ideas as well as leaders and thinkers. If this path is not followed, West fears: "Black people will become even more isolated as a community and the black freedom struggle will be tarred with the brush of immorality" (*Race Matters*, p. 78).

In other words, West equates the work of such coalitions as projects directed toward the common good. The equation of a synthesis of the historical leftist organizations with a new civil rights movement is not nearly as new as some of West's rhetoric indicates. In fact, Maulana Karenga emphasized the idea of a synthesis of the best of socialism and black thought two decades ago. West's idea of the marriage of prophetic Christianity with socialism goes back more than one hundred and fifty years to the pre-Marxist thought of one of Marx's mentors, Henri Saint-Simon (see Saint-Simon, *The New Christianity* 1830).

West's advocacy of the Americanness of Africans in the United States seems to be more a matter of principle than of practicality. Thus, for him, Africans are to be morally bound to expand their focus from their own plight to concern themselves with the plight of women, homosexuals, and poor people, regardless of race. Such advocacy is certainly commendable since there are Africans who are women, homosexuals, and poor. But Africans do not have to abandon nationalism in order to express concern about, and sympathize with, *les miserables* of other nations. Are Irish nationalists required to abandon their nationalism in order to prove they are concerned with oppression against women? Are Jewish supporters of the Israeli nation accused of antifeminism or homophobia just because they are Israeli nationalists?

C o n c l u s i o n

The position advocated by West in some respects resembles the solution proposed by Harold Cruse in *The Crisis of the Negro Intellectual* (1967), an essay from which West quotes. In that place Cruse asserts:

> American group reality demands a struggle for democracy among ethnic groups, rather than between two races. What is called a racial struggle over civil rights is, in reality, the contention in America among several different ethnic groups of which Protestants and American Negroes are only two. (p. 458)

I read Cruse to mean that we should transform the racial struggle into an ethnic struggle so that we can pursue our objectives as do the various European ethnic groups in the United States. Certainly, he cannot mean that the condition of the African population is like the condition of the European ethnic or religious groups which he identifies as the white Anglo-Saxon Protestants, Catholics, and Jews in America. Therefore, Cruse suggests the necessity of a constitutional convention to provide the basis for a society that permits Africans to function as an ethnic group. In essence Cruse's theory seems to fit well with the position of Frederick Douglass and E. Franklin Frazier, who made a distinction between "integration" and "assimilation." Frazier favored integration, which he viewed as a process of desegregation that would remove the barriers against equality for Africans while still allowing some internal integrity to "negro life."

Although West is ambivalent about the position, his call for including "the best of black nationalism" such as Maulana Karenga's "Kawaida Theory," "Garveyism," and "the best of Malcolm X (his notion of psychic conversion)," indicates that he can live with some "black nationalist insights," as long as the "insights" are not offensive to the potential European American allies. That is the real problem.

All serious African Nationalism offends most Europeans, whether they are conservative, liberal, or Marxist. This is especially true of highly educated Europeans or European intellectuals. Pan African Nationalism is a direct threat to their intellectual traditions. Anglo-Saxon Protestants and European Catholics trace their intellectual lineage from Homer, Socrates, and the Bible through Charles Martel, Thomas Aquinas, Galileo, Machiavelli, Bacon, Locke, and Hegel. Jews have their heritage from Abraham through Josephus to Spinoza and Marx. The construction of these traditions involved at critical points the fabrication of African inferiority and history which African nationalism must refute in order to stop the campaign to deform the African heritage.

This African challenge offends European scholars and makes them uncomfortable. Though Europeans intellectually curse each other out, if an African courteously suggests that some Jews got rich selling Africans, then African nationalism is lambasted. Thus, the dialogue which West and his fellow Afro-American intellectuals advocate is a far-fetched dream, even if it were desirable on theoretical grounds. Other African intellectuals who tried and failed in this regard include W. E. B. Du Bois, Richard Wright, Chester Himes, Ralph Ellison, James Baldwin, and Harold Cruse. Even though they continually failed to hold interracial peer dialogues, most continued to try because they either did not know of any other thing to do, or they did not have the courage to pursue topics which the children of their oppressors found offensive.

What West calls "the best of Black culture, (such as) jazz and the prophetic Black church," are those elements of the traditions of Africans in the United States which whites enjoy and allow. So, the image which West advances as the "African American" culture, would consist of the ideals of Thomas Jefferson (minus his slave holdings and *Notes on Virginia*), the Constitution of the United States (as amended and interpreted by European American office holders and minus the unfavorable decisions), the Calvinist's Christianity of the American protestant, (minus their white supremacy), and the pragmatic ideas of Emerson and Dewey (despite their detachment from slavery and segregation). In other words, the basic framework of this African American culture is European American. To this framework would be added a dab of color—Negro preaching in the form of the eloquence (but not the profundity) of Martin Luther King, Jr., and, of course, the only truly "American" music, jazz. [One should also throw in "rap" and the slam dunk (I think black basketball players invented that).]

West realized that even this benign "African American" subculture cannot flourish unless a miracle occurs. Therefore, the African American intellectuals and leaders must get some help, not only from the feminists and the gays, but also, and above all, from the Marxists.

One other point which West argues is that the nationalists' approach, which, according to him, is based primarily on "Black rage," has a suicidal tendency in both the individual (i.e., Denmark Vesey) and group senses. In his own words:

> The inability of Afro-American Christianity to produce a millennialist tradition is a tribute to Black Christians—for as great and heroic it may sound in books, it would have resulted, more than likely, in either wholesale genocide for Black people or disabling despair and overwhelming self-destruction among Black people.

Thus, the mild cultural identity of the African-American church is not only morally desirable, but it is also practical for West. Our argument, however, is that teaching Africans the truth is not necessarily depressing, nor will it result in slaughter should Africans resist white supremacy. For two hundred years we have had a splendid example of an alternative—the Haitian Revolution. Is menticide preferable to biological genocide?

There are alternatives to continuing the Sambo subculture as a part of American pluralism. We can choose from a variety of proposals concerning getting out of this mess. We may pursue the possibility of establishing a homeland on the continent of our origin, as an autonomous member of a United States of Africa; we may launch a campaign to divide this country into a number of autonomous city-states or even partition the territory into an African state and one or more non-African states; or we may investigate the feasibility of repatriation of European Americans. As long as we have to fight, let us set some noble and bold objectives.

It becomes apparent that Cornel West's location is flexible. He appears to be more comfortable in the petition mode (West, pp. 7–11, 23). But in this analytical role as a scholar, he often slips into the collaboration mode and provides a useful anatomy of the oppressed community (in the best tradition of slave rebellion research). Furthermore, from time to time, he echoes the rhetoric of the rebel tradition. Such an inherently contradictory position characterizes many so-called African intellectuals and is a problem for all Africans who specialize in speaking about the mess we are in. However, because he is a philosopher, one would expect West to be less ambivalent about his position.

It is clear that Cornel West has responded to E. Franklin Frazier's charge, "we have no philosophers or thinkers who command the respect of the intellectual community at large." Indeed, he has not only read Hegel, Kant, and James, but he has "reflected upon the fundamental problems which have always concerned philosophers" (Frazier 1973, p. 60). Nonetheless, he has evaded the African heritage and connection, in relation to Africans in the frigid diaspora of the Western Hemisphere.

R E F E R E N C E S

Bernal, Martin. 1987. *Black Athena: The Afroasiatic Roots of Classical Civilization*. Vol. I. The Fabrication of Ancient Greece 1785–1985. New Brunswick: Rutgers University Press.

Bracey, John Jr., et al., eds. 1970. *Black Nationalism in America*. New York: Bobbs-Merrill.

Cruse, Harold. 1967. *The Crisis of the Negro Intellectual*. New York: William Morrow.

Delany, Martin. 1960. *Condition, Elevation, Emigration and Destiny of the Colored People of the United States*. New York: Arno Press.

Diop, Cheikh Anta. 1986. "Nile Valley Executive Committee Interviews Diop," *Great African Thinkers*. Vol. I Cheikh Anta Diop. Editors Larry Williams and Ivan Van Sertima. New Brunswick: Transaction Books.

Ebony Readers Polls. 1991, 1992, and 1993; *Time*/CNN Poll. Feb. 16–17, 1994, published in *Time*, 28–94.

Ernst, Frederick A., et al. 1991. Readers Polls. *Ebony*, 18–19 (April). "Condemnation of Homosexuality in the Black Community: A Gender-Specific Phenomenon?" *Archives of Sexual Behavior*, Vol. 20, No. 6, 579–585.

Frazier, E. Franklin. 1973. "The Failure of the Negro Intellectual" in *The Death of White Sociology*. Ed. by Joyce Ladner. New York: Vintage Books Random House.

Garvey, Amy Jacques, ed. 1992. *Philosophy and Opinions of Marcus Garvey*. New York: Macmillan.

hooks, bell and Cornel West. 1991. *Breaking Bread: Insurgent Black Intellectual Life.* Boston: South End Press.

Hume, David. 1987. *Essays: Moral, Political, and Literary.* Indianapolis: Liberty Classics.

Karenga, Maulana. 1980. *Kawaida Theory: An Introductory Outline* Inglewood: Kawaida Publications.

Locke, John. 1952. *The Second Treatise on Government.* New York: Bobbs-Merrill.

Montesquieu, Charles. 1949. *The Spirit of the Laws.* New York: Hafner.

Thompson, Anderson. 1975. "Developing An Afrikan Historiography." *Black Books Bulletin*, vol. 3, (Spring).

de Tocqueville, Alexis. 1945. *Democracy in America.* New York: Vintage Books.

Walker, David. 1965. *David Walker's Appeal.* New York: Hill and Wang.

West, Cornel. 1982. *Prophesy Deliverance!: An Afro-American Revolutionary Christianity.* Philadelphia: Westminster Press.

—. 1988. *Prophetic Fragments.* Trenton: Africa World Press.

—. 1993. *Race Matters.* Boston: Beacon Press.

Wiley, Ed III. 1992. "Intellectual Pursuits." *Black Issues in Higher Education*, No. 15, (May).

Wobogo, Vulineda. 1976. "Diop's Two Cradle Theory and the Origin of White Racism." *Black Books Bulletin*, 4:4 (winter). 20–29.

Wright, Bobby E. 1984. *The Psychopathic Racial Personality and other Essays*. Chicago: Third World Press.

12

A Loose Cannon in Search of Losing Canons

According to Manning Marable, a scholar of African descent, Henry Louis Gates is "profoundly at odds with the Afro-centric position" (Wiley 1965, pp. 12–15). This general impression is shared by Arthur Schlesinger Jr., a scholar of German American descent, who identified Gates as one of the "serious Black scholars" who regards Afrocentricity with skepticism (Schlesinger 1991, p. 53). These impressions among African and European American intellectuals are supported by recent statements attributed to Gates which have appeared in newspapers and popular magazines. Such explicit indictments of African-centered thought, however, were avoided in his publication, *Loose Canons: Notes on the Culture Wars,* (1992), in which one might expect him to articulate his criticism in a disciplined fashion. Since such was not the case, our task is more difficult. We have to identify the explicit conclusions which Gates allegedly stated and, through inference, connect these statements with their antecedents in his "scholarly" discourse.

This task is complicated because, in *Loose Canons,* Gates has presented a partial autobiography as an integral part of his discourse. Thus avoiding the charge of *ad hominem* in our reading of this work is virtually impossible. Four mass-media-published articles attributed to Gates provide us with the gist of his gripes against what he identifies as the "Afrocentric movement." The first article cited here was published in the fall of 1991 and the last in the winter of 1994. Sometime after the first article and before the third, Gates finished the essays and commentaries published in *Loose Canons*. We may, therefore, conclude that the thoughts in the scholarly work are connected to the media statements.

In the first article Gates implied that there is good and bad Afrocentricism. He states the problem:

> Surely all scholars of Africa and its diaspora are, by definition, "Afrocentric," if the term signals the recognition that Africa is centrally in the world, as much as the world is in Africa. But this is a source of the problem: all Afrocentrists, alas, do not look alike. ("Beware of the New Pharaohs," 1991, p. 47)

The term Afrocentrism is without exception used to identify the bad version in the later articles. In a second article, Gates, through a web of innuendo, insinuation, and guilt by association, cleverly connects the Afrocentric movement with the Nation of Islam and both to the "new anti-Semitic" movement ("Black Demagogues and Pseudo-Scholars," 1992, Op-Ed page). He has laid out his definition of the phenomenon. According to Gates, Afrocentrism is advocated by demagogues in:

> The bid of one Black elite to supplant another...in the raging battle of who will speak for black America...they know that the more isolated black America becomes, the greater their power. (Op-Ed page)

Gates recognizes the struggle between African-centered thought and its opponents as an intellectual civil war. Gates, however, misses the point of the war. Contrary to Gates' assertion, it is not so much to determine who will "speak" for black America as who will speak with and guide the instruction and reeducation of Africans in the United States. Will it be the new "African 'hyphen' American" Black Studies elite and its white American sponsor, or the champions of African civilization? The larger struggle is a war of liberation from the tyranny of the culture of Western civilization with its Siamese twin, white supremacy.

The upshot is that Gates feels that "black writers, intellectuals

202

and religious leaders" who are taking an unequivocal stand on the issue of the "isolationist agenda" of the Afrocentric movement must continue to do so because "the moral credibility of our struggle against racism stands in the balance." Thus Gates characterized this vaguely defined group as fighting against "racism" as well as bad Afrocentricism, which he views as reverse racism.

Since Gates' explicit criticism of African-centered thought constitute a series of media blurbs rather than a logical scholarly analysis, I will attempt to summarize his allegations. He finds two basic flaws in "Afrocentricism."

1. Afrocentrism has created a "segregated ghettoized" discipline. The proponents of this doctrine advocate exclusion of nonblacks from the teaching and study of the discipline. They are anti-Semitic. They associate with a bad crowd, for example Minister Farrakhan and the Nation of Islam. Moreover, the Afrocentrists are guilty of opposing "trans-racial cooperation" ("Demagogues," Op-Ed page). According to Gates, this discipline is furthermore enforced by "thought police" ("New Pharaohs," p. 47). Finally, the members of the discipline do not engage in internal criticism.

2. Afrocentrism produces "shoddy" scholarship. The proponents attempt to "rediscover a lost cultural identity—or invent one that never quite existed" ("New Pharaohs," p. 47). They advance "dubious theories" such as "the relation of melanin to humanitarian impulses" and "bogus theories" such as 'sun' and 'ice' people. Thus Afrocentrism has created "racial ideologies" which are inverted versions of the worst racism of the past few centuries. These are "racial fantasies" projecting "blackness as an ideology or religion." Such theoretical attempts are based upon the "shaky grounds of self-esteem." Finally, the Afrocentrists read and endorse bad books. In this regard, Gates cites Dr. John Henrik Clarke's introduction to *The Iceman Inheritance* by Michael Bradley and a student newspaper's recommendations of "The Protocols of the Elders of Zion" and the Nation of Islam publication, *The Secret Relationship Between Blacks and Jews* ("Black

Demagogues," Op-Ed page).

Gates' indictment is spiced with a few identities. He mentions Dr. Leonard Jeffries, and alleges that Conrad Muhammad and Khalid Muhammad are his "cohorts" ("Black Pharaohs," p. 47). He identifies Dr. John Henrik Clarke as the "great paterfamilias of the Afrocentric movement" (Gates) and connects Minister Louis Farrakhan to the movement. In Schlesinger's diatribe, Gates is quoted as asserting, "I am certainly not in the same camp as Molefi Asante and all those guys" (Schlesinger 1991, p. 53). Gates, however, does not analyze Asante's works or the scholarly research of Dr. Clarke, Cheikh Anta Diop, or Théophile Obenga. None of the criticism and charges against those individuals who are singled out, or the movement in general, are explained with scholarly documentation, therefore the indictment appears to be frivolous and without standing as a serious discourse.

Certainly Gates should be aware of the doctrinal and organizational differences between the African-centered movement and internal criticism. I must also point out that proponents of African thought have been severely critical of white supremacists and their Negro colleagues, including Gates and his cohorts. But speaking of internal criticism, where is Gates' internal, negative criticism of Cornel West, Anthony Appiah, and others?

In *Loose Canons*, Gates wages his battle against the African-centered discourse through the time-tested strategy of nonrecognition. The most notorious historical use of the ploy is the original U. S. Constitution which avoided any mention of slavery or Africans, and yet fully empowered the national and state governments to maintain the chattel slave system for "three score and 10 years." In more recent times the policy of diplomatic nonrecognition of Red China was less successful. Gates' use of the strategy is quite clever. He weds "Afrocentrism" to cultural nationalism and then proceeds to battle against the easier target of white supremacy which has paraded throughout the twentieth century as a right wing conservative monopoly. The trick is performed in the introduction to the discourse *Loose Canons* in which he equates multiculturism (his position) with cultural pluralism and then asserts:

> Cultural pluralism is not, of course, everyone's cup of tea. Vulgar cultural nationalists—like Allan Bloom or Leonard Jeffries—correctly identify it as the enemy. These polemicists thrive on absolute partitions: between "civilization" and "barbarism," between "black" and "white," between a thousand versions of Us and Them. But they are whistling in the wind. (p. xvi)

By joining one of the most well-known advocates of African-centered discourse with one of the most arrogant white supremacists, Gates pulls an "old Black Marxist" trick by implying that Afrocentricists are black conservatives. Thus, every blow against white supremacy is supposed to injure "Afrocentricism." The obvious ploy convinces no one but those who are already the enemies of African thought.

From this battleground, Gates states the case for African-American studies to lead academia toward multiculturalism. The crux of Gates' cultural pluralism can be seen in this statement:

> I look forward to truly comparative programs of comparative literature that embrace the languages and literatures of Yoruba, Urdu, or Arabic as well as the traditional European literatures. I think we should design a required Humanities Course that's truly humanistic—with the Western segment comprising a quarter or a third—in addition to the traditional Western Civilization course, so that students can begin to understand the histories of civilization itself, in a truly comparative manner. Such an embrasive posture honors the best, the noblest traditions and ambitions of the academy. And while I've decried cultural nationalism, I hope you'll permit me to bow to it in citing something Ishmael Reed has said on the subject of multiculturalism. He said it's possible here "because the United States is unique in the world: *the world is here*." (p. 116)

In other words, Gates' curriculum reform still leaves "Western Civilization" dominant by making it a course of its own plus one-third of the multicultural course. The question which emerges is why is

Gates willing to settle for so little? In order to shed some light on the question, which he neither answers nor even raises, one must take a few glimpses at the man's concept of his life and work.

In *Loose Canons*, Gates presents himself as a son, husband, and father. His mother appears as the parent of strength "who gives him his voice" which, in turn, is the foundation of his calling as an English teacher (pp. 41–42). His father comes across as a weaker big brother, exhibiting the survival wisdom of Southern black men during the segregation era (pp. 132–133, 147–148).

Although he introduces his wife simply as a white woman (p. 148), he wants his daughters to grow up "with Black middle-class values as common to them as the air they breathe" (p. 149) and he wonders whether they will identify themselves as "African Americans" or perhaps "Africans." Gates views himself as one:

> Who understand(s) the costs, and the pleasures of achievement; who care(s) about "the race," and who is determined to leave a legacy of self defense against racism in all of its pernicious forms. (p. 149)

In showing these personal snapshots, Gates demonstrates his identification with the black experience. In signifying on the "trope of race" he invokes the overworked trope of the frustrated black man trying to secure a taxi in New York (pp. 38, 147). Another trope common to upwardly mobile blacks is name and place dropping. In this regard, Gates injects his voyage to Cambridge on the liner Queen Elizabeth II, where he encountered Wole Soyinka (pp. 83, 88, 126).

It is in this context that Gates justifies his calling, his basic intellectual methodology, and this autobiographically oriented discourse. His goal is to be a first-class citizen in what he calls "the republic of Western letters," (p. 36) an idea he borrowed from Alexander Crummel. As such, he realizes that he must accept his dual appointment and contribute his talents not only to this chosen field of English, but also to Black Studies. Without apparently realizing the real significance of such an assignment, Gates feels "fortunate" that "the accident of birth" enabled him "to teach at" a white research institution, rather than at a "Black school" (p. 145). Indeed, for him the secondary assignment in Black Studies has proved a boon:

For a woman or person of color, there has never been a more exciting and rewarding time to be in the academy than today. More women and Black people are tenured than ever before, and more occupy tenure-track positions.

We are in the midst of a renaissance of Black scholarship, both individual and collective. (p. 121)

Gates defines his role on that basis:

My task, as I see it, is to help guarantee that Black and so-called Third World literature is taught to Black and Third World and white students by Black and Third World and white professors in heretofore white mainstream departments of literature, and to train students to think, to read, and to write clearly, to expose false uses of language, fraudulent claims, and muddled arguments, propaganda, and vicious lies—from all of which our people have suffered just as surely as we have from an economic order, in which we were zeros and a metaphysical order in which we were absences. These are the "values" which should be transmitted through critical theory. (p. 80)

Such a statement is sure to make one a candidate for tenure in a "White" university. Gates' professed interest in the *Loose Canons* project, which seems to divert him from his primary focus, becomes a bit clearer from this perspective. He put it thusly:

The essays collected here are the attempts of a critic of literature and culture to examine the implications of nationalistic eruptions and the politics of identity for the future of American society and culture, for our university and public school curricula, and, to be sure, for literary and cultural studies themselves. Perhaps it should seem anomalous that I, a person whose first scholarly passion is the recovery and editing of "lost" and ignored texts, should find myself preoccupied with these questions. And yet, what is often referred to loosely as the "multicultural" movement traces its origins in the academy to the birth of Afro-American Studies in the late 1960s. (xii)

This articulation of multiculturalism is designed to enhance Gates' usefulness to the republic of Western letters as one who can defend it against its cultural nationalists enemies, which implicitly include the bad Afrocentrists.

Because of his gratitude for the opportunity to "teach at" a "white research" institution, Gates aggressively submits to the republic's mandate that U.S.-born Africans must be a part of American society and a part acceptable to European American authority. In his search for "lost" and ignored texts and the African American canon, he accepts the guidance of Theodore Parker, a nineteenth-century European-American intellectual who proclaimed that the "Lives of Fugitive Slaves" were the only authentic forms of American literary texts (*Loose Canons*, p. 23). Such a historical construction enables one to submit to the literary role enlightened European Americans permit Africans to play. This is similar to the perception that jazz and its associated musical genre are the only authentic "American music." According to this fantasy, African American subculture is more American than the European American subcultures. But the "petitions" and other pleading texts (i.e, "slave narratives") of enslaved Africans were written not only to Americans, but also to Europeans who they knew held power over their destiny. Thus, the autobiographies of enslaved Africans were not peculiar to the "American" experience, they were demonstrations of worldwide white supremacy oppression of African humanity. Africans have alternatives to accepting the permitted cultural roles just as they had alternatives to submission to enslavement.

In pursuit of this "lost" canon, Gates exposes what he considers the deep secrets of the African experience in the diaspora. He shares with academia: "Those human emotions that we share with everyone else, and that we have always shared with each other, when no white people are around" (p. 147). Indeed, he invokes the trope "when no white people (are/were) around" (p. 133) to authenticate his discovery of the real black vernacular which, for him, is the root of the African-American literary tradition (p. 33). This urge to share intimacies across racial boundaries is in conformity with the direction of his personal and public lives, as well as his philosophy.

Gates liberates himself from some of the judgements of the African literary tradition of Africans born in the United States. This enables him to reevaluate Phyllis Wheatley and find for her a positive contribution to a proud African American heritage. He also elevates the trope of the "talking book" to an indispensable position in the foundation of the African American canon. His reading suggests that "slave narratives" such as *Equiano's Travels* were futile attempts by captured and oppressed Africans to write themselves out of slavery and into humanity. According to him the texts signified upon the European doctrine of the nonhumanity and natural slave status of Africans.

Gates' focus on the talking book trope is a demonstration that the meaning of a text is in the mind of the reader.

> the talking book trope is the tendency for the African authors of these texts to portray themselves as illiterates when captured and who upon observing whites reading books thought the books were speaking. Thus they tried to talk to the books themselves and finally learned to read and write. (pp. 64–66)

Equiano's narrative presents another line of thought. In his poem which is appended to the cited edition, there is a reference to the trope "Ethiopia" which points to the oppressed Africans "signifying" on the English biblical traditions. As such the European reader to whom the petition is directed is warned about the retribution of God for the sin of enslavement throughout Equiano's narrative. In texts following Equiano's, the trope is revised by the invocation of the biblical passage "Princes shall come out of Egypt, Ethiopia shall soon stretch out her hands unto God" (the *Holy Bible, King James Version*, Psalm 68:31 was evoked in this context). The passage was used as a veiled threat by Reverend Richard Allen in 1893, four years after Equiano's publication and two years after the start of the Haitian Revolution it was used as an instruction and call to arms by Prince Hall in 1797; as a prophesy and severe warning in David Walker's *Appeal*, published in 1829; and it closed out the nineteenth century as a charge by Martin Delany to the African world community to renew and reconstitute African civilization. Thus a prophesy of doom was delivered to eavesdropping Europeans.

Henry Louis Gates is truly a loose cannon to whom the order "loose cannons" (an imperative) has been a major preoccupation. The texts which his assault leaves standing are the petitions and pleas by oppressed African authors for deliverance tendered to their masters. The intended readers of such texts are Europeans of power, whether slave owners, governors, rich whites, or the docents of academia. The texts he tries to destroy, through the strategy of public nonrecognition and covert violence, are those where Africans communicate with other Africans. These texts were authored with no whites around in terms of directives. They were not intended for the eyes of the oppressor, although the authors knew that whites would nonetheless get access to them because of the existence of Africans who were willing to share "black talk" with white folks.

These African-centered texts contain a canon that Gates and his cohorts want desperately to lose. Only if they destroy or hide this canon can they become the spokespersons "for African-Americans" which their European American masters expect them to do.

This is the *significance* of Gates exposing the trope of the "signifying monkey" derived from oral traditions and used as the title of one of his major works (*The Signifying Monkey*, 1989). This trope is defined as the base for the African American literary framework. Gates connects the *Signifying Monkey* with the European defined "trickster" deities of West Africa. From this perspective he signifies upon his friends and enemies through discourse as well as silence (which appears to be an oxymoron, but is in fact quite strident). In this "seminal" work, Gates also ignores another oral tradition which Africans often recite to each other "when no white people are around." That one is "Shine," a tale about an African seaman who abandons the sinking Titanic after warning the white captain of the impending danger. As Shine swims toward shore, various representatives of European power over Africans beg him to save them by offering the symbols of the treasured white world: wealth, status, prestige, power, and white sexuality. The last verse of the version that I recited at Phyllis Wheatley (N.B.) High School in the Fifth Ward, Houston, Texas went something like this:

The captain's daughter ran upon the deck
her dress in her hand and her drawers round her neck.
She said Shine Shine please save me
and all my good White—is yours for free.
But Shine said there's— on land
There's —on the sea,
But the—in Harlem is
good enough for me
and Shine swam on.

By rejecting an offer of the most valuable possessions of the white world, "Shine" abandons a sinking ship and represents a tradition of independence and defiance which is unacceptable to the European masters. By contrast, the *Signifying Monkey* is welcomed by the authors of the continuing tradition of Western civilization/white supremacy. "Shine" is unacceptable to Gates as the foundation of the African-American canon because it threatens his chosen hybridity in his intimate, as well as his intellectual and professional, life.

Gates implies that he is involved in the multicultural wars. He is fighting on the side of multiculturalism and cultural pluralism. He should be aware that Diane Ravitch calls herself a multiculturalist and that Arthur Schlesinger Jr. is a proponent of cultural pluralism. Gates also implies that he opposes vulgar cultural nationalists like Alan Bloom. However, the real intellectual battle is the war between the champions of African-centered thought and the defenders of Western civilization. Gates is definitely on the side of the defenders.

211

References

Delany, Martin. 1991. *The Origin of Races and Color*. Baltimore: Black Classic Press.

Equiano, Olaudah. 1967. *The Interesting Narrative of the Life of Olaudah Equiano or Gustavus Vassa, the African*. London: Heinemann.

Frazier, Thomas R. 1970. *Afro-American History: Primary Sources*. New York: Harcourt, Brace and World, Inc.

Gates, Henry Louis. 1989. *The Signifying Monkey*. New York: Oxford University Press.

—. 1991. "Beware of the New Pharaohs." *Newsweek* (23 Sept).

—. 1992. *Loose Canons: Notes on the Culture Wars*. New York: Oxford University Press.

—. 1992. "Black Demagogues and Pseudo Scholars." *New York Times* (20 July) Op-Ed page.

—. 1993. "Black Intellectuals, Jewish Tensions." *New York Times* (14 April).

—. 1994. "Black Studies: Myths or Realities." *Essence* (February).

Hughes, Langston and Arna Bontemps, eds. 1958. *The Book of Negro Folklore*. New York: Dodd Neal.

Jones, Leroi and Larry Neal, eds. 1968. *Black Fire: An Anthology of Afro-American Writing*. New York: William Morrow.

Schlesinger Jr, Arthur. 1991. *The Disuniting of America: Reflections on a Multi-cultural Society*. Knoxville: Whittle Direct Books.

Walker, David. 1965. *David Walker's Appeal.* New York: Hill and Wang.

Wiley, Ed. III. 1992. "Intellectual Pursuits." *Black Issues in Higher Education,* No. 15, (May).

PART IV

THE CHAMPION OF
AFRICAN-CENTERED THOUGHT

13

Cheikh Anta Diop and the Evocation of African Intellectuals

Then Falsehood said to the Nine Netchers:

Let Truth...be blinded in both eyes,
and let him be given to me as a door-keeper in my house

And the Nine Netchers did what he asked. Now many days after this, Falsehood raised his eyes to see, and he observed the Virtue of Truth, his elder brother. Then Falsehood said to two servants of Truth:

Take your master and throw him to a savage lion...

Then the young man seized him and took Falsehood to court before the Nine Netchers. He said to the Netchers:

Judge between Truth and Falsehood, I am his son and I have come to avenge him.

(translated by M. Lichtheim)

The Kemetic story of the abuse of Truth by Falsehood symbolically anticipates the life work of Cheikh Anta Diop. He found his father, Truth, shackled and abused, and he set out to avenge him. Diop saw African Heritage slandered and dethroned, with an impostor in its place, and he dedicated himself to the overthrow of the impostor and the reenthronement of the African Truth.

Diop called us forth. His evocation was the evocation of a Master teacher who, like a Good Father, instructs not only in precept, but in deed, thus obeying the command *ded Maat—ir Maat* (Speak Truth—Do Truth). It is Cheikh Anta Diop's calling forth in word and action which I wish to examine in this paper.

After explicating the evocation, this essay will review the major ideas put forth by Professor Diop and the methodology which he used to bring the ideas into concrete existence. The last section will trace the development of his work and the foundation laid for the work of those who would heed his call.

The Evocation

Cheikh Anta Diop was totally involved in the struggle to transform the situation in which African peoples exist. He was concerned with the "condition, elevation...and destiny" of Africans (to paraphrase the title of one of Martin Delany's works). According to his own testimony this labor consumed the great African scholar for forty years, from his young manhood as a student in Paris until his death in his native country in 1986.

For Diop, the problem was the "cultural alienation" of African peoples (Moore 1986, Vol 1, pp. 267–269); a cultural alienation which Diop, in *Great African Thinkers* (1986), forcefully described in the following way:

> We have been brainwashed. Do not forget that we have become an amnesic people from the sole fact that for almost 2,000 years, in differing degrees, we have been dominated. There was a reversal of the situation in Egypt with the

arrival of the Persians, as you know. After the Persians there were the Greeks, then the Romans, then the Arabs. And the domination continues. The historic consciousness of African peoples has dimmed and we have become progressively an amnesic people cut off from our history. (Finch 1986, vol. 1, p. 237)

The final stroke, however, was the near fatal blow delivered by the modern European scholars including:

The succession of dishonest Egyptologists, armed with a very determined scholarship (who) have perpetrated a crime against science which is done by subscribing to a deliberate falsification of human history. Upheld by all of the western countries, this ideology based on intellectual and moral fraud easily won out over the true scientific tenets...The new Egyptological ideology, born at the opportune moment was used to support the theoretical bases of the imperialist ideology. That's how it was able to muffle the voice of science so easily; by *veiling historical truth with falsehood.* It was propagated with the aid of extensive publicity and taught globally. It had both the material and financial means necessary for its own propagation.

Thus imperialism, as the hunter of prehistory, killed the being, first spiritually and culturally, before seeking to destroy it physically. The negation of history and of the intellectual accomplishments of Black African people is the cultural and mental murder which has already taken place and has paved the way for genocide here and there in the world. So that...the distorted perspective caused by the blinders of colonialism has so thoroughly altered the vision of intellectuals concerning the African past that we experienced the greatest difficulties, even with Africans...One can scarcely imagine what must have been the level of alienation of Africans of the past. (Diop 1991, *Civilization or Barbarism,* p. 163)

This criminal triumph of falsehood over truth is the evil which Diop pledged himself to avenge. Diop's vision was to create a new

African who:

> Will have felt another man born within him, moved by an
> historical conscience, a true creator, a Promethean bearer of
> new civilization and perfectly aware of what the whole
> world owes to his ancestral genius in all domains of science,
> culture and religion. (p. 167)

In order to create the new African who will become a creator,
Diop asserts, "we must restore the historical consciousness of the
African peoples" (p. xv).

The reawakened Africans would then create a new African reality
and be a major factor in rescuing the world from the pessimistic
prospects facing the world as a result of the flaws in the scientific
worldview which now prevails and dominates the consciousness of the
intellectual community. The basic task in this regard is the
reestablishment of the ancient Egyptians as "Black people." The
establishment of this idea as a fact of African and world consciousness
and as a working scientific concept, was for Diop the accomplishment
of his life's work (p. 162). In order for this fact to be fully operational,
a total offensive against the mentacidal project of the "dishonest"
Egyptologist had to be waged. Thus, the foundation laid through the
vocation of Diop was only the launching pad for the campaign.

Diop envisioned a massive project to restore African culture to its
people. He explains this in response to a question asked during an
interview:

> I consider culture as a rampart which protects a people, a
> collectivity. Culture must, above all, play a protective role;
> it must ensure the cohesion of the group. Following this
> line of thinking, the vital function of a body of African
> human sciences is to develop this sense of collective
> belonging through a reinforcement of culture. This can be
> done by developing the linguistic factor, by reestablishing
> the historical consciousness of African and black peoples so
> as to arrive at a common feeling of belonging to the same
> cultural and historical past. Once this is attained, it would
> become more difficult to 'divide and rule' and to oppose
> African communities one against the other. My feeling is
> that such is the role of a new body of African human

sciences, provided it does not depart from a strictly scientific terrain. This is most important; never to depart from the path of science. (Diop 1976, vol. 4, pp. 30–37)

Such a project must be the work of a group of leaders and intellectuals who commit themselves to the vocation of restoration of African historical and cultural consciousness. The model *par excellence* for such leaders was Diop himself, who acted as one truly called to his profession.

The Challenge to the African Scholar

This project to cure the amnesia of African peoples and restore African historic consciousness was to be led by African scholars. This is the core of the army which Diop evoked. The appeal was set forth in the introduction to some of his publications, and in numerous conversations he engaged in and interviews he granted African scholars.

In an interview which appeared in *Black Books Bulletin* in 1976, he called for a generation of scholars who would become well-trained pluridisciplinary specialists or at least masters of one discipline who would form competent scientific cadres of the black world. Earlier he had advocated: "The formation of teams, not of passive readers, but of honest, bold research workers, allergic to complacency and busy substantiating and exploring ideas expressed in our work" (Diop 1974, *African Origins,* p. xiv). He felt that the work called for "a generation of scholars" who would "become well trained *pluridisciplinary* specialists" or at least "masters of one discipline" who would "form competent scientific cadres of the black world" (p. 239).

While the appeal to African scholars in general was cordial, he did warn those reluctant to join this endeavor. In *African Origins of Civilization,* he chided the skeptical historians by asserting: "The African historian who evades the problem of Egypt is neither modest nor objective, nor unruffled; he is ignorant, cowardly, and neurotic" (p. xiv).

In a similar fashion he cautioned the African philosophers who dismissed the profundity of traditional thought by advising them not to separate themselves from the "historical framework" of "African cosmogonies." This is because "no thought...can be developed outside its historic terrain." Therefore the "young (African) philosophers must...quickly arm themselves with the intellectual means necessary to renew contact with the source of philosophy in Africa" and stop exhausting themselves "without knowing it slicing the air with cutting blows of the sword" (Diop 1986, p. 164).

While Diop called forth the African scholar, in no uncertain terms, he also occasionally appealed to white scholars. While such an appeal was typically tacit, many of his statements commend some of his teachers, intellectual heroes, and the "group of honest Egyptologists whose intellectual integrity and even courage one cannot emphasize too much" (p. 162). This rather subdued appeal to white scholars was ensconced in a call for debate with the Egyptologists. The pursuit of these two groups was evidence of Diop's conviction in the ultimate success of the project.

The African Diaspora Connection

Professor Diop made a special appeal to African Americans and "West Indians." He invited African Americans to form research teams, suggesting that our contributions might be decisive. In an interview, he asserted, "African-Americans must help us create a strong African state" (p. 295). He went on to point out that, even though they are part American, African Americans are of African ancestry as whites are Americans of European ancestry. Thus, on the basis of cultural kinship, African Americans have an "African cultural citizenship." Diop proclaimed that Africa was open to African Americans and that our interests was mutual.

When I met Cheikh Anta Diop fifteen years ago he immediately challenged me to modify the course of my research interests to include the study of Kemetic civilization, especially its language. He insisted that I learn *Medew Netcher*. After my conversion, he kept in constant contact with me and my progress and sent me copies of his latest works. Once, when I had not responded to his last communication for some months, he wrote me a letter in French and chided me for not keeping in touch. I was a soldier in his army and he had to see that I was manning my post.

I suspect that Diop's special concern for younger historians was also due to the inspiration he received from Africans of the diaspora. His one hero seems to have been Aimé Césaire, the great revolutionary poet from the French Caribbean. In his student days in Paris, Diop was spellbound by the conviction of Césaire and by his ability to expose the "cultural alienation among blacks." Césaire was also totally committed to reviving "the lost cultural personality of colonized black societies" (Moore 1986, vol. 1, p. 267).

A curious aspect of Diop's work is encountered in this diasporic connection. Césaire was only vaguely aware of the work of African American thinkers who, had put forth the same arguments for more than a century. Diop himself was not even vaguely aware of this work before he began to dialogue with us rather late in his career.

The irony of such communication gaps can be more fully appreciated when one realizes that most of the themes emphasized by Diop had been argued by Martin Delany almost one hundred years before Diop's works germinated. Diop was not at that time even aware of George G. M. James' *Stolen Legacy,* which paralleled his early work in terms of both time and ideas.

Ideas and Methodology

The following four ideas of Dr. Diop and his basic methodological thrust covered roughly forty years of his life work. Whatever differences one finds are matters of emphasis and not of quality.

A. *The Intellectual Restoration of Kemet*

The restoration of Kemet (ancient Egypt) to the African heritage was the beginning and the central chord of Diop's vocation. This theme contained or was connected with all of his other arguments. His arguments about this theme covered several assertions.

1. *Ancient Egypt was a Negro Civilization.* Diop

insisted on this fact in an early work and his cultivation of this fact spanned his career. Feeling that the Egyptologists were most dishonest in this regard, his basic position was that, by all the standards of phenotypical identity used in antiquity as well as today, the Kemites were black Africans. Thus, Kemet was black in origin and came from Kush. It was without compromise black in population.

2. *Kemet was the initiator and decisive influence on the major aspects of Greek, Hebrew, Moslem, and Christian civilizations.* Thus, the African people of Egypt were the inventors of the basic sciences, including mathematics; the philosophical and theological concepts; the architectural designs; the engineering technologies; and complicated surgery and medical practices.

3. *Kemet must be cultivated as the classical civilization of Africa.* As he put it in the preface to the English edition of *African Origin of Civilization* (1974): "The history of Black Africa will remain suspended in air and cannot be written correctly until African historians dare to connect it with the history of Egypt. In particular, the study of languages, institutions, and so forth, cannot be treated properly; in a word, it will be impossible to build African humanities, a body of African human sciences so long as that relationship does not appear legitimate" (p. xiv).

Thus, Kemet, was for him what ancient Greece was to the Europeans. "Imagine, if you can, the uncomfortable position of a Western historian who was to write the history of Europe without referring to Greco-Latin Antiquity, and try to pass that off as a scientific approach" (p. XIV). In other words, Kemet was the matrix out of which the new African civilization was to be reborn.

B. *The Cultural, Historical, and Linguistic Unity of Africa:*

The major premises was the idea that Africa is united culturally in all major aspects of human activity and that such unity has persisted through time. Thus, the black worldview was established first by the Kushites and transferred to Kemet, where it was developed to a remarkable profundity and later disseminated throughout Africa. This is also true of the languages of Africa. Biologically and culturally, transnationally and dischronically, the African peoples were one.

C. *The Two Cradle Theory*

Perhaps the most exciting of Diop's analytical concepts was the argument that world history could not be properly understood until historians abandoned the attempt to universalize the stages of historical evolution and accept the reality of the two cultural cradles which nurtured the two conflicting basic worldviews, that later were to become the major driving forces of modern history. Thus Diop offered his "Two Cradle Theory" as a more valid framework for understanding the past. In his earlier works, he emphasized the fundamental opposition between the nomadic, paternalistic, aggressive ethos of the Indo-European peoples *versus* the sedentary, maternalistic, peaceful worldview of African peoples. This emphasis, though modified in his later works, was not by any means abandoned.

D. *The African Human Sciences*

The call to the African intellectual is coupled with the mandate to develop the African human sciences. Diop constantly called for such in his early works and reemphasized this in one of the first of a series of interviews with African Americans. This was a clear call for restoration of an African intellectual agenda which would enable us to finally free our minds and achieve what E. Franklin Frazier found wanting, that is, intellectual independence. Diop himself echoed the sentiment when he queried in *African Origin*: "How does it happen that all modern

Black literature has remained minor, in the sense that no Negro African author or artist, to my knowledge, has yet posed the problem of man's fate, the major theme of human letters?" (p. xvi) The creation of a body of human sciences would, in effect, be a declaration of independence from the corrupting effect of the European intellectual tradition.

E. Methodology

It is in the area of research that Diop felt he made his major contribution. Certainly, by the time he finished *Civilization or Barbarism*, his last major work, Diop knew that others before his time had rigorously argued for the blackness of Kemetic people and for most of his other ideas. Therefore, he stated in the book's introduction: "For us, the considerable new feat, is less having stated that the Egyptians were a Black people, than having contributed to making this idea a fact of African and world historical consciousness, and especially, a working scientific concept: this is what our predecessors had not succeeded in doing" (Diop 1991, p. 162).

Making "an operational scientific concept" of Kemet's blackness, both biologically and culturally, is the summation of Diop's methodology. Because of his selection and commitment to the scientific method, he utilized physics, mathematics, and archaeology, and plied his trade through history, sociology, and linguistics.

Because of his insistence on scientific method, by both word and example, Diop is held in high regard by many African scholars. Dr. Diop was adamant that the project of African rehabilitation required scientific rigor. This emphasis requires African historians to consider the scientific methodology of Cheikh Anta Diop from several angles.

In order to counter extensive brainwashing and in keeping with the intimidating prestige of science, Dr. Diop believed that only a rigorous scientifically verifiable argument could accomplish the task. The reliability of honest scientific procedures cannot be questioned, therefore only scientific proof should convert African peoples to the truth. In addition, only scientifically based investigation can guarantee that the necessary ideas are authentic. Other bases of propagation of the faith are too subjective to insure the integrity of ideas. Diop was intolerant of some of the ideas which were put forth as authentic African characteristics and historical truths. This criticism applied to those who "flirt with Kemetic Culture" as a diversion, rather than seriously return to it as a source of redemption, and to Eurocentric Africans who accepted the European myth about Africa.

Diop's insistence on a strictly scientific method should not obscure the overriding utilitarian use of that method. In other words, Diop's devotion to science was not for the sake of science. Much more important is the practice of taking the scientifically supported arguments into the arenas of politics, education, and scholarly debate. Thus, in terms of the methodology of Cheikh Anta Diop, the process of evoking the African scholar and battling against the European intellectuals for the rescue of the African heritage formed a working discipline similar to the profession of a soldier.

This utilitarian attitude can also explain the apparent acceptance by Diop of materialism. Some writers go so far as to suggest in some of his statements an acceptance of Marxist methodology, but while Marx has probably influenced most twentieth-century thinkers in one way or another, including Diop, there is ample evidence that Diop was sufficiently independent to eclectically use methodological ideas without becoming a devotee. Such is the case with his insistence on finding a material base for certain explanations.

In *Civilization or Barbarism*, Diop critically analyzes the "materialistic" school of Greek philosophers after pointing out that the thought of Plato, Aristotle and some other Greek philosophers was very similar to ancient Egyptian deep thought. Diop notes:

> things change radically with the Greek materialistic school; the principles, the laws of natural evolution become intrinsic properties of matter, which no longer necessitate coupling, even symbolically, with any divinity; they are self-sufficient. Likewise, any primary cause of a divine nature is rejected; the world was never created by any divinity; matter has always existed.
>
> Even though this thought was the logical development of the materialistic component of Egyptian cosmogony, it did sufficiently deviate from its Egyptian model to become

identifiably Greek. Atheistic materialism is a purely Greek creation; Egypt and the rest of Black African seem not to have known it. (p. 328)

In other words, for Diop, one branch of Greek philosophy corresponded to the Northern Cradle of his Two Cradle Theory. This trend was reinforced during the Renaissance and became dominant in the early European modern age, according to Diop.

The Vocation

However compelling Dr. Diop's direct evocation was, his works expressed the challenge that converted his disciples to the calling. Thus, to fully understand the *peret kheru* (evocation), one needs to briefly trace out his fulfillment of the project.

In his first major work, Diop refuted the arguments of the dishonest Egyptologists and set forth his scientifically based thesis, concerning the biological and cultural origins of the Kemites. This rigorous work inspired the African intellectual world and infuriated the European intellectuals who had advanced the philosophical conspiracy to establish the doctrine of white supremacy and black inferiority, both biologically and culturally.

The rigor in which he garnered the evidence for the biological identity of Kemites was awesome. Highlights of Diop's pursuit includes the 1974 UNESCO symposium on "The Peopling of Ancient Egypt and the Deciphering of the Meroetic Script" and the publication of his article, "The Origin of the Egyptians" in the second volume of the *General History of Africa*. His work with the assistance of his closest disciple Théophile Obenga stopped a considerable body of Egyptologists, and especially the younger generation, from the blatantly asserting that the Kemites were white. Presently some Egyptologists either proclaim the irrelevance of race, profess to not know the race of the Kemites or claim that the Kemites were mixed. While Dr. Diop was not completely satisfied on this point at least he was found *Maa Kheru* (True of Voice) at his final initiation in 1986.

Diop's works precisely focused on the relationship between Greek philosophical ideas and ancient Kemetic deep thought. This was his special concern in the penultimate chapter of *Civilization or Barbarism*. In chapter 16, his focus was the relationship of Greek philosophy to science. Some of the reaction to the work of Martin Bernal is evidence of the effectiveness of Dr. Diop's work in this regard. Indeed one can say that his earlier statement on this issue in *African Origin* has been vindicated: "It is impossible to stress all that the world, particularly the Hellenistic world, owed to the Egyptians. The Greeks merely continued and developed, sometimes partially, what the Egyptians had invented" (p. 230).

In this regard, the thorough investigation of the origin of these philosophical ideas was a decisive answer to the African philosophers, like Hountonji, who so arrogantly reject the profundity of ancient African thought. Obenga's and my forthcoming works in this regard are testimonies to the effectiveness of the Diopian call, although I have criticized a few of my mentor's thoughts on the subject.

Diop's call for the elevation of Kemet as the classical civilization for Africa was so consistently pursued that it has become reality for the thousands of Africans, especially the scholars and members of associations such as ASCAC. Over the last few years thousands of African Americans have made and continue to make pilgrimages to and hold conferences in Kemet. This is a testimony to Diop's work, and a testimony to eloquent mobilization of Dr. Yosef ben-Jochannan.

Diop's persistent use of the Kemetic worldview, language, social organization, and concepts of governance to explicate the culture of the whole of Africa has convinced us that Kemet is indeed the classical African civilization. Furthermore, his arguments about the prospects for a viable African future, articulately put forth in *Black Africa: The Economic and Cultural Basis for a Federated State,* have caused us to lower our buckets into that deep well to find wisdom models for the reconstruction of a new African civilization.

This latter theme overlaps with Diop's pursuit of establishing the cultural unity of Africa, a point which is well-outlined in his works *Precolonial Black Africa, Civilization or Barbarism* and *The Cultural Unity of Black Africa.* In his analysis of precolonial Africa, Diop started to develop an analytical framework for explaining the "sociological laws" of African societies and systems of governance. This framework established the historical factors which inhibited successful revolutionary movements within African societies as contrasted with the institutional revolutionary traditions among Europeans, especially marked among the Greeks. The difference was primarily attributed to the fact that African society was based upon hereditary vocational craft divisions (castes), while European society was based upon economic class divisions determined by the distribution of wealth. The analysis was also a major feature of his last major work, *Civilization or Barbarism*, in which he greatly expanded the analytical framework.

As a result of his rigorous analysis, Diop firmly believed that African societies were moving towards large nation states before the massive brutal intrusion of the European imperialistic enterprise. He also believed that the impact of Islam was not nearly as devastating *vis `a vis* traditional African society as was the European invasion. Indeed, he theorized that Islam may have been used to promote nationalism, a conclusion which has been brought into question by some of those who follow his theories.

On the basis of this historical cultural unity, Diop hoped that the future leaders of Africa would build a powerful, federated Africa so that Africans could regain their former position as a major world force. Such a unified Africa could save both Africa and the world.

A final note on this point is Diop's high regard for the African traditional culture, which enabled Africans to survive the two thousand year attack on African peoples and their culture. To his strong cultural foundation was attributed the propensity of Africans in the diaspora to heed his message.

Diop was perhaps less consistent in the development of the "Two Cradle Theory" than the other themes mentioned in this paper. In the beginning, the idea was the mainstay of his historiography. He asserted:

> The history of humanity will remain confused as long as we fail to distinguish between the two early cradles in which Nature fashioned the instincts, temperament, habits, and ethical concepts of the two subdivisions before they met each other after a long separation dating back to prehistoric times. (p.111)

This theme is more fully developed in *The Cultural Unity of Black*

Africa, where he employs the theory to destroy the Eurocentric assertion about a uniform cultural evolutionary pattern which established European societies as more advanced than African societies. Eurocentrists had ludicrously claimed that patriarchy and monogamy were more advanced types of family than was African matriarchy.

Indeed, in that work Diop compared all of the fundamental categories of culture and developed a much more factually based explanation for the conduct of racial agendas than the doctrines of European superiority and white supremacy. The theme was also echoed throughout *Precolonial Black Africa,* though less explicitly and less emphatically. He also used the concept in *Civilization or Barbarism* in a context similar to his earlier formulation to contrast African and European societies.

However, in this last work, especially in the chapter on philosophy, Diop seems to modify the principle in two important ways. First, in pursuit of the *Stolen Legacy* doctrine, Diop asserts that practically all of the metaphysical and ontological principles of Greek philosophy were taken from the Kemites. This includes the concept of the four basic elements, the law of opposites, and the reincarnation of the soul. While it is clear that ideas such as the immortality of the soul and the uncreated universe were "stolen" from Kemet, it is less clear that the enumerated ideas came from Kemetic thought. The Greeks who studied in Kemet may have mistakenly interpreted what they heard in this regard. I suspect that those notions are more the product of the Eurasian worldview because they are congruent with the fundamental Eurasian philosophical and theological alienation implicit in the characteristics of the Aryan Cradle so clearly articulated by the young Diop.

Second, Professor Diop, who had apparently been shocked by the rapidity of the rise of a "Capitalistic Class" in postcolonial Africa, suggested more than once that the original African matrix might not be as strong as the original statement of the theory suggested. On this point he said: "Once you change the social environment, even a Black man who has been conditioned by a communitarian life-style can become the most individualistic and self-centered being". (Moore 1986, vol. 1, p. 268).

A statement in the chapter on philosophy of his last major work was the basis for his projection of the opportunity for a new world synthesis. This statement seems to contradict the original formulation and ignores an alternative that is consistent with the Two Cradle Theory. Here is the way he explained the idea:

> All the specific traits of the African societies analyzed in *Unité Culturelle de l'Afrique Noire* have no permanence; they are very profound traits, but not sealed up for good. Nature, the material conditions that made them possible, can reshape them by changing themselves; thus I do not plead for a petrified African psychological nature; the sense of solidarity so dear to the African could very well be replaced, when conditions are modified, by an individualistic greedy behavior of the Western type. (Diop, *Civilization or Barbarism*, p. 362)

In my opinion, the explanation of the abandonment is based upon the earlier statement which attributes the change in the worldview of individual Africans to changes in the *social* (not natural) environment. The destruction of viable African societies, and the brainwashing of significant members of those societies, has resulted in a Europeanized African who is a robot blindly carrying out the directions of his master.

The development of a foundation for the African human sciences was perhaps the most enduring contribution of Cheikh Anta Diop. This is so even though none of his works are specifically denoted or designed to accomplish that task. In response to this apparent vagueness, Diop asserts:

> This idea follows the proposition that ancient Egyptian culture enjoys a position vis a vis present day African cultures analogous to the role which Greco-Latin culture plays in regard to contemporary western culture. Could you imagine a western scholar researching in western history without referring to Greco-Latin culture? Could his work be considered as scientific? The same applies to African scholars in respect to ancient Egypt. This is why I say that as long as we ignore ancient Egyptian culture, the oldest evidence of an African civilization, we will be unable

to create anything in the domain of the social sciences that could be considered as scientific. It is only by a systematic reference to Egypt that we can introduce a true historical dimension to the social sciences, whether the field be linguistics or any other. For instance, why not replace the study of Roman law in our law schools with the study of Egyptian jurisprudence?

The same applies to philosophy. Ancient Egypt was at the origin of an elaborate philosophical system, and not a mere cosmogony as most still hold. (Diop 1976, vol. 4, p. 8)

When we follow the development of the Two Cradle Theory as an analytical framework which explains the sociological principles of stability and change applicable to African and European societies, we get a glimpse of Diop's vision of the discipline. His works in linguistics are further evidence of his development of the idea. In his final work he concluded with the explications of the theories and methods necessary for the foundations of the African human sciences.

Conclusion

Cheikh Anta Diop was truly the most inspiring leader of African intellectuals in the twentieth century. He challenged scholars of Africa and the African diaspora to commit themselves to the task of recovering the hidden African past. His words were impressive but his deeds were even more compelling.

The questions before us now are: Can we rise to his challenge? Can we develop the skills? Can we stand the work load? Can we submerge our egos and paranoias so that we can work together in trust?

I assert that: Yes we must. If African people are to be revived and if we are to retake our fame, perhaps the most appropriate memorial would be to continue to develop the African human sciences and bring them into being as a body of disciplines. To do this in the truly Africa tradition we should first of all name them. A suggested start in this regard is to call the deep thought of Africa (what the Greeks call philosophy) *Medew Netcher* (Divine Speech or Theology). We could then call the general method of discourse *Medew Nefer* (Good Speech).

The suggested terminology comes from the vocabulary of our classical African language and is consistent with African denominations for deep thinking. Furthermore, this is totally consistent with the evocation and vocation of Chiekh Anta Diop, *Maa Kheru.*

R E F E R E N C E S

Diop, Cheikh Anta. 1974. *The African Origin of Civilization: Myth or Reality.* Westport: Lawrence Hill.

—. 1978. *Cultural Unity of Black Africa.* Chicago: Third World Press.

—. 1986. "Nile Valley Executive Committee Interviews Diop." *Great African Thinkers.* Vol. 1: Cheikh Anta Diop. Editors Larry Williams and Ivan Van Sertima. New Brunswick: Transaction Books.

—. 1991. *Civilization or Barbarism: An Authentic Anthropology.* New York: Lawrence Hill. Introduction and chapters 1 and 2. Translated by Edward F. Taylor and reprinted in *Great African Thinkers.* Vol.1: Cheikh Anta Diop (161–225). Editors Larry Williams and Ivan Van Sertima. New Brunswick: Transaction Books.

Finch, Charles. 1986. "Further Conversations with the Pharaoh." *Great African Thinkers.* Vol. 1: Cheikh Anta Diop. Editors Larry Williams and Ivan Van Sertima. New Brunswick: Transaction Books.

James, George G. M. 1976. *Stolen Legacy.* San Francisco: Julian Richardson Associates.

Lichtheim, Miriam. 1976. "Myth and Falsehood." *Ancient Egyptian Literature,* Vol. II. Berkeley: University of California, Berkeley Press.

Madhubuti, Haki R. ed. 1976. "BBB Interviews Cheikh Anta Diop." *Black Books Bulletin.* 4:4 (Winter).

Moore, Carlos. 1986. "Interview with Chiekh Anta Diop." *Great African Thinkers*. Vol. 1: Chiekh Anta Diop. Editors Larry Williams and Ivan Van Sertima. New Brunswick: Transaction Books.

14

Cheikh Anta Diop
Without Compromise

Two centuries ago some of the leaders of what has come to be known as the Haitian Revolution, after a brilliant and successful battle against the plantation owners and their army, were lured into negotiations by their enemies. The negotiation offer was first turned down by the architect and commander in chief of the revolution, Bookman Dutty, who saw no reason to negotiate since the enemy was virtually defeated. But some of the brothers around him opted for a shortcut, or the easy way out, and decided to negotiate. As a show of good faith, these brothers had to set up Bookman, who was speedily assassinated. Then, when these "moderately responsible" brothers offered to continue the negotiation, the Colonial Army demanded their unconditional surrender. The brothers had been deluded by what the hero of the revolution, Jean Jacques Dessalines, would later call the "Phantom of Liberty."

At the beginning of the conflict, both sides fought under French flags because Toussaint L'Ouverture, who had been among the compromising leaders, identified his country as the Black France. Napoleon Bonaparte, on the other hand decided that in order to firmly establish white supremacy, the Blacks had to be put back in their proper place—slavery. So, in the beginning of 1802, his army invaded the island with massive force. The ex-slaves, however, were equal to the occasion and again beat back the French. When the French general offered to negotiate, Toussaint jumped again at the opportunity and fell victim to the "Phantom of Liberty," this time over the strong objections of Dessalines. The results were fatal for Toussaint; the French set him up through flattery, kidnapped him, took him to

France, threw him into a cold prison cell, and starved him to death. Fortunately, Dessalines resumed the struggle and led the Haitian people to victory, "without compromise." When Dessalines took over after the kidnapping of Toussaint, he tore the white center from the red, white, and blue tri-colors of the flag, and later gave the Haitian people their own flag consisting of two broad stripes, one black and one red, signifying the union of people of African descent.

It is appropriate that we recognize and celebrate such a significant achievement of an African people. Our historical and cultural heritage is, indeed, a deep well from which we can draw the inspiring waters of renewal and victory. The Haitian Revolution is important to the situation in which we find ourselves at this time. Although many of us are unaware of it, we are in the midst of a war, perhaps the greatest intellectual conflict of world history. This is the war to liberate our historical and cultural memory from the most vicious intellectual assault ever perpetrated on humankind; it is a war to free the African mind.

The defenders of Western civilization were slow in recognizing the effectiveness of the African-centered campaign, but once they did, they launched an academic and journalistic blitzkrieg designed to wipe our project from the face of the earth. This deafening onslaught, led by generals such as Arthur Schlesinger Jr., has made more noise than damage and so far it has failed. Now it seems that the defenders are offering to negotiate. Similar to the white supremacist regime in South Africa, the defenders of Western civilization want to compromise in order to retain as much white supremacy as possible.

To begin with, they want us to accept their definition of our movement. They have identified a moderate to conservative wing represented by Henry Louis Gates, a liberal or radical wing typified by Molefi Asante, and an extreme fringe epitomized by Leonard Jeffries. In order to negotiate, we have to denounce Jeffries and embrace Gates.

Our position should reflect the spirit of the French subtitle of Cheikh Anta Diop's last major work, *Civilization ou Barbarie: Anthropologic sans Complaisance*, which is translated by Dr. Leonard Jeffries as *Civilization or Barbarism: Anthropology Without Compromise* (Diop [1981] 1991). The subtitle reflects the position Diop took at the beginning of his vocation. As one of the African intellectuals in post-war Paris, Diop was converted to the restoration of African civilization by Aimé Césaire. When the French intellectuals, reacting to Césaire's powerful declaration of intellectual independence, offered to negotiate, they wanted Césaire to admit that Africa had received some benefits from French colonialism. Césaire's response was an uncompromising reaffirmation of his indictment as expressed in his great poem, "Return to My Native Land."

The offer to negotiate was then made to Léopold Senghor, who uttered the well-known sentence, "Emotion is Negro and reason Greek." Diop's bitter rejection of Senghor's compromise earned for Diop a life of political persecution in his native land during Senghor's long presidency. Diop recognized that the arena was the theater of war, although the battles sometimes may be fought in classrooms and university auditoriums. Our only alternatives are, as Bookman and Dessalines asserted, "Liberty and independence, or death." There is no compromise. If we reject Jeffries today, we will be destroyed tomorrow; our cause will be flawed. Leonard Jeffries is not on the extreme fringe, as a recent *Newsweek* article alleged, he is at the center of our struggle. His utterances have been maliciously distorted, as would be any of ours, provided we were the direct targets of the day.

The first premise of Professor Diop's lifelong project involves answering the following question: Why did European scholars refabricate history by denying that the authors of the great Nile Valley civilization were black? The Africanity of the Kemites had been accepted as self-evident by the recorders of both pillars of modern European culture (Western civilization) the classical Greeks and the ancient Jewish people. One of the linguistic facts supporting such an assumption, to which Diop constantly pointed, is the word *Kemet* itself. *Kemet* was the word most commonly used by the citizens of the Nile Valley civilization to identify their country and themselves. The root of this word means "black" (Faulkner 1976, p. 286).

Modern Egyptologists assert that Kemet means "the black land" in reference to the fertile soil of the banks of the river Nile, which was considered the country proper. These Egyptologists stress that this term Kemet or black land is contrasted with the term desert which they say means the "Red Land." The root *dsrt* does indeed mean "red," however whether either term should be attached to the word *land* is another matter. The generic determinatives, which convey the category into which the word fits, suggest a different reading. The determinative attached to the spelling of *kmt* (Kemet) is that for a settled and developed locale, probably referring to an urban area. Thus a possible translation would be "black town" or "black community." The determinative for *dsrt* is that for hills, sometimes connoting a foreign nation. Thus, a possible translation could be the "red hills." If these translations are reflective of the meaning of the terms, then the meaning of the contrast may be as much in the determinatives as in the root words; the reading may be The Black *Community* versus the Red *Hills*, stressing the ancient contrast between the settled life in Kemet, as opposed to the nomadic life in the desert. Desert life was expressed in the Instruction for Merikare:

Lo the miserable Amu (Western Asian)
He is wretched because of the place he's in...
Its paths are many and painful because of hills
He does not dwell in one place
Food propels his legs
He fights since the time of Horus (the beginning of time).
(Lichtheim 1976, vol. 1, p. 104)

If this reading is reasonable then the term *kmtyw*, which the Egyptologists insist is the correct reading of the spelling *kmt* with the determinative for people, may well mean those who are of Kemet, that is, those who are of the black community. Such a reading settles the question of ethnicity of the people of Kemet.

As previously mentioned, the blackness of the Kemites was generally assumed by the world before the modern European scholars concocted "the most monstrous falsification in the history of humanity" (Diop 1974, *African Origin*, p. 43). In addition, their blackness has been the foundation of modern African-centered thought for more than two centuries, especially among Africans of the diaspora.

In 1828 David Walker, following the guidance of his mentor, Reverend Richard Allen, made the Nile Valley connection which has withstood the test of time among modern African teachers and leaders. In his *Appeal* (1965), David Walker said:

The Egyptians were African...such as we are...some of them yellow and others dark...a mixture of Ethiopians and the natives of Egypt...about the same as you see the colored people of the United States at the present day. (p. 47)

And he continued by suggesting that his readers:

Take a retrospective view of the arts and sciences—the wise legislators—the pyramids and other magnificent buildings—the turning of the channel of the river Nile, by the sons of Africa or Ham among whom learning originated and was carried thence into Greece. (p. 48)

David Walker taught that identification with a study of Kemetic civilization was a necessary phase of our liberation. This position was taken before the modern European fabrication had become completely formulated.

What the European scholars did in the middle of the eighteenth century was to put forth the philosophical necessity for the doctrine of white supremacy. This doctrine was invented to elevate the Europeans to a level of cultural superiority and, to justify three hundred years of the most brutal assault ever perpetrated on humanity.

This scheme did not erupt in the eighteenth century; there was a long history of anti-African ideas which had been incubated in theological circles among certain non-African peoples. For example, the idea of the "curse of Ham" had been cultivated among some Talmudic theologians during the Babylonian Diaspora (Drake 1990, p. 28–30). This tradition worked its way into Arabic thought before and after the advent of Islam (Drake 1990, pp. 150–164 and Khaldun 1967, pp. 59–64). Readers of antiquity also find racially negative statements against Africans among the Greeks (Harris 1987, pp. 15–16).

There are other antecedents embedded in the thought of some pre-eighteenth century modern European thinkers. Francis Bacon, for example, referred to the "Foul ugly Ethiop" (Bacon 1955, *New Atlantis*, p. 570). He, nonetheless, advised that Europe's superiority resulted "not from race but art" (p. 538). Before the eighteenth century these and other antecedents were apparently still scattered and uncoordinated.

During the decade in which David Walker formulated the African-centered project, a European sage, Georg Wilhelm Friedrich Hegel, put the finishing touches on the intellectual framework for their white supremacy scheme. As put forth by Hume and Montesquieu, the hypothesis had one near fatal flaw. The ancient Greek thinkers who they were adopting as the founders of Western civilization had proclaimed profound respect for and gratitude toward the ancient Africans who, according to Greek intellectuals, contributed many great ideas to the world. How, then, could one allege the innate inferiority of African peoples?

Hegel's solution to the nagging question of the Kemetic connection was to separate Egypt from Africa, remove Africans from ancient Egypt, and then to remove Africa from world history (Hegel 1955, *Philosophy of History*, p. 99). Thus, most scholars need not concern themselves with the study of Africa which was relegated to the field of anthropology, which itself emerged as the study of primitive peoples.

The African-centered project, which sought to nullify this evil scheme, was laid out by David Walker, and was significantly expanded by other African thinkers in the diaspora such as Hosea Easton, Henry Highland Garnet, and Martin Delany. It is in this context that we should further consider Diop's contribution. Diop examined the role of the doctrine in the context of the development of Egyptology. As a scholarly pursuit, Egyptology came on the heels of Napoleon's pre-Haitian conflict—the invasion of Egypt.

Napoleon brought with him to Egypt an army of French scholars who began the groundwork for the establishment of Egyptology by incarcerating the "antiquities" of the Africa civilization. Diop captured the heart of the matter in his first major work. He explained:

> The birth of Egyptology was thus marked by the need
> to destroy the memory of Negro Egypt at any cost and

in all minds. Henceforth, the common denominator of all these theses of the Egyptologists, their close relationship and profound affinity, can be characterized as a desperate attempt to refute that opinion. (Diop 1974, *African Origin*, p. 45)

Thus, one of the essential steps in our continuation of the African-centered project is liberation from the discipline of Egyptology which has been involved in this heinous conspiracy. This, the thrust of Diop's call for the establishment of the "African Human Sciences," is, in part, the implication of Asante's concern with Afrocology and was a premise that Maulana Karenga and I shared when we issued the call for the first ASCAC conference. We were pushing toward the establishment of the disciplines of Kemetic Studies and Kushitic Studies. This is also why I often have to correct moderators who introduced me as an Egyptologist.

Diop scored the most significant victory in relation to the question of the identity of the Kemites when he forced representatives from the discipline of Egyptology into the battle of Cairo in 1974 (UNESCO). Diop had demanded such a meeting under the auspices of UNESCO's International Scientific Committee for the Drafting of a General History of Africa. The symposium on the peopling of ancient Egypt was dominated by Dr. Diop and his able assistant, Dr. Théophile Obenga. They forced the attending Egyptologists to admit that Kemetic culture and language were African and that the people were not white, although those defenders of Western civilization would not take final steps and admit that the authors of Kemetic civilization were Black. That final point is substantially where the battle presently stands.

Some among the older league of Egyptologists, such as Miriam Lichtheim, still defiantly assert that the Kemites were not black. The newer league either evades the problem, such as Bruce Williams (Williams 1985, pp. 29–45) or offers a compromise, such as Frank Yurco, who suggests that the Kemites were mixed, and Martin Bernal, who "gives" us a few black pharaohs.

By giving up the claim that Kemet was white, while still insisting that Africans cannot claim it, some European scholars are attempting to compromise. For us to allow them this luxury would be tantamount to snatching defeat from the jaws of victory.

Inspired by our pioneers and elders such as Diop, George G. M. James, Chancellor Williams, John Henrik Clarke and Yosef ben-Jochannan, we, over the past thirty years, have been effective in the battle arena. Through research, published works, institutional teaching, community-based classes, study tours, organization building, public lectures, and other activities, we have recruited and organized our army. We are ready to continue the battle from high ground. Like Piankhi's liberation forces, our army includes "artists and builders," physicians, lawyers, plumbers, accountants, computer experts and people from all walks of life. In other words, our ranks are deep; if one should stumble, there are many other replacements.

The battle over the identity of the Kemites is the foundation of the larger project—the restoration of African civilization. The two hundred years invested in the project is obviously not merely an exercise in intellectual ecstasy. Diop, perhaps more than any other African thinker, clearly articulated the necessity of the connection with Kemet. The reconstruction of history, which is demanded in the struggle to allow *Maat* to return to her throne, requires the acceptance of Kemet as the classical African civilization. Diop compared the situation to the connection between present day Europe and ancient Greece: "Imagine, if you can, the uncomfortable position of a western historian who were to write the history of Europe without referring to Greco-Latin Antiquity" (*African Origin*, p. xiv).

Indeed, Diop sternly lectured those of us in the arena of scholarship: "The African historian who evades the problem of Egypt is neither modest nor objective, nor unruffled; he is ignorant, cowardly, and neurotic" (p. xiv).

The current campaign, the struggle to establish African-centered education, to use Wade Nobles' term, brings us face to face with the ghosts of the eighteenth-and nineteenth-century European philosophers and discipline builders, with the Egyptologists of the twentieth century, and with a broad front of scholars and political leaders of European descent who will defend Western civilization and its hidden major premise, white supremacy, at any cost.

The defenders have begun to unite on the defense strategy. It is no longer possible to distinguish the hard-liners from the soft-liners. They have rallied behind the leadership of a female field marshal, Daine Ravitch. They have called out of retirement the venerable Mortimer Alder who created the *Great Books of the Western World* project. They have commissioned one of their most popular, aged, American historians to launch a learned attack on the African-centered scholars. The news media has been mobilized to scandalize the ideas and personalities involved in the African-centered project. They have formed several organizations and tapped the resources of the think tanks, foundations, and major business corporations, including the Heritage Foundation, Federal Express, Whittle Press, and the National Association of Scholars. They have also made an appeal to what they label as the "serious" and "respected" black scholars (Schlesinger 1991, p. 53), thus initiating that time-tested strategy of white supremacy, the attempt to create a civil war among the Africans.

Unity is at the center of the European battle plan, the hard-liners and soft-liners have rallied under the banner of cultural pluralism. The soft-liners are professing pluralistic multiculturalism; the hard-liners are softening on the rejection of multiculturalism. Even the hard-liner Arthur Schlesinger Jr., who otherwise scorns the "Multicultural Zealots" (p. 66) and accuses them of evil intentions, supports Diane Ravitch's statement that "the United States has a common culture that is multicultural" (Ravitch 1990, p. 18).

What the African cultural education is promoting now, with some success, is the dissemination of a cultural configuration significantly different from the white supremacist one which has, until now, prevailed. Although the African-centered approach teaches from an African historical perspective, it nonetheless teaches about the various cultures of the world. This teaching, however, is significantly different from the multicultural approach established by Hegel. In his *Philosophy of History* (1956), Hegel examined the cultures of the world and subordinated all of the non-European cultures to the one of the Germanic peoples. After examining African cultures, he expelled them from history altogether. Neo-Hegelians, like Schlesinger and Ravitch, are presently attempting to pull the same stunt.

In conclusion, let us draw from the Kemetic deep well and evoke the spirit of Kamose, the pharaoh who delivered the first decisive blow against the Hyksos who, for many years, had humiliated Kemet through conquest of the Delta. On the eve of launching his offensive against the usurpers, Kamose consulted the Great Council which advised him to compromise. With a disappointed heart, Kamose rejected their advice and asserted: "As for this advice of yours...he who divides the land with me will not respect me [therefore] I will fight against the foreigners [and] victory will come" (Pritchard 1969, p. 232). Indeed it did come, and it will come to us again, if we continue the struggle without compromise.

R E F E R E N C E S

Asante, Molefi. 1990. *Kemet Afrocentricity and Knowledge.* Trenton, New Jersey: Africa World Press.

Bacon, Francis. 1955. *Novum Organum. Selected Writings of Francis Bacon.* Ed. by Hugh G. Dich. New York: Modern Library.

Carruthers, Jacob H. 1985. *Irritated Genie: An Essay on the Haitian Revolution.* Chicago: Kemetic Institute.

—. 1977. "Writing for Eternity." *Black Books Bulletin,* 5:2.

Clement, Elizabeth and Irene, D'Almula, translators. 1986. "Nile Valley Executive Committee Interviews Diop." *Great African Thinkers.* Vol 1. Editors Larry Williams and Ivan Van Sertima. New Brunswick: Transaction Books.

Diop, Cheikh Anta. 1974. *The African Origin of Civilization: Myth or Reality.* Westport: Lawrence Hill.

—. 1978. *Black Africa: The Economic and Cultural Basis for a Federated State.* Westport: Lawrence Hill.

—. 1978. *The Cultural Unity of Black Africa.* Chicago: Third World Press.

—. 1978. *The Peopling of Ancient Egypt and the Deciphering of the Meroetic Script. UNESCO.*

—. 1981. *Civilization ou Barbarie Anthropologic Sans Complaisance.* Paris: Presence Africaine.

—. 1981. "The Origin of the Ancient Egyptians" *General History of Africa,* Vol II. G. Mokhtar. London: Heinemann.

—. 1987. *Precolonial Black Africa*. Westport: Lawrence Hill.

—. 1991. *Civilization or Barbarism: An Authentic Anthropology*. New York: Lawrence Hill.

Drake, St. Clair. 1990. *Black Folks Here and There*. Los Angeles: Center for Afro-American Studies, University of California, Los Angeles. Vol. 2..

Faulkner, R. O. 1976. *A Concise Dictionary of Middle Egyptians*. Oxford: Griffith Institute.

Finch, Charles S. 1986. "Further Conversations with the Pharaoh." *Great African Thinkers*. Vol. 1: Cheikh Anta Diop. Editors Larry Willliams and Ivan Van Sertima. New Brunswick: Transaction Books.

—. 1986. "Meeting the Pharaoh." *Great African Thinkers*. Vol 1: Cheikh Anta Diop. Editors Larry Willliams and Ivan Van Sertima. New Brunswick: Transaction Books.

Harris, Joseph. 1987. *Africans and Their History*. New York: New American Library.

Hegel, Georg Wilhelm Friedrich. 1956. *The Philosophy of History*. New York: Dover.

Hume, David. 1987. *Essays: Moral, Political and Literary*. Indianapolis: Liberty Classics.

Jeffries, Leonard Jr. "Civilization or Barbarism: The Legacy of Cheikh Anta Diop." *Great African Thinkers*. Vol. 1: Cheikh Anta Diop. Editors Larry Willliams and Ivan Van Sertima. New Brunswick: Transaction Books.

Khaldun, Ibin. 1967. *Muqaddimah: An Introduction to History.* Translated from the Arabic by Franz Rosenthal, and edited by N. J. Dawood. Princeton: Bollingen Series.

Lichtheim, Miriam. 1976 *Ancient Egyptian Literature,* Volume 2. Berkeley: University of California Press.

Moore, Carlos. 1986. "Interview with Carlos Moore" (for Afriscope: Africa's Political Unity et al.) *Great African Thinkers.* Vol. 1: Cheikh Anta Diop. Editors Larry Willliams and Ivan Van Sertima. New Brunswick: Transaction Books.

Moore, Shawna. 1986. "Interview with Cheikh Anta Diop," (for *Black Books Bulletin*). *Great African Thinkers.* Vol. 1: Cheikh Anta Diop. Editors Larry Willliams and Ivan Van Sertima. New Brunswick: Transaction Books.

Montesquieu, Charles. 1949. *The Spirit of the Laws.* New York: Hafner.

Pritchard, James R. ed. 1969. *Ancient Near Eastern Texts.* Princeton: Princeton University Press.

Ravitch, Diane. 1990. "Democracy and Diversity: Multicultural Education in America." *American Educator* (Spring).

Schlesinger, Jr. Arthur. 1991. *The Disuniting of America Reflections on a Multi-Cultural Society.* Knoxville: Whittle Direct Press.

Toure, Mamadou. 1991. "Cheikh Anta Diop: The Man and the Political Question in his Work. A Continental Vision of the Future." Unpublished manuscript.

Walker, David. 1965. *David Walker's Appeal.* New York: Hill and Wang.

Williams, Bruce. 1985. "The Lost Pharaohs of Nubia" and "Latest Research on Nubia: A Letter to the Editor" in Ivan Van Sertima, ed. *Nile Valley Civilizations: Journal of African Civilizations.*

PART V

TOWARD THE RESTORATION
OF AFRICAN CIVILIZATION

15
African-Centered Education

All educated Negroes suffer from a kind of slavery in many ways far more subversive of the real welfare of the race than the ancient physical fetters. The slavery of the mind is far more destructive than that of the body.
—Edward Wilmot Blyden

The state of black education is indeed bleak if current reports are correct. The future, according to these reports, is even more dismal. The desegregation process has left the public school system in metropolitan America in a shambles. The economic crisis has visited disaster upon chaos. Nearly thirty years after the *Brown v. Board of Education* case, the comparative quality of education for blacks is not significantly different from that which prompted the U.S. Supreme Court in 1954 to find that black children received an inferior result from public education. This would suggest that the inferiority of black education to white education is endemic and exists in bad times as well as relatively good times.

This conclusion seems to support the prediction advanced by De Gobineau in 1850 that blacks are naturally inferior to whites and education will only widen the gap. Indeed, the statistics of recent years seem to indicate that at grade one, the differences between black children and white children are insignificant, but by eleventh grade blacks seem unbelievably disadvantaged. What this general trend suggests is that the American education process deeducates black students.

The impact of this deeducation is heightened by the back to

basics movement, the construction of educational assistance programs, and the decline of Black Studies curricula at the college level. The deeducated black child who may get out of high school will find it virtually impossible to get into college.

Thus, while the present crises in education are dismal, the fact that "the crisis" in black education is chronic is even more depressing. Even this is only the surface of the problem—the tip of the iceberg as they say.

The real crisis can be clearly seen only when black education works as it is designed; that is when it succeeds. Let us consider Carter G. Woodson's appraisal of the educated or rather miseducated Negro, who has been driven mad through European education:

> The only question which concerns us here is whether these educated persons are actually equipped to face the ordeal before they unconsciously contribute to their own undoing by perpetuating the regime of the oppressor...The so-called modern education, with all its defects, however does others so much more good than it does the Negro, because it has been worked out in conformity to the needs of those who have enslaved and oppressed weaker peoples. For example, the philosophy and ethics resulting from our educational system have justified slavery, peonage, segregation and lynching...The Negro thus educated is a hopeless liability of the race (pp. xi–xiii)

> When a Negro has finished his education in our schools, then, he has been equipped to begin the life of an Americanized or Europeanized White man, but before he steps from the threshold of his alma mater he is told...that he must go back to his own people from whom he has been estranged by a vision of ideals which in his disillusionment he will realized that he cannot attain. (p. 5)

> Even if Negroes do successfully imitate the Whites, nothing new has thereby been accomplished. You simply have a larger number of persons doing what others have been doing. The unusual gifts of the race have not thereby been developed, and an unwilling world, therefore continues to wonder what the Negro is good for. (p. 7)

Like the deeducation of the Black masses, the miseducation of the blacks who do "succeed" is not accidental. This truth can be seen only in historical perspective just as defacto segregation can be seen only in historical perspective because the current evidence is virtually absent.*

The beginnings of this miseducation go back to the beginnings of the exploration of the African coast by Europeans who had been hemmed in by Arabic power for six hundred years. In 1481, when the Portuguese arrived at the Congo-Ngola area, they initiated the process of miseducation of blacks as an instrument of exploitation. The Portuguese invaders persuaded the royal and noble families of the area to send their sons to Portugal for a European education. When these sons returned with Christian names, they began directing African society in the interest of the Portuguese. The physical slavery which the Portuguese started was facilitated by the mental slavery of the African leaders who had been educated by the Europeans. This model has endured for five hundred years as the most successful method by which Europeans defeat, control, exploit, and annihilate Africans.

In the eighteenth century, an African was given the European name of Jacques Elisa Jean Captein, and a degree in theology. He wrote his thesis in defense of slavery and spent his life as a priest to those who had been kidnapped and locked up in a slave factory awaiting shipment to the Western Hemisphere as chattel. We are often presented a picture of prohibitions against educating the black slave, lest he catch the idea of liberty. There are two things wrong with the alleged wisdom. First, blacks didn't need "education" to want freedom—we always want it, however illiterate. Second, European education was the best method of pacifying the African, though it never seemed to pacify or civilize the European. Many whites, like Benjamin Franklin and the Quakers knew this and that's why Negro education finally received the endorsement of the establishment and

---

*Documentation for this historical sketch can be found in Jacob H. Carruthers. "Black Intellectuals and The Crisis in Black Education," in: Mwalimu J. Shufan, *Too Much Schooling, Too Little Education.* 1992. Trenton: Africa World Press.

the Southern white supremacists after the Civil War. The decision to put the Black masses into a modified chattel slave system after the Civil War was coupled with a consensus on the need for sending blacks to school—at least some of the time. As the president of a white university said at the Mohonk Conference on the Negro Question in 1890: "I believe if they (Negroes) are not educated then they will become a dangerous element to the community liable to be thrown at any moment into the hands of demagogues who may use them for bad purposes" (Barrows 1969, p. 132).

✳✳ There were two Mohonk conferences, one in 1890 and the other in 1891. This is the place where the leading white educators and ministers met to hammer out a consensus on Negro education. No blacks were in attendance—none were invited, but the conference thought they had successful meetings and more importantly they—those white men— plotted the course of black education that still exists today! That pattern was later transferred to Africa by the British. Many of them shared the opinion of Reverend James Pike who, claiming to be a friend of the Negro and an advocate of the abolition of slavery, nonetheless, asserted that the problem of Negro education was not how to teach them reading and writing, indeed they learned that all too readily. Rather, the problem for Pike and many aware Whites was how to teach the Negro proper manners and respect for his new role as a worker.

That's what "Negro" education was and is about, regardless of the great debate between Booker T. Washington and W.E.B. Du Bois. While the black men of educational theory were arguing about the advantages and disadvantages of liberal versus vocational education, the white men of educational power were effecting a mental slave system to better control the new physical slave system.

In view of these realities, it is indeed surprising that many black leaders want to improve the educational system. Certainly a system with a record like that deserves destruction, so that black people can build a new educational system that will not deeducate our masses and miseducate our leaders.

At the beginning, I equated the crisis in black education in America with the rise of European directed education for people living in Africa. Let us not forget that association because the endemic crisis we speak of is worldwide wherever Europeans have been in charge of Africans and the education of Africans. But what about education before the Europeans conquered us? There are those (even among us) who feel that European oppression was a step up for us—because we were totally ignorant before we were discovered by them.

A F e w P a g e s f r o m t h e B o o k o f A f r i c a n E d u c a t i o n

Most of us are ignorant about African education before the European invasion. Some of us have read the accounts of the European explorers, soldiers, adventurers, missionaries and administrators. A few have read the reports of the European-trained anthropologists. To some extent there have been a few debates on the virtues of the "informal," "practical" education system in "pre-colonial" Africa. A smaller group has examined the great African Koranic universities and extolled their virtues in comparison with the mediocrity of Western education. All of this, though, leads to a false impression of indigenous African education. The data are too fragmented; the explanations are either from outsiders or, if by natives, from an outside perspective because the latter have been trained by European methodology; or *A la* Islam about societies already corrupted by outside influence. In order to get a handle on African education, we need to look at education in ancient Egypt because it is here that we find primary data from Africans themselves. It is true that a great deal of the education was apprentice or practical education designed to pass on the various occupational skills, for example, brick masonry, baking, farming, gold smithing, barbering, shoe making, carpentry, fowlery, and ranching. But in ancient Egypt and other parts of Africa there was a tradition of formal education which centered upon literacy and the ability to read and write.

This type of education may be called scribal education. It was through scribal education that the civilization produced its priests, civil administrators, physicians, artists, scientists, astronomers, and architects. It is through the scribes that we learn of that great black civilization of antiquity.

We discover that the process of education was founded on the family model. In other words, instruction was conceived of as the teaching of a parent to a child, or a father to his son. The foundations for the instruction was the moral guidance that the father, as a responsible elder, was obligated to pass on to his children. Such teaching was the exemplary model of Good Speech which, according to Ptahhotep, the great prime minister of the Fifth Dynasty, was as rare as "precious stones." Good Speech was the possession of the truly educated man, and as a Ninth Dynasty pharaoh said, it is more powerful than anything, including weapons. Thus, education consisted essentially of teaching Good Speech because speech was the highest visible manifestation of man's unique nature. Good Speech was the balance—because the heart and mind of man gives direction to the tongue which commands the body's limbs to act.

Good Action, which is the real test of a person, thus, is the result of articulate speech, which in turn results from keen judgement, mental and moral insight. Such wisdom is handed down from the ancestors to the elders to the children in the eternal educational process. As one sage put it "no one is born wise."

The other end of the learning process is the listening son. Listening is not just hearing, but in the deeper sense, it is obedience. Thus, education represents the Good Speech of the father (good in form and substance) and Good Hearing of the son (good in the sense of hearing and reception of the teaching).

Let us now glance at the explanation of this aspect of educational philosophy by Ptahhotep:

If you listen to my saying,
All your affairs will go forward...
Every man teaches as he acts,
He will speak to the children,
So that they will speak to their children:
Set an example, don't give offense,
If justice stands firm your children will live.

(Lichtheim 1975, vol. 1, p. 75)

The truly educated man is a person of balance—in other words, he is cool. He moderates his temper. He controls his ego. Above all, he is a listener. When he does speak after effectively controlling this urge to blurt out and react emotionally, he speaks with power and he is listened to. If this discipline does not exist, then skills cannot be effectively learned, or if half learned they cannot be used to good ends. Just as balance (the operational definition of weighing and allocating) is the core of distributing the material things that sustain life and make good living possible, so balance in a man enables him to do the right thing that leads to individual and public happiness.

✳✳ The balanced and cool man who possesses Good Speech always exhibits exemplary conduct. He knows how to act *toward* his elders and superiors, his peers, and those who are under his authority or area of responsibility. He knows how to distinguish the proper modes of behavior from situation to situation. He is always restrained and becomes effective by indirection. That is, rather than directly confronting another with a delicate problem, the educated African uses examples and third parties to bring the point across. Again, listen to the teachings of a father to a young son who is being sent to the Per Ankh (the house of life), or the university:

> I'll make you love scribedom more than your mother,
> I'll make its beauties stand before you;
> It's the greatest of all callings
> There's none like it in the land. (p. 184)

As indicated in the passage, higher education was a greatly sought value among the Black people of the ancient Nile Valley civilizations. The children of rich and poor alike were dedicated to the god of wisdom and education, Jehewty. The people were taught that among all people, writers were able to achieve a life beyond death that was more certain than those who merely built elaborate tombs because the ideas of the writers live in a society long after tombs crumble and other material things rot away.

It is in this context that the teaching of reading, writing, arithmetic, and other skills was achieved. Good form and content were achieved primarily by having the students read and copy exemplary "classic" models. Through such drills the pupils learned not only how to read and write but what to read and write about. Even more importantly they encountered the ideas of the great men of antiquity and thus were able to become wise while in the process of picking up the skills. Thus, going back to basics is an African educational movement, when we truly understand our basics.

The Case For Restoring African Education

In view of the dismal projects of Eurocentric or European-centered education for our black youth, we ought as a matter of common sense consider an African-centered education. (I will dismiss without comment the absurd notion that a universalistic curriculum is the solution.) Let us now make the case a bit clearer.

The endemic crisis in black education is at the base of the process which Bobby Wright calls "Menticide." Menticide is the most sophisticated phase of the war strategy of the white supremacists against the black race. If we lose that war, there will be no more problems in black education, no more black education, and no more blacks. Black intellectual awareness of the genocidal plan for blacks is not new. Martin Delany warned about it over a hundred years ago. He pointed out that this plan has been in progress for two thousand years. Edward W. Blyden called attention to it in 1872 when he asserted: Some have reveled in the prospect of hearing some fine morning of "The Last of the Negroes!" If we are to win the war against white supremacy, if we are to live, then we must take education away from our enemies. We must build true African education on a life-giving base. Only an African-centered education offers such a base.

An African-centered education can only be built on the foundations of traditional African concepts of education. These traditions must be modified to reflect contemporary concerns and issues, but the return to the African view of the universe is imperative. When that worldview is restored, the problem of African liberation will become clear and, thus, the agenda and curricula of African education will be given the direction that seems so elusive at present.

The African view of the universe is based upon the truth that man, nature, the universe, and God are in harmony. There is no alienation. The basic mode of human action is cooperation, peace, and

260

building great projects. This is diametrically opposed by the European or rather Aryan worldview which sees man as alienated from God, at war with nature, and surrounded by an indifferent universe.

The Europeans, since 1440, have been reorganizing the world. The world we now live in was organized by them. They conquered the lands of all continents and unilaterally redesigned the social and biological modes of existence. They changed the course of rivers, removed mountains, and built deserts. They created scarcity in the land of abundance. They moved populations from one continent to another. They created new races. They established themselves as the master race and all others as their servants. They made what they like good and everything else bad.

In order to liberate ourselves we must take the world and then reorganize it according to our worldview. Only then will mankind be allowed to live in harmony with the universe. Only then will we be truly free.

Notes on What We Should Teach Our Youth or Africanizing the Curriculum

If we accept the premise that the present-day education of our youth both deeducates and miseducates them, we then should examine carefully what is taught in the schools and strive carefully to supplement, augment, repudiate or reject those teachings that continue to drive black people mad. But most urgently, we really have no alternative but to Africanize the curriculum.

To begin with, we need to establish new time and space orientations. One may say that black people are forced to live in white time. This is indeed ironic when we consider that the operational definition of time which is used in today's world was given to the Westerners by the Africans of the great Nile Valley civilization. Observe the 365-day year came from Egypt and has endured and replaced all other types of years. The same is true of the 24-hour day divided into 12 hours of daylight and 12 hours of night. This is true also of the 12-month year which has determined celebrations and business arrangements for thousands of years. Why, then, must we now submit to the European-imposed concept of year. In truth, as well as from our perspective, the greatest historically significant year was the *Sep Tepy* (the first time), that is, the unification of Upper and Lower Egypt. This event, which occurred over 6200 years ago, resulted in the birth of the greatest nation of antiquity, gave civilization as we know it to the world. The black nation Kemet, or Egypt as the Eurasians called it, introduced to the northern continent writing with a phonetic alphabet, a numbering, counting and mathematical system, written drama, novels and stories, higher spirituality, medicine, architecture, history, science and art, among other things. In other words, the birth of Kemet made what we call history possible. Why not, then, let that be our day one and thus we are now in the sixty-second century of history. Think of what such a change will do in the restoring of racial sanity!

We encounter the same imperative in spatial orientation. One day some Eurasians drew a picture of the various lands in the world. They put their own lands at the top of the picture and the African lands at the bottom. Thus they arbitrarily equated North with up and South with down. How ridiculous for us to accept a picture of the world that puts white on top of black.

Our ancestors, the ancient Kemites (i.e., Egyptians) equated up with South and down with North. Upper Kemet (Egypt) is in Southern Egypt and Lower Egypt is in the North. The Nile flows down from the Equator to the Mediterranean Sea. Pharaoh Jehewty-Mose asserted: "My southern boundary is at the top of the world." Quite possibly the Kemites considered the Equator as the top of the world. This is very interesting because Africa is the only continent which is nearly equidistant from the Equator, that is, about one-half is in the Southern Hemisphere and half is in the Northern Hemisphere. Eurasia (Europe is merely a peninsula of the largest land mass, more than half of which is caked with ice and snow much of the year) is totally in the Northern Hemisphere as is North America. Australia is totally in the Southern Hemisphere, while South American is a Southern continent, except for a tip which is in the northern half. Thus, Africa can be said to be the central continent; it is the land of balance, the two poles being equidistant from the center of Africa. Until we turn the world right side up, we will always stand on our intellectual heads as we view the world upside down. Think of the psychological benefits of such a healthy spatial view.

Another area of necessary change is in the conceptualization of historiography. Western historiography is based upon the records of Eurasian warfare and conquest. It has been so since the time of Herodotus and before, even back to Hesiod and Homer. On the other hand, before the Eurasian invasion, the annals of Africa were dominated by records of peace time projects; the building of irrigation systems and channels; the erection of great temples and roadways. Warfare was a minor concern for the ancient Egyptians before the Eighteenth Dynasty—and was primarily a matter of national defense at that. Expansionism did not really affect the nation until the nation became corrupt in the Eighteenth Dynasty.

While we cannot ignore the ethos of conquest and dominion that the Eurasians have thrust on the world for the last twenty-five hundred years, we can commit ourselves to a restoration of the true principle of human activity. Thus, when we write a history of the Western Hemisphere to replace American history, we will base it upon the early African migrations such as the one which brought constructive techniques and knowledge to the indigenous inhabitants. The monuments that bear the unquestionable imprint of African presence are monuments of peace and prosperity, not conquest and humiliation. When we deal with that part of history since the European invasions initiated by Erikson and Columbus, we will focus on the independent African communities which existed side by side with the settler colonies. These free and independent African communities were established by Africans who had been kidnapped in Africa by the Europeans and their flunkies. They were placed on ships destined for the Western Hemisphere. Some of the ships were taken over by the blacks and crash landed in the islands. The blacks thus established communities in the areas since they had no way of getting back home. Other communities were established by those who ran away from the slave markets and plantations. Indeed, some escaped the ships when they docked. These free African communities were the bastions for the liberation struggles that were waged from the early 1500s until chattel slavery was destroyed by the masses of Africans. The "Abolition" by the whites was only a formal act reflecting an "act accomplished." Such a framework for a history of the Western Hemisphere would revolutionize the development of the racial psyche of black youth.

We must teach and stress the importance of a classical language, *Medew Netcher* and contemporary African languages. This is true also of literature and drama. As George G. M. James put it, we must stop quoting Plato and start quoting Ptahhotep. In the areas of math and science, we would teach the Egyptian system of arithmetic along with the one now used. We would point to the scientific medical and architectural knowledge of sages like Imhotep. In other words, we would Africanize the curriculum as a preparation for Africanizing the world.

The only way we can restore life and sanity to the African race is by such a level headed unilateral move. The major thrust of our educational efforts is to restore to health a strong positive African personality. I close with a statement Edward Blyden made regarding African personality:

> It is sad to think that there are some Africans, especially among those who have enjoyed the advantages of foreign training, who are blind enough to the radical facts of humanity as to say, 'Let us do away with the sentiment of race. Let us do away with our African personality and be lost, if possible, in another race.'

> This is as wise or philosophical as to say, let us do away with gravitation, with heat and cold and sunshine and rain. Of course the other race in which these persons would be absorbed is the dominant race, before which, in cringing self-surrender and ignoble self-suppression, they lie in prostrate admiration. Some are really in earnest, honestly thinking that by such means they will rise to the cloudless elevation of Olympus or reach the sublime heights of Parnassus, but the verdict of spectators is that they qualify themselves for Bedlam. There is, only then, one fatal influence against all this teaching, and that is, The Whole Course of Nature. Preach this doctrine as much as you like, no one will do it, for no one can do it, for when you have done away with your personality, you have done away with

yourselves. Your place has been assigned you in the universe as Africans, and there is no room for you as anything else. (Blyden [1893] 1971, pp. 200–201)

R E F E R E N C E S

Barraws, Isabel G., ed. 1969. *Lake Mohonk Conference on the Negro Question.* New York: Negro Universities Press.

Blyden, Edward W. 1971. "Study and Race" (written in 1893). In *Black Spokesman: Selected Published Writings of Edward Wilmot Blyden,* ed. by Hollis R. Lynch. London: Frank Cass and Co.

—. 1971. "Letter to Governor Hennessy, Freetown, December 1872." In *Black Spokesman: Selected Published Writings of Edward Wilmot Blyden,* ed. by Hollis R. Lynch. London: Frank Cass and Co.

Brown v. Board of Education of Topeka. 1954. 347 U.S. 483.

Carruthers, Jacob H. 1980. "Reflections on the History of the Afrocentric Worldview." *Black Books Bulletin.*

—. 1972. *Science and Oppression.* Chicago: Kemetic Institute.

Kenyatta, Jomo. 1961. *Facing Mount Kenya.* London: Secker and Warburg.

Lichtheim, Miriam. 1975. *Ancient Egyptian Literature,* Vol. I. Berkeley: University of California, Berkeley Press.

Lomotey, Kofi. 1990. Introduction. In Kofi Lomotey, ed. *Going to School: The African-American Experience.* Albany, NY: State University of New York Press.

Nkrumah, Kwame. 1967. *Challenge of the Congo: A Case Study of Foreign Pressures on an Independent State.* New York: International Publishers.

Shujaa, M. J., ed. 1992. *Too Much Schooling, Too Little Education.* Trenton: Africa World Press.

Woodson, Carter G. [1933] 1969. *The Mis-education of the Negro.* Washington, DC: The Associated Publishers.

Wright, Bobby. 1981. "Black Suicide-Lynching by any Other Name is Still Lynching." *Black Books Bulletin.*

16

Institution Building
An Imperative for Africans in
the Twenty-First Century

> I will make a work in the temple of the Creator....It is in this place that ˊmy perfection will be remembered....Doing what is valuable is perpetuity....A (person) who is invoked (through) works cannot be destroyed....The things of eternity cannot perish.
>
> (translated by James Allen)

It is with the above cited proclamation that the pharaoh whom the Greeks called Sesostris dedicated one of the most beautiful chapels in the history of humankind. The structure was one of the first monuments in that great temple complex, Karnak, located on the Nile River in what is today called Upper Egypt.

Whenever the African authors of the greatest civilization of antiquity established a temple, they built for eternity. Thus each temple became an institution. While such establishments were dedicated to the Creator, they were not merely places of worship, they were, above all, places of learning and service. They were educational institutions and social service organizations. They were institutions in the classic sense of the term.

When one visits the Nile Valley Antiquities, one does not merely view the ruins of great buildings which are themselves awe-inspiring, one also sees the material evidence of institutions that vitalized and continually renewed a civilization that lasted more than four thousand years, and inspired the development of most of the civilizations that we consider a part of world history.

Those traditions are exemplary models for those of us who would dare attempt the establishment of institutions for African people today. (I am using the terms African to refer to people of African descent, including African Americans. Likewise, I use the term European to refer to people of European descent, including those we call white Americans.)

I will focus on three concerns relative to "institution building" by African people. First, let us review what is called "The Crisis of Institution Building Among Modern Africans." Next, I will discuss the general directions and prospects for successful institution building by African people. Finally, I will share a model which may provoke you to raise questions about your own origins.

C r i s i s   o f   A f r i c a n   I n s t i t u t i o n   B u i l d i n g

The closing of the Egyptian temples by the order of Emperor Justinian in the fifth century anticipated and symbolized the "2000 seasons" of the attempt to destroy African civilization. In the name of "the only true religion," or "higher civilization," or "progress," century after century has witnessed the dismantling, deforming, and defaming of African institutions, a necessary precondition for the more perfect exploitation of African peoples and resources.

This perennial onslaught has been waged not only by foreign invaders, but also by African converts to the alien cultures. This attack has been intense and unremitting, both on the African continent and among those Africans of the diaspora who were dragged into the Western Hemisphere. The campaigns waged by the colonial usurpers and slavemasters against African people stand out as the most brutal wars of biological and cultural genocide ever conducted. This is the context in which we must understand the crisis of institution building among modern African peoples.

The most critical African institution, the family, has been a special target in this unrelenting warfare. The African family is the foundation of African culture and its destruction is the most passionate objective of what is called "Western civilization." The concept of the "Vanishing American Family" which was aired on television a couple of years ago provides an example of the attack. Its generic form is the attack on African matriarchy, insisting that mother-centered families cannot exist in the modern world! The emphasis on the "engineered" gender war (black women against black men), as per exploitation by movies such as *The Color Purple*, is another example of the continuation of that war. The publicity surrounding the myth of the "black underclass" is an attempt to divide the African American community along family class lines and to obscure the genocidal thrust of neowhite supremacy. The constant bombardment of African governments with the necessity of birth control, a clever way to destroy African families (no birth control, no foreign aid), is a sophisticated demonstration of the genocidal agenda. Ironically, Africa is the most sparsely populated continent in the world; and even more ironically Africa is potentially the most richly endowed continent in relationship to resources that could be used to support human life.

The attack on African institutions is accompanied by a superimposition upon African communities of alien organizations. In fact, most of the so-called "accepted" and "responsible" organizations in modern African communities have a European format. The purpose, as well as the modus operandi, of these groups is defined in Eurocentric terms. Any deviation from the European form is castigated as "primitive" and "irresponsible." These modern organizations then operate from within the African community and continue the attack on the African tradition.

Ironically, it is these very Eurocentric African institutions that are continually in crisis today. They are chronically financially strapped when their European sponsors choose to withdraw support. They are usually embroiled in leadership brawls because of competing Eurocentric ambitions. They often fail and wind up in economic social and political bankruptcy. Indeed, recent history is littered with the hideous ruins of atrophied and irrelevant black organizations.

Some of these organizations have arisen for good cause and have made substantial progress under the circumstances. Others exist merely because some simplistic Negro said, "they got one so we need one too."

One of the inherent weaknesses of these limited purpose imitation organizations is that they often have a secret purpose of integrating with their white counterpart as soon as "they stop treating us so bad" or "as soon as they accept us." Indeed the *raison d'etre* for many of these black organizations is white rejection of black members, or some other manifestation of what is called white racism.

The major problem with such organizations is that they are only quasi-institutions. They do not spring from the fertile soil of African culture. They are hybrid and are thus generally sterile. The real crisis of many modern African institutions is that they are anti-African. They are designed to destroy African life (consciously or unconsciously) and ironically they suffer the same fate they were created to cause. They are indeed like the African slave traders who, after they had captured scores of Africans and brutally marched them to the sea in shackles, were themselves thrown into the slave ships by their would-be paymasters. How condign can a reward be?

Directions for Institutional Revitalization

How can we begin to change this sad story? Let me begin by sharing an invitation first issued by the pharaoh with whose wisdom we started.

> Come back to Kemet
> Come back to the Black Community
> See the Cradle City
> It's the place where you came into existence
> Kiss the ground at the great gate
> And mingle with friends
> (my translation from Erman 1909)

That invitation was sent by the Pharaoh Sesostris to an African named Sinuhe who had left his home and adopted a foreign country. Sinuhe was a young man who held a high government post. But during a time of trouble he had run away and taken refuge in a foreign land. The powers in this foreign land welcomed him because he was such a well-educated and cultured man. He became a valuable producer in this new land. He helped them fight their enemies. And so he lived in this adopted land and thought it was a good place—it was something like America.

Then one day he was faced with the jealousy of a native citizen of that land and nearly lost his life and fortune in a duel with his adversary. Although he won the fight, he realized that he was in a strange place and did not really belong. Then he wanted to go back home. So he sent a message to the pharaoh. He apologized for having left. He begged forgiveness and indicated he was willing to do penance if only he would be allowed to return. The pharaoh, without hesitation and without any preconditions, sent him the invitation!

"Come back to the Black Community."

What African builders need is to go to the deep well of our classical civilization and draw the fresh fertile water to nourish our fledgling organizations. While our organizations must deal with the problems that confront us today, they do not have to be condemned to the structure and spirit dictated by the authors of our plight. Let us build institutions that are not only designed to meet the immediate problems caused by the vicissitudes of white supremacy, but let us also establish institutions for eternity. Let us build for perpetuity.

Let us recover and restore our classical civilization so that it serves us like the classical civilizations of other people serve them. Every great European institution is molded in part in the image of the ancient Greek-Roman civilization, including the United States of America and the Republic of South Africa. Every great Jewish project is enriched by the idea of the classical culture of the Torah, including the modern State of Israel. Every organization in the Moslem world harkens back to the classical Islamic civilization of the Middle Ages, including Iran.

Our classical Nile Valley civilization is even more appropriate for us. In the first place it is more ancient and achieved greater accomplishments than any of the others. In the second place, it was an inspiration and model for later cultures. In the third place, it brought the African world to the highest point of perfection thus far.

It is therefore fitting and appropriate that we restore our classic civilization. It is the deep well from which we must draw the waters of

273

African revitalization. There we will find the exemplary models for our institutions. This is the place we must go if we are to stop borrowing from the ideas of our oppressors.

When we begin to erect our institutions after an African pattern, then we will begin to reconstruct African life. We will change the spirit of African life from that of "one day we will be developed and become like them" to the spirit of "let us build on the heritage of our parents so that we can truly endow our children." It is the eternal spirit that imbues an organization with perpetuity.

This African model, working within modern African institutions can be seen historically in the free and independent African communities of the Caribbean and South America. These communities were called Maroon societies by the Europeans. Some of them existed for four hundred years and others still exist today. Their longevity and success is due to the fact that they were modeled after African communities. Among the most successful ones was the Palmares Republic which lasted for more than a century as an independent nation in South America. Another was Haiti which freed itself from slavery through the greatest revolution in modern history.

We can also see the model in other organizations and movements: After the Civil War the African Methodist Episcopal Church, under the leadership of Bishop Henry McNeal Turner, who started a back to Africa movement; after World War I, The Universal Negro Improvement Association and African Communities League under Marcus Mosiah Garvey advocated return to Africa at least in a spiritual sense. In more recent times we saw that African spirit in the black student movement in this country during the 1960s, with its emphasis on Black Studies and African Liberation Month; the same spirit inspired the rebirth of the South African revolution when the African students revolted against the language and culture of their white supremist oppressors and initiated the Black Consciousness movement. The problem is to keep this African orientation alive in the face of overwhelming odds. This can be done only by conscious and deliberate study and periodic renewal.

Indeed, this African worldview has been kept alive. We can trace it back to the beginning of the nineteenth century in this country. Paul Cuffe started a back to Africa movement in the early 1800s. David

Walker, a few years later, connected his revolutionary philosophy with the heritage of ancient Egypt. In the 1850s, Martin Delany, a contemporary of Frederick Douglass, who was the first to proclaim that we were "a nation within a nation" and "Africa for African people" contributed a comprehensive historical framework on the unity of African peoples and their history.

This is the stream from which the organizations which I represent get their fertility. The Association for the Study of Classical African Civilizations has as its major objective "The Restoration of African Civilization." We first came together as scholars attempting to network about our common interest, the study of African life and history. We soon discovered that in order to accomplish our goals we could not afford to limit ourselves to the format of a conventional, professional organization. Many African Americans and other Africans, besides professional scholars, want to study African life and history. Our scholarship agenda must therefore compete with many other needs of the one thousand African people from all over the world who have joined our ranks in the last four years. We founded the organization in 1984, and last year we took nearly one thousand of our members to Egypt for a historic homecoming celebration. Our annual conventions are not merely conferences for professionals to read papers and try out new theories, they are celebrations of our African heritage, they are renewals that hopefully will continue to produce new cycles of creativity and productivity, like the annual Nile floods did in ancient Egypt.

An African Way of Thinking about Speech

Your direct interest is in the domain of Speech. Like most Black associations it grew out of the need for African professionals to take over the control of the theory and methodology of their profession from the European or white experts. Some of you may have resented the arrogance, irrelevance and irreverence of the white professionals toward African Speech. Others may have revolted because of the demeaning way the white experts treated the black experts. Whatever the case, you came together around contemporary African interests.

That's a good starting point. But where do you go from there? In order to go forward, you first must *go back to the Blackland,* to the deep well of African heritage.

What you find at the center of the African worldview, at the foundation of the deep thinking of African culture is the exaltation of Speech. For the ancient Egyptians speech, was the gift of God to humanity. In fact, they called their language, *Medew Netcher* or "divine speech." For them, "good speech" was the equivalent of what the ancient Greeks later termed logos. In the Kemite's perspective, the world came about through the creative word and the human world was maintained through good speech.

In the oldest textbook on pedagogy in the world, the *Instruction* of Ptahhotep, the Egyptian sage equated good speech with wisdom and governance. That text also includes an insightful commentary on good listening or hearing. The legendary divine creator and guardian of speech, Jehewty, whom the Greeks called Thoth or Hermes, was the exemplary model that African parents held before their children to inspire them to a higher life. As one popular Egyptian tale put it, "Do not stammer because it is a person's speech by which one is saved!"

The Master teachers in the *Per Ankhs* (that is the House of Life as the Egyptian universities were called) were considered the earthly guardians of the civilization. Their profession, that is, the teaching of Good Speech through the medium of Good Speech, was the highest calling.

Good Speech consisted not merely of proper pronunciation, enunciation, grammar, syntax, and so forth. It included these, but more significantly good speech was wise speech, ethical speech, profound speech. Therefore, the teachers of speech, oral and written, were not just technicians or narrow professionals, they were above all the transmitters of the tradition, the keepers of the culture. Their more recent counterparts in West Africa are call griots, an aspect of African life popularized by Alex Haley in his novel, *Roots.*

This model from the deep well of our classical civilization should suggest a way to think about our work; a way to connect it with eternity; a way to renew and revitalize your organization; a way to direct it toward the true service of African people. It is the challenge of the twenty-first century. So I again invite you as Sesostris did Sinuhe:

Come Back to the Black Land
See the Cradle City (that is African people)
It's the place where you came into existence
Kiss the ground at the great gate
And mingle with friends (and your African ancestors)!

R E F E R E N C E S

Allen, James, trans. "The Berlin Leather-Roll." Unpublished.

Erman, Adolph, ed. 1909. Literarische Texter des muttleren. Reicher: Leipziz.

17

Speaking About Kemetic Theology

L et us begin with the Greek connection, not as an effort to reiterate the thesis of the *Stolen Legacy*, but because the word theology is deeply embedded in the Greeks intellectual contribution to the world. This essay will identify the origins of their concept of theology and then to look at how that connects with African thought. Let us then consider a statement from the *Metaphysics* of Aristotle.

> As more arts were invented and some were directed to the necessities of life, others to recreation, the inventors of the latter were naturally always regarded as wiser than the inventors of the former because their branches of knowledge did not aim at utility.
>
> Hence, when all such inventions were already established, the sciences which do not aim at giving pleasure or the necessities of life were discovered. And first in the places where man first began to have leisure. That is why the mathematical arts were found in Egypt for there the priest caste was allowed to be at leisure.
>
> All men suppose what is called wisdom is to deal with the first causes and the principles of things. Theoretical kinds of knowledge are more of the nature of wisdom than the productive. (Aristotle *Metaphysics*, p. 981b)

Another statement from Aristotle is further explaining the connection:

It is no new, or even recent, discovery of political science that the state should be divided into classes. To this day, it is the case in Egypt. In Egypt, the system is believed to have been introduced by the legislation of Sosostres. The division of classes originated in Egypt. Egypt bears witness to the antiquity of political institutions. Her people are recognized as the most ancient of all races, and from time out of mind, they have had a legal code and a regular system of government. We ought, therefore, to make good use of what has come down to us from the past and merely supplement its defects. (Aristotle 1962, *Politics*, p. 1329b)

A validation for Aristotle's thinking is given with this statement from Plato, who was Aristotle's teacher. Plato introduces the Egyptian connection in the beginning of the *Timaeus* which some think is his most profound work. Plato tells a story of an Egyptian priest giving a lecture to Solon, the archetype of wisdom. The priest says to Solon:

Then as to wisdom, observe how our laws from the first made a study of the whole order of things extending even to prophesy and medicine which gives health. Out of these divine elements, deriving what is needful to human life and adding every sort of knowledge which would attend to them. (Plato 1949, *Timaeus*, p. 3)

What Plato did was recognize Egyptian wisdom as the foundation of Greek philosophy. Plato merely echoed the universal Greek opinion concerning the source of their most profound knowledge.

I note that connection because the word that I want to emphasize is theology, both in terms of denomination, that is the word *theology* itself, and in terms of the science or the branch of knowledge which it treats. Theology which was derived from the wisdom of ancient Egypt became a separate discipline for the Greeks. It is quite difficult to try to abstract out of ancient African thought anything that we could say is theology in the narrow sense because of the original synthesis of knowledge in the African culture. But, *theos* is a Greek word which means divine or God and *logos* is a Greek word which means, in its fundamental and radical interpretation, speech with the connotation of

280

reasoning or intelligent speech.

Theology means divine speech to the Greeks. It concerned what they called "first principles." In other words, had Aristotle named the science that is called metaphysics, he probably would have called it either theology—that is, "divine words," "first principles," "first science" —or "first philosophy," which he identifies in "Book Six" of the *Metaphysics*. Whatever the case, we can see that the concept of divine speech has such a word to word, idea to idea relationship to the thought of the ancient Kemites (Egyptians) that we can rightfully put it in the category of the stolen legacy. We do not know exactly how Aristotle or any of the others developed theology, but we can say that three thousand years before they started talking about divine speech, the ancient Kemites had already developed the concept in perhaps its highest form to this date. I will, therefore, focus on divine speech, or what the ancient Kemites called *Medew Netcher.*

Medew Netcher is the language that was written by the ancient Kemites (that is the ancient Egyptians) and the language that the Greeks called hieroglyphs, or sacred inscriptions, because it is the language that is inscribed on the walls of the temples and tombs, and written on the papyrus. But the term hieroglyphs is simply a technical identification; the deeper meaning of *Medew Netcher* is embedded in the texts of the ancient Kemites themselves.

The most profound explanation of it is found in a text that was written about two hundred years before the first of the pre-Socratic Greek philosophers came on the scene. The Shabaka text was transcribed during the regime of Shabaka, in what is called the Twenty-fifth Dynasty or the so-called Nubian Dynasty. During this period, the people from the southern part of the northern Sudan came down to liberate Kemet (Egypt) from its foreign occupiers. The liberators attempted, over a one hundred year period, to restore that long and beautiful ancient tradition. While rebuilding the old order, the Kushites (Nubians) made several significant contributions to the articulation and the reconstruction of the ancient Kemetic ethos. One of them is contained in a text that was dictated by the Pharaoh Shabaka, who even the Egyptologists admit was a pure African. I am going to let ancient Africa speak for itself because Africa has been spoken for by others for far too long. The Egyptologists assert that the text was something that Shabaka copied from another source. In the text, Shabaka asserted that it was a copy of something written a long time ago; but Kushites and Kemites always based what they did on the sayings of the ancestors. They, however, always extended the ideas for contemporary meaning and so we can say that these ideas are a contribution of Shabaka's generation.

The text contains an epistemological statement which is very important because Africans have been accused of having no epistemology, or an epistemology that is based upon the category of fantasy, which Carl Spight laid out so well. (I might point out that Carl's analysis was absolutely brilliant. He laid modern science out. He brought it to court, examined it, and found the basis for the indictment of it. Now we have to go back to something on which we can begin again.) Let us begin then with the Shabaka statement of epistemology. It says:

> The seeing of the eyes, the hearing of the ears and the sniffing of the nose report to the mind, which makes every understanding come forward. As to the tongue, it repeats what the mind has planned, thus all divine powers were created. For every divine speech came about through what the mind planned and the tongue commanded, thus all labor and all crafts are made, the actions of the hand, the motions of the legs, the movement of the limbs, according to this command which is planned by the mind and comes forth on the tongue and creates the performance of everything. Thus, it is said of the creator, he made and created the principles and from his everything came forth—all good things; thus, the creator was satisfied after he had made all things, that is all divine speech. (my translation from the transcription of the *Medew Netcher* text in Breasted *The Philosophy of a Memphite Priest.*)

The text explains the essence of the creative word as far as the ancient Kemites were concerned. For them, speech was the "it" of understanding and the "it" of knowledge. In other words, speech was epistemology. Speech was the essence of humanity. Speech was what the creator gave to humanity to negotiate. When you look at humanity and observe humanity, in its human form, acting as human, then you observe it acting through speech. You can influence other people in various ways, through physical force or through meting out pleasure, but if you wish to deal with them "qua-human," you must deal through speech. Speech is humanity when humanity is at its best. This was the profound belief of the Kemites or the ancient Africans. As they may have put it, the mind thinks, the tongue commands, and the limbs obey. To put it in a more exalted fashion, they had a formula that appears in the tombs which reads: When you are fully developed, when you have achieved your full humanity, you are filled with three essences.

The first is *Sia*, exceptional comprehension—that is you see clearly, you understand, you perceive and comprehend clearly. The second is *Hu*, authoritative utterance; you speak articulately and thus, your speech has the force of a command and everything complies because the command is based on *Maat* (truth). Finally, you have *Heka*—the follow through. According to the Egyptologists *Heka* is magic. More properly it is extraordinary power which results from a clear mind and an articulate tongue; then you have extraordinary power to accomplish those things you desire in a very efficient manner. Africans viewed the human process in the indicated order. The order is important because if you have the body moving before the command comes, then you have stupidity. When the tongue wags without the benefit of the mind, silliness is the product. So the sequence has to be in correct order. Therefore, *the word* truly creates because if you consider the relationship of the three, from thought to action, speech is the mediator. From an epistemological standpoint, the Kemites preceded Francis Bacon who could not improve on Kemetic wisdom. In fact, Bacon simply restates what the Kemites had stated two thousand years earlier: Knowledge begins with sensory perception.

To understand this epistemology, reflect on the process of thinking. Once you start speaking, whatever your thoughts before you started speaking, you can not go back to that any more and get a grasp on things. That is one of the reasons most people cannot remember things that happened before they were two or three years old. Once you start speaking, you think in speech. When you think about all of the so-called mental processes, you are really talking to yourself. That is why speech was at the center of everything for the Kemites. They recognized that thought was first, but they knew it was impossible to conceive a thought without (silent) speech. That is why Jehewty, the God of wisdom, was also the God of speech and articulation. This is also indicated through the Kemetic philosophy of education. The product of education was Good Speech, as was the process of education.

For the Kemites, all sciences were divine speeches. All systems of knowledge and wisdom were divine speech. When you can speak correctly about an object of inquiry, you have internalized that object. Whether those events are natural events or human-made events.

Regarding the first principles of Kemetic thought, let us follow the wisdom of letting the Kemites speak for themselves. All systems of knowledge are based upon assumptions regarding the origin of the cosmos and mankind. Most sciences go back to cosmic events. When studying Kemetic observations of cosmic events and human experience, you get two contradictory impressions. On the one hand, because of the perpetual recurrence of celestial phenomena, you get the impression of eternity—what is, has always been and always will be. And yet there are certain human experiences that suggest just the opposite—that everything is destined to go out of existence, especially human life itself. The thinkers in Kemet recognized the paradox of the contradiction and they dealt with it in a very practical manner. They analyzed the concept of time, which they had organized around the cycles of the sun. Long before they fully developed their system of thought (or articulated it), they developed the notion of the 365 day year based upon what man perceives to be happening regarding the sun. The resultant calendar gave them the idea of time, and thus they tended to equate time with the sun. In fact, most of the words that deal with time in the language have a determinative of the sun. And so, the question that they put to the paradox was this: When was the first time the sun came up? That is the operational meaning of the question about the origin of the universe.

If one can say time started, then it started the first time the sun came up. The sun's cycle is eternal. Therefore, the sun represents both time and eternity. And that is why *Re* (the sun) was such a powerful symbol of divinity for them. Now we can divide the explanation into a consideration of divine speech about the eternal and divine speech about time. Divine speech about the eternal begins with the notion that there is a primordial uncreated universe—no beginning and no end—that preceded time, that will exceed time and that continues while time is going on. It is difficult to talk about some of these things.

They divided this preexistence, or this eternity, into four couples. The concept of the couples is very important because it suggests there is one original principle of being: maleness and femaleness. Thus they had four divine couples whom we will call *Nu* and *Nunette*, *Hehu* and *Hehut*, *Keku* and *Kekut*, and *Tenemu* and *Tenemut*—man and woman, male and female.

Nu and *Nunette* represented waterness—that is the primeval water which has some characteristics that are important. One is incessant movement: from a standpoint of humanity, meaningless movement; and also fluidity with all of its characteristics. That is one of the features or aspects of eternity. Another is *Hehu* and *Hehut*, or infinity, that is, no limit in time, and so this eternity was also limitless. The third is *Keku* and *Kekut*, which means darkness; but I think darkness in the sense of uniformity similar to Hegel's statement "all cows are grey at night." That means uniformity. And I think that is what is meant here, that everything is together. Things are difficult to distinguish in darkness. Until the light shines on something, you cannot tell what it is; you just see a lump out there. Finally, *Tenemu* and *Tenemut*, words the Egyptologists do not have a definition for; therefore, every Egyptologist can give his own definition. Although I am not an Egyptologist, I will say that I think it means the unknown. It simply means that the totality is basically unknown, and only a small part of it is knowable. This, in sum, is the eternal world: the world that always has been and always will be. It is also the world that has the potentiality of everything that is, that we recognize as created, or that we recognize as reality.

It is out of this world, and only out of this world, that the coming into being comes into being. It is called *NuNu* (waterness), which was the base of universal creation. The concept was tied to their experience with the Nile which covered the earth during the flood season. It is out of the very lack of form, lack of foundation, incessant movement, inertia, and fluidity of the flood waters that stability and life come. That is the only place it can come from—the water. The water brings

285

forth what appears to be its opposite and that is solidity. In like manner, out of infinity, time and limit emerge as moments of this infinity; not as cancellations of it as Hegel would put it. There is no contradiction, limit is just simply moment development within infinity; you can come from eternity and emerge into time and return from time into eternity. Next there is total uniformity. The Kemites always said, in most of the serious formulas, that the end was as the beginning and that all things are one. Therefore, in the beginning and in the end, everything is one—in between you have variety and distinction. Though variety and plurality may seem to be contradictions of unity, nonetheless, in Kemetic thought, the occurrence of plurality is just a moment of unity. Finally, there is the unknown aspect of eternity. The totality of existence will basically remain unknown; only a fraction of it will ever become known to man. That which is known comes from that which is unknown, but it does not cancel out the unknown. The unknown is still out there, but you know a little something, that which perhaps is revealed or that which is given by the creator.

The next level is the relationship of the eternal to the temporal. The Kemites called the beginning of the world *Sep Tepy* or the very first occasion. What happened on the very first occasion was explained by them in the *Pyramid Texts* and the so-called *Books of the Dead*, which is more properly called the *Book of Coming Forth by Day*. Accordingly, on the first occasion, *Kheper*—that is the self-created one—came into existence and brought all things that came into existence into existence. Let me discuss that for a moment. *Kheper* is the beetle (sometimes you see people wearing scarab or beetle rings). The Nile was a reminder of the great primordial substance—water. And when the Nile flood came, everything went out of existence. Everything was completely inundated and the people recognized this as the beginning of fertility and new life; so they waited until the Nile receded so they could go back and redraw the boundaries and bring the world back into existence. As the Nile receded and reached the level of the earth, one of the happenings they noticed were millions of beetles coming out of the slime. These beetles rolled a little ball between their legs, and the ball became red hot, looking like the sun itself. At a certain point, little squiggly things began to emerge from the ball. This seemed like spontaneous generation, or self-creation. Thus, the name for the beetle—*Kheper*—became the word for self-creation or vice versa. But what is *Kheper?* In my definition *Kheper* means "happening."

Thus on the very first occasion, "happening" came into existence and brought all of the happenings into existence as a happening. But *Kheper* is an aspect of the sun and so after coming into being, after self-creating, then *Kheper* begins to create. *Kheper* in this sense must be androgynous, that is female and male. The sun is *Kheper* in the morning, as a beginning or a happening. The sun is *Re* at midday, at full potency bringing life and giving life to everything. Finally, the sun is *Atum* at dusk, which connotes completion, or when the whole world has come into view. Then *Atum* creates two others by self-copulation, because in the beginning the creator is one, containing both female and male principles. The Creator then, after having impregnated itself, sneezes and Shu comes into being (*Shu* is pronounced *shwoo*, like a sneeze). At the same instance, the text indicates that *Atum* spits and creates *Tefnet*, which means "she who is of spit." The universe came into existence through procreation and not through artificial creation. Creation did not come through art as we understand it nor through molding and taking some material and forming the world. It came from the body of the self-created Creator as the text says. And therefore, God and the universe are one. The Creator proclaimed "from one I became three." This, incidentally, is the first idea of trinity. And so here we have the beginning of the creation. The divine twins *Shu* and *Tefnut* give birth to *Geb*, the earth, who is male, and *Nut*, the sky, who is female. In the beginning they were one, reflecting the principle of unity, but immediately at birth they were separated. What is discovered upon their separation is that their oneness in this case was symbolized as copulation. They were so united to each other that it was impossible to know one from the other until they were separated. When they separated, the rest of the world came into existence. *Geb* and *Nut*, in turn, gave birth to *Osiris* and *Isis* and *Set* and *Nephtys*. That is, two more divine couples were born and these two divine couples were the progenitors of human kind. Thus, we have an unbroken chain between creator and mankind through procreation. Humankind is indeed the progeny of God, that is, human beings are the children of God in the sense of being blood relatives. In other words, people contain the substance of the Creator, that is, the life force of the Creator, the core is distributed among all creatures. So all creatures are divine. There is no alienation between humanity and God. God did not merely create humanity, God procreated human beings. It was a natural chain. Thus, this idea of creating became the core around which individual human life is organized.

In the individual human, there are several essential elements. Four of them are: *Khet,* or the body which comes into being at conception (it begins to function) and goes out of existence at the point of what we call physical death (it ceases to function). Then there is the *Ba,* that is, the personality, that which hangs around for a long time after you die, and is always associated with you, cannot be separated from you, and it lasts as long as there is somebody that remembers you. Once the people who remembered you die then your *Ba* also leaves. That concept is widespread in Africa through concepts like "the living dead." Each individual also possesses the *Ka,* that is, that which is truly alive in you. The *Ka,* the "life force," leaves the body at death and goes to heaven and waits for the rest of the individual. Joining the *Ka* is problematic and depends upon the state of that other essential part of the individual that is the *Ib,* the heart or mind. The heart/mind symbolizes the real individual. That is the aspect of the individual which is morally responsible. The heart/mind is symbolically weighed on the scales of *Maat* (Justice) to determine whether the individual will join with the *Ka* and have everlasting life. The individual and the *Ka* are separated forever and go out of existence when the heart is not in accord with *Maat.*

An interesting aspect of creation is the fact that *Maat* is always there from the beginning because it is recognized as the creative substance that the creator spits out—the *Tef* of *Tefnut* whose alter ego is *Maat.* The text indicates that the occurrence of *Maat* is not a separate event but that all aspects of the creation occur simultaneously. In human speech, we relate the story as though the various aspects occur one after another; however, everything comes into existence on the very first occasion. The text tells us that before the Creator himself can come into existence, He must be infused with *Maat;* He must be filled with *Maat;* He must ingest *Maat;* and He must be surrounded by *Maat* or He cannot come into existence. There is no notion of an arbitrary creator. The Creator must be true and right. Human kind must also be internally and externally guided by *Maat*. When the individual dies and goes to the judgement bar, he or she has to be what they call *Maa Kheru* (true of voice), which is the title of one of the great books of sacred knowledge. Thus, when you go before judgement, and the judges ask whether you have lived according to *Maat*, your answer is yes. Of course, the answer has to be the truth, thus you are *Maa Kheru* (true of voice). Then and only then will you be allowed to join your *Ka* which is already in heaven.

The upshot is that there is no fundamental alienation in the Kemetic worldview. Eternal life is guaranteed from the beginning to the end. There is no separation between God and humanity. There is no cosmic hostility, no inherent warfare. Everything is one in the beginning and in the end it comes back together. Thus, at death you return to your maker. When you go back to your maker, you do not have to have the great revolution and the great arising as envisioned by the Hebrews, Persians and Greeks. After life on earth, you automatically go back to the Creator, if you lived according to the principles of the universe. That is what is essential about the African viewpoint that you find all over Africa. This teaching is put forth in divine speech, which is generally called theology. Divine speech in this sense encompasses all ways of thinking.

At the human level, what you receive from your teacher in order to negotiate social life is *Medew Nefer* (Good Speech). Education is good speech. You are instructed through Good Speech and the test of whether you have attained it is whether you possess Good Speech. Good speech is also synonymous with wisdom. Therefore, everybody is evaluated by how well they speak. It is not only how "proper" they speak, but also how profound and moral the content. As one of the texts asserts, Good Speech may come from the mouth of the girls who grind grain as well as from the highly educated.

Good Speech itself is based upon something else that people often overlook. Once you become articulate you tend to think that you must say something all the time! But good speech is dependent upon good listening. You must first of all be silent and listen, because you cannot speak "good" unless you have first listened "good." And you cannot continue to speak "good" unless you continue to listen "good."

However "good" you speak, you must balance this activity with "good" listening.

Medew Netcher, that is, divine speech, contains the totality of human knowledge. In it is contained what the Greeks termed theology, epistemology, and ontology. The book of *True Voice* was the epitome of divine speech; it taught how to get from this plane to eternal life. It was, perhaps, the most important book because it dealt with the cosmos and answered the problem confronting other civilizations, such as fundamental alienation.

The Kemites had other great books. One was a book of mathematics, which is called very arrogantly by the Egyptologists, *The Rind Mathematical Papyrus*. Let us read part of the prefatory statement from that book which begins, "the first calculation of entering into things; the knowledge of all existing things, all mysteries and all secrets." In other words, what this mathematical papyrus introduces are formulas for solving various quantitative problems. Cheikh Anta Diop has analyzed this book in his last work *Civilization or Barbarism*. The work has many formulas and it relates those formulas to the general problem of epistemology.

There are also several books of medicine, one of which is called the *Ebers Papyrus* by the Egyptologists. The introduction of the text identifies it as a book of illnesses of the body. Thus, the book is a component of divine speech. As indicated above, in the field of ethics there are books of the instructions such as *The Instruction of Ptahhotep*. Each book is a "divine speech." Each one contains fundamental knowledge. One is in the area that we would identify as theology, a book of speaking the truth; another is in the area of mathematics, a book of calculation; and one is in the area of medical sciences, that is, a book of medicines that cure the illnesses of the body; finally, another is in the area of ethics, that is, the book of teaching Good Speech.

Formulas of ancient Kemet provide connection between the divine world and the human world that prevents the African mind from being pessimistic, characterized by and obsessed with fundamental alienation and the struggle against metaphysical alienation which is the basis of "modern" science and modern thought in the European context. One Kemetic formula reads "may the king give a blessing to Osiris, the Great Divinity, and may he in turn give a thousand jugs of water, a thousand loaves of bread, and a thousand of everything that is good and pure for the soul of the person who is seeking entrance into eternity." *The Book of Coming Forth by Day* instructs that a person going before the judgement must always show that he or she has given bread to the hungry, water to the thirsty, and clothes to the naked. That is a way of showing the connection between humanity and divinity. The giving of life by God and its repetition by human beings guarantees eternal life.

When we look at it, the main element which frustrates modern science and all of the non-African modes of deep thinking is resolved in the African worldview. Ultimately, time and eternity are united. You come out of time and go back into eternity. The divine curse of humanity was always "the problem for the Greeks" and the Babylonians. They thought that when time ended for them as individuals, it was all over: thus, there was ultimately no reconciliation between humankind and God.

I will close with that dynamic idea from Kemetic wisdom, that the Creator gave life, power, and health, and therefore, the command to humanity is to give life, power, and health.

Further Reflection on Kemetic Theology

I have spoken about the role of divine speech, or *Medew Netcher,* in ancient Kemetic thought. I emphasized the idea that divine speech, or theology, is the thought of African people. As we see through the experience of the ancient Kemites, it is a wisdom about the highest things which associates speech with what we call, in the European philosophical framework, metaphysics and ontology. That is, speech is, in fact, the way to obtain wisdom about *Maat* which connotes, among other things, the entire divine order. Furthermore, Good Speech is the essence of human life. Speaking good is the measure of the human individual. To paraphrase and extend Descartes' famous assertion, we may say "I speak and therefore, I think and therefore, I am."

I would first like to mention the impact of Kemetic thought on inner Africa. I use "inner Africa" as a term which identifies the rest of Africa. According to Diop, Kemet was to inner Africa what Greece was to inner Europe. Hunter Adams, in some of his earlier essays, demonstrates quite clearly that the Dogon system of thought and cosmology was very much related to the cosmology of Kemet. Diop, noting Hunter's work, explored the connection more exhaustively in *Civilization or Barbarism*. Diop's work is a profound probe into the real relationship between the thought of Kemet and thought of the rest of Africa. It should be read because it is a synthesis into Diop's earlier thoughts on the cultural unity of what he called "Afrique Noir."

One thing we can say without detailing the research, is that the profound respect for the "word" throughout Africa is undeniable. Throughout Africa one finds the concept of the word. Notice, for example, the way African people treat personal names. The name is sacred, which is why the naming ceremony is necessary. If you do not have a name, you do not have a personality. You cannot be incorporated into the community if you do not have a name.

(In his analysis Diop warned us that we have to be careful when we look at the expression of African wisdom in recent times because a great deal of it has become fossilized. According to Diop, the last few centuries of oppression and repression caused a degeneration throughout African life.)

I would also like to discuss the impact of the Kemetic system of thought on the world outside Africa. I want to approach the influence from the standpoint of history. I agree with Carl Spight that we must master the paradigm of the European because it encompasses us, it imperils us, and it has brutalized us; so we must become physicists and political scientists, and so on. We must also, in mastering the European paradigm, remember that we have to understand the history of it, how it came to be as it is.

In the fifteenth and fourteenth centuries, B.C., the wisdom of Kemet was the most prestigious wisdom of the world because, at the time, Kemet was the leading nation. Kemet had imposed upon the world a system of international order that is not unlike the system that the northwestern Europeans are trying to impose on the world today. It is clear that Kemet was the imperial power in terms of culture, even though their imperialism was much more benign than contemporary imperialism, if imperialism can indeed be such. And so, it is understandable that the world of antiquity, which is most familiar to us in the literature, is a world that was impressed by all of the good things that flowed out of Kemet. When we look at the ancient Greeks, it is understandable that they sent their sages to study at the feet of the Kemetic priests. There is no mystery about that, because everybody thought that the greatest wisdom was in Kemet. The Bible reveals the same respect. Abraham went into Kemet as an uncivilized nomad and came out with a higher degree of morality after being chastised for prostituting his wife. We can agree with George G.M. James and assert that to the extent that the ancient Greeks did not admit that they got good ideas from Africa, they stole them. That is, they committed plagiarism, and plagiarism is an act of theft.

Let us hasten to point out that the Greeks did not get all of their ideas from Kemet. Some of their thoughts were non-African, including some of their core concepts. Indeed, Africans should not want to claim responsibility for everything that Plato thought; some of it belonged to his Greek ancestors, so, let us be clear about the *stolen legacy*.

One of the things that I believe the Greeks did not steal from Africa, but is absolutely the most determinative thing about their thought, is what I call the metaphysics of alienation: the profound belief that man is alone and that man is confronted by hostility from the Creator, nature, and from all other individual men and women, especially women. Speaking of the gender problem, it was Pandora in Greek cosmology who brought real trouble to the world when she opened her box.

Whatever the Greeks borrowed or stole they re-formed. Because of the tenacious hold of metaphysical alienation they had to restructure what they stole; out of that restructuring came an intense desire to dominate nature. This is seen in the very early period of Greek literacy in the works of Hesiod who asserted "the Gods hide the good things," therefore, competition and strife are the essence of progress. That idea has not changed in two thousand years. When Francis Bacon laid out the rationale for the modern European scientific project, he said it is the "glory of God to conceal a thing, and the glory of Kings to search it out." He continued by asserting that the greatest ambition of mankind is to establish dominion over nature. Thus, the earlier modern philosophers like John Locke had to go to war against human nature itself, which resulted in, among other things, a rationale for taking the land away from African people and a doctrine for justifying slavery.

This is the real objective of the European scientific project that I call the "science of oppression." It is a science that works for the master and which produces a master's mentality. The question I was confronting at the time I made that formulation was, whether African people ought to be celebrating and extolling this science, and saying "if we could just take his science, we could solve our problems." I agree that we must master modern science, but we have to understand where it came from, what it does and has done to us, and what it does to humanity in general.

Finally, we need to look at where we are. That is, where do we go from here? One of the concerns that we must deal with implicitly is whether this is something which is good for African people. My point is that we are about an Afrocentric synthesis and the development of a methodological and theoretical framework to reorganize this world. In other words, we are in the process of creating a new world order, because the world order which was created under the metaphysics of alienation has begun to destroy the world. We must replace it with a methodology and metaphysics that restores the world and gives light to everybody. As the divine speech taught us at the beginning of our history, it is necessary that human beings, like the Creator, give life and power and health. We should examine everything that we do by that command. If our actions support life and power and health, then they are right. If not, then we ought to stop that line of action.

REFERENCES

Aristotle. *Metaphysics: Basic works of Aristotle.* Ed. by Richard McKeon. New York: Random House.

—. 1962. *Politics.* Translated with an introduction by T. A. Sinclair. Baltimore: Penguin Books.

Bacon, Francis. 1955. *Novum Organum. Selected Writings of Francis Bacon .* Ed. by Hugh G. Dich. New York: Modern Library.

Breasted, James. "The Philosophy of a Memphite Priest." 39 Zeitschrift fur. agyptische Sprache und Altertums-kunde. Bund (Shabaka Text Translation) 39–45.

Carruthers, Jacob H. 1984. *Essays in Ancient Egyptian Studies.* Los Angeles: University of Sankore Press.

Plato. 1949. *The Timaeus.* New York: The Liberal Arts Press.

Spight, Carl. 1987. "Science." Unpublished lecture (April). Ohio State University Press.

Index

297

Prophetic Fragments, 173
Race Matters, 175
Wheatley, Phyllis, 168, 209
When Egypt Ruled the East (Steindorf and Seele), 70
White Question, 155–168
White supremacy, 94, 95, 114, 177–183, 202, 205, 241, 242, 245
    beginning of, 6–7
    and communist movement, 33
    defined, 183n
    and New Orthodoxy, 5
    psychological effects of, 139
    in South Africa, 156–157
    and Western civilization, 4
    winning against, 260
Wiley, Ed III, 176, 201
Williams, Bruce, 243
Williams, Chancellor, 22, 244
    The Destruction of Black Civilization, 10, 25, 70
Wilson, Joan P., 119
Wilson, John A., 67, 109
Wolin, Sheldon, 77–78
Woodard, Maurice, 77
    Blacks and Political Science, 75
Woodson, Carter G., 132, 164, 166, 254
Work European attitudes about, 35–49
Worldview
    African v. Asiatic, 22–24
    African v. European, 260–261
    Aryan, 34
Wright, Bobby, 53–54, 260
    The Psychopathic Racial Personality, 54
Wright, Richard, 169, 194

X
X, Malcolm, 186, 188, 191